THE RISE OF MULTINATIONALS
IN CONTINENTAL EUROPE

The New Business History Series
Series editor: Geoffrey Jones, Professor of Business History, Department of Economics, University of Reading

In recent years business history has emerged as an exciting and innovative subject. A new generation of business historians has moved away from former preoccupations with commissioned histories of individual companies towards thematic, conceptual and comparative studies of the evolution of business. The pioneering studies of Alfred D. Chandler Jr on the rise of big business have inspired much of this work, but there is also a growing dialogue between business historians and their counterparts in business policy, management studies and industrial economics.

The *New Business History Series* is the successor to the former Gower Business History Series, which played an important role in the 1980s in encouraging thematic studies of such topics as the rise of multinationals, the evolution of marketing and the relationship between business and religion. The New Business History Series aims to build on and develop this innovative role by publishing high-quality studies in the 'new' business history.

The Rise of Multinationals in Continental Europe

Edited by

GEOFFREY JONES
Professor of Business History
University of Reading, UK

HARM G. SCHRÖTER
Free University of Berlin,
Germany

Edward Elgar

Published by
Edward Elgar Publishing Limited
Gower House
Croft Road
Aldershot
Hants GU11 3HR
England

Edward Elgar Publishing Company
Old Post Road
Brookfield
Vermont 05036
USA

A CIP catalogue record for this book is available from the British Library

A CIP catalogue record for this book is available from the US Library of Congress

Printed and Bound in Great Britain by
Hartnolls Limited, Bodmin, Cornwall.

ISBN 1 85278 544 6

Contents

v

Tables

Figures

Contributors

Greta Devos, University of Antwerp

Ben P.A. Gales, University of Groningen

Peter Hertner, European University Institute

Fritz Hodne, Norwegian School of Economics and Business Administration

Geoffrey Jones, University of Reading

Angelo Montenegro, Milan

Ulf Olsson, Stockholm School of Economics

Harm G. Schröter, Free University of Berlin

Keetie E. Sluyterman, Center for Business History, Erasmus University

Richard Tilly, University of Münster

Preface

This volume continues the tradition of the *New Business History Series* in exploring a major theme over the long run. The enormous literature on multinationals in the contemporary world is often Anglo/American-oriented or, more recently, concerned with Japanese corporations. We hope this volume will add both historical and continental European dimensions to the literature.

The chapters in the first part of the book, in particular, are designed as surveys rather than as research articles, though they all contain the products of new research. The last decade has seen a proliferation of literature on the history of international business, which is now large and difficult for all but specialists to keep up-to-date. The recent publication of collections of essays on this subject, such as Mira Wilkins (ed.), *The Growth of Multinationals*, Aldershot, 1991, and Geoffrey Jones (ed.), *Multinational and International Banking*, Aldershot, 1992, is one indication of the perceived need for this material to be gathered together in a more accessible form. This volume is offered as a further contribution to making recent historical work on multinationals accessible to a wider audience.

We believe that the book covers the experiences of a wide range of European countries. However, we are disappointed not to have an essay specifically devoted to French multinationals. We commissioned such a study from a leading French business historian, but sadly pressure of other commitments prevented the delivery of his contribution on time. We have attempted to portray the outlines of French direct investment in Chapter 1.

The book is a collective effort. As editors, we would like to thank our contributors for agreeing to become involved in this project. We would also like to thank the economic research institutions in Hamburg and Kiel and the Department of Economics, Reading for their academic and other support. At Reading, Lynn Cornell typed many of the chapters and helped prepare the book for publication. Her contribution to the project was considerable. Finally, we would like to thank Fabienne Debrunner and Verena Schröter for their patience and assistance.

Geoffrey Jones (Reading)
Harm Schröter (Berlin)

PART 1
NATIONAL SURVEYS

1 Continental European multinationals, 1850–1992

Geoffrey Jones and Harm G. Schröter

European multinationals past and present

This book examines the historical evolution of multinational enterprises (mnes) owned in continental Europe from their origins in the mid-19th century until 1992. In the 1960s, when the concept of the 'multinational' was first defined by economists, such a study would have seemed rather marginal. The mne was then regarded as virtually synonymous with American corporations. These enterprises were seen as either useful transferers of American management skills and technologies to less advanced economies in Europe and elsewhere, or as aggressive and highly-mobile predators which could be controlled only with difficulty.[1]

From the perspective of the 1990s, it is evident that the pre-eminence of American multinationals was a transitory phenomenon. Business historians have shown that multinational business had its origins as much in Europe as in the United States, and that this origin can be dated to the mid-19th century. The United States was only a modest source for multinational investment before the First World War, with the great majority of world foreign direct investment (fdi) originating from Europe. Meanwhile, in recent years, American international business activities, though still growing in absolute terms, have both shrunk in relative importance and declined in competitiveness. During the 1980s, in particular, American-headquartered corporations lost world market share in many, if not all, industries. Japanese and South Korean companies have often replaced them, but so have European-owned firms in a range of sectors.[2]

During the 1980s, in fact, ownership of the world's multinationals became concentrated in a 'triad' of the United States, Japan and the European Community (EC), which together accounted for around four-fifths of total outward stocks and flows of fdi. In 1980 the United States was still the single most important home (and host) for fdi in the world economy. By 1988, however, the EC had reached parity with the United States in terms of stock, while both it and Japan exceeded the United States in terms of flows (see Table 1.1).

The importance of EC-based multinationals in the contemporary world economy makes a historical study of their origins and growth both timely and important,

Table 1.1   Outward fdi from the EC, the US and Japan, 1980–89 (US$ billion)

	Stock of FDI		Flow (annual average) outward	
	1980	1988	1980–84	1985–89
EC[1]				
Billion dollars	153	332	18	39
% world total	33	34	41	37
USA				
Billion dollars	220	345	14	18
% world total	46	35	31	17
JAPAN				
Billion dollars	20	111	4	24
% world total	4	11	10	23
World[2]				
Billion dollars	474	974	44	105

Notes
1. The EC figures do not include Ireland, Greece and Luxembourg. They *exclude* intra-EC fdi. Including intra-EC fdi gives an outward stock of US$ 203 billion (39 per cent) in 1980 and US$ 492 billion in 1988 (44 per cent), and raises the flow to US$ 22 billion (47 per cent) in 1980–84 and US$ 59 billion (47 per cent) in 1985–89.
2. This figure excludes intra-EC fdi.

Source
UNCTC, *Directory of Transnational Corporations*, New York, UNCTC, 1991.

especially as so little has been written on this subject. Lawrence Franko published a pioneering study of *The European Multinationals* in 1976.[3] Since then, there have been several studies on individual countries, but these have often been written in national languages. This volume brings together some leading historians of European multinationals, and presents their work, sometimes for the first time, in English.

As in the earlier Franko study, the United Kingdom is not specifically included in this book. In a contemporary perspective, this looks odd, for during the 1980s the British economy became ever-more closely integrated into that of the rest of the EC, despite the wishes of the government of Margaret Thatcher, which continued to look towards the United States as a model and mentor. The United Kingdom has also been traditionally the largest foreign direct investor in Europe, so to exclude it from a study of European multinationals represents in some respects a considerable distortion. Yet the process of convergence between Britain and the rest of Europe has been slow. In terms of ownership patterns, corporate govern-ance structures, the degree of cross-shareholding between firms and the role of capital markets, British business has been, and remains, closer to the American than the continental European 'model'. In addition, the history of British-based multinationals has already been explored.[4] This book, as a result, concentrates on continental European multinationals, but the focus is not restricted to members of the EC in 1992.

This book is organized in two parts. Part 1 discusses the long-run evolution of mne based in a number of European countries. The Part 2 offers case studies of individual multinationals and sectors. The purposes of the remainder of this chap-ter are to place these essays in a wider context; to highlight points of international comparison; and to offer guidance on the many topics which could not be included in this book. It includes a brief review of the main theories currently used to explain the development of mne. There is then a discussion of the dimensions of continental European multinational investment over the last century and a half. Subsequently, the evidence offered by our authors is assessed to explore whether there has been a distinctive continental European 'model' of mne.

Concepts and models

It would be superfluous to duplicate the many literature surveys and textbooks which discuss the modern theory of the mne. The following paragraphs confine themselves to a brief survey of the main concepts used in the following chapters which, it is hoped, will be of use to non-specialists.

The most wide-ranging attempt to explain the phenomenon of the mne is the 'eclectic paradigm' developed by Dunning.[5] This is not an economic theory as such, but a framework which draws on a number of – in some cases competing – economic theories. It develops the basic premise that a multinational needs an advantage to produce and compete successfully in an unfamiliar foreign environ-ment. It is suggested that multinationals have *ownership* advantages, which can derive from, among other things, technology and marketing skills, and managerial and financial factors. Multinationals utilize their ownership advantages by estab-lishing production in sites that are attractive owing to their *location* advantages. Locational factors can include trade barriers, relative labour costs, host govern-ment policies, and market size and growth. Multinationals retain control over their networks of assets because of the *internalization* advantages of doing so. Transac-tions costs theorists suggest that the market is costly and inefficient for undertak-ing certain types of transactions, so companies may reject the market and organize these transactions within the firm itself. Internalization advantages arise from the greater ease with which an integrated firm is able to appropriate a full return on its ownership of distinctive assets.

Internalization theorists such as Casson have sometimes claimed that internali-zation can alone explain the growth of multinationals, and that 'ownership advantages' are not a necessary part of the explanation.[6] The fundamental insight of transactions costs theorists is that markets have inherent imperfections, primarily because of the problems of bounded rationality and a tendency to opportunism. Multinationals use hierarchy as a way of eliminating market transaction costs. Internalization is concerned with intermediate product markets, and most applications of transaction cost theory of the multinational have explored the internationalization of one particular type of input – knowledge.[7]

Both the eclectic paradigm and internalization theory help to explain the development of multinationals over time. As Cantwell has recently argued,[8] the two approaches are not so much rivals as seeking to answer different questions. Internalization theory endeavours to explain why mnes in general displace intermediate product markets in general. To explain why one firm displaces another, or why the firms of one nationality grow at the expense of others, then the concept of ownership advantage needs to be introduced. Business historians can use the concept of ownership advantages to explain, in part, national differences in the level of outward fdi, and in the industries in which it occurs.

A second observation about both the eclectic model and internalization is that they were developed to explain multinationals of the classic United States type, which predominated in the world economy between the 1950s and 1970s. These were very large firms, which had gone abroad after growing to a large size in their domestic market. Generally, their subsidiaries were wholly-owned and they were fully integrated. Their ownership advantages lay in proprietary know-how and specific managerial competences, and their international expansion could be readily explained in terms of the internalization of knowledge. The problem, as Hennart has recently cogently argued,[9] was that this was only one type of fdi. The models need adjustment and modification when faced with different time periods, and the experience of countries beyond the United States.

The work of two other authors, A.D. Chandler and Michael Porter, is reflected in this book. Both are American and based at Harvard Business School. Neither is explicitly concerned with the mne, yet their writings are full of rich insights of use to those studying international business.

Chandler has fundamentally shaped modern thought on the historical development of large business corporations. His methodology is that of a historian, reaching conclusions from detailed empirical research, though his explanation for the existence and growth of firms has obvious parallels with the transactions cost literature. In *Strategy and Structure* and *The Visible Hand* he related the rise of large corporations in the United States from the late 19th century to changes in markets and technologies. He argued that the development of professional managerial hierarchies within a multi-divisional corporate structure was critical to success in the mass production and science-based industries which began to appear in the decades before the First World War.[10]

In *Scale and Scope*, Chandler applied his model beyond the United States in a comparative study between that country, the United Kingdom and Germany.[11] He showed that the firms that succeeded in the new industries of the late 19th century were those that developed their organizational capabilities by making a threefold – and interrelated – investment in manufacturing, marketing and management. These firms were thereby enabled to exploit the full potential of economies of scale and scope, and to become first-movers in their industries. According to Chandler, British firms were disadvantaged in this process because of the persistence of family or personal capitalism, which meant that the growth of modern managerial hierarchies was stunted. German business, however, did make the threefold investments, notably in such industries as chemicals and machines. A distinctive form of 'cooperative managerial capitalism' developed, shaped by a very different environment from the United States, especially in regard to the lack of an anti-trust legislation and closer contacts between banks and industrial enterprises.

The Chandlerian perspective deepens and broadens our understanding of the 'ownership advantages' possessed by firms. His work highlights the critical importance of management and organization in generating such advantages. For instance, the importance of research and development in the growth of German chemical and other industries has always been known, but Chandler shows that the fundamental competitive advantages of the German firms lay not in their research expertise, but in the professional managerial hierarchies which made possible the investment in research in the first place.[12] At a more general level, Chandler provides a framework for understanding why the United Kingdom's industrial performance progressively deteriorated from the late 19th century, and why Germany became the industrial powerhouse of Europe. In other words, a framework for understanding sources of national competitive advantage.

Given their concern with specific firms and industries at specific moments in time, it is not surprising that business historians have been attracted to the recent work of Porter, an economist who has all but abandoned conventional economics. In *The Competitive Advantage of Nations*, Porter sought to explain variations in national competitiveness between countries and, more specifically, why some countries are competitive in some industries and not in others.[13]

According to Porter, despite the globalization of business in recent decades, the fundamental influences on competitiveness remain in the national economy. His main concept is the 'diamond' of competitive advantage. The 'diamond' represents the interaction of four determinants. These are the ability of economies and industries to create factor advantages by upgrading investment, research and skills; the quality of home market demand; the proximity of competent suppliers and 'clustering' by closely-related industries; and the intensity of local competition, which for Porter is probably the single most important factor.

The Porter 'diamond' is not a model of mne. Indeed, he can be criticized for barely noticing the importance of multinationals in the world economy. However, it is extremely useful in identifying many of the explanatory variables behind country-specific explanations of the changing, or unchanging, pattern of international production by firms.[14] The essays of this volume reveal strong historical continuities in multinational investments of the countries concerned and several authors make explicit use of Porter to explain these patterns.

The large literature on the theories of the mne and international production, on the growth of the modern industrial enterprise and of international competitive advantage, have provided powerful analytical tools for those seeking to explain the historical development of multinationals. There remains no consensus between the different approaches, which is not surprising given the complexity of the subject. As Dunning has recently observed, 'because the motives in foreign production are so different, no one model can hope to explain equally well each and every kind of multinational activity'.[15]

Dimensions over time

Over 20 years ago, in a pioneering study, Mira Wilkins traced the evolution of American multinationals from the 19th century.[16] She discovered that, as early as the 1850s, Colts, an American gun manufacturer, had built a factory in Britain, but it had failed. The first sustained American multinational investment had come in the following decade, when Singer Sewing Machines built a factory in Glasgow, Scotland, in 1867. During the following decades many more American companies, especially in the machinery and food sectors, built foreign factories. By 1914 Wilkins showed that over 40 American companies, including such well-known names as Coca Cola, Gillette, Heinz, Quaker Oats and Ford had factories overseas.

The first students of the history of non-American multinationals had believed that it had been very limited before the First World War. Writing in 1974, John Stopford could only locate 14 British manufacturing multinationals active before 1914.[17] As a result, he focused his analysis on why British manufacturers had been apparently slower than their American equivalents to become multinationals. In fact this proved not to be the case. New research established that the first British manufacturing multinationals had developed at least in the 1880s. By 1914 there were probably hundreds of British-owned multinationals operating factories in other countries of Europe, the United States and the settler countries of the Empire. The pioneer British multinationals included some of that country's largest companies, such as Lever Brothers (soap), J. & P. Coats (cotton thread) and Dunlop (tyres).[18]

Coincidental with this research on the history of British multinational manufacturers, economists re-examined the structure of foreign investment flows in the 19th century, and made a startling discovery. It had long been believed that these capital flows had been overwhelmingly portfolio in nature. Svedberg, and later Dunning, re-examined the evidence, and concluded that, in fact, a high percentage of international investment in this period had been direct – involving management control as well as capital investment. Dunning suggested that the stock of accumulated fdi in 1914 amounted to $14 302 million, or over a third of total world foreign investment.[19] This had particularly dramatic implications for the United Kingdom, the world's largest foreign investor before 1914. This investment had long been cast as portfolio and *rentier* in nature: much of it was now recast as direct.

The problem remained of the corporate form taken by this now substantial amount of 19th century fdi, for it seemed strange that historians had overlooked the existence of extremely large numbers of 'multinationals' active in the world economy. It became apparent that this early fdi had taken a variety of institutional forms, some of which had subsequently disappeared from the world economy. Wilkins's development of the 'free-standing' concept was a particularly important advance. She demonstrated the existence before 1914 of thousands of British-owned 'free-standing' companies, which did not grow out of domestic operations, but were formed to manage a single investment. Typically these ventures maintained a tiny office in Britain which supervised the overseas business. This form was quite unlike American multinationals, but it was, she claimed, the 'typical' form of pre-1914 British fdi. And it was the activities of these companies that made Britain, according to Dunning, by far the world's largest direct investor.[20]

It has long been evident that the nations of continental Europe were also important sources of fdi before the First World War,[21] and the following chapters add rich new empirical data, but they also point to the considerable difficulties in quantifying the extent of this multinational activity, especially as few countries collected data on fdi before the Second World War. The Dunning estimates given in Table 1.2 must, as a result, be regarded as, at best, orders of magnitude.

The historical estimates for individual European economies in Table 1.2 must in particular be regarded with caution. The 1914 figures look particularly suspect. Wilkins has suggested that the Dunning estimate for German fdi in that year 'greatly underestimated the activities of German business abroad'.[22] She would raise the level of German direct investment to higher than that of France. Schröter, in Chapter 2 of this book, suggests that a figure of US$2600 million rather than US$1500 million is more plausible. The figures for 1938, and indeed later, must be treated with almost equal caution. The Swiss estimates are particularly dubious for, as Schröter observes in Chapter 3, the first official figures on fdi for that country were published only in 1985.

Remarkably little is known, also, about French fdi before the Second World War, and this makes any statistical estimate of dubious worth. It is generally agreed that France was the world's second largest capital exporter before 1914, but it has been assumed that much of this was portfolio. However, it is not unlikely that if the structure of French investment was re-examined in the same way as has been done for the British case, a different picture might emerge. Wilkins found a 'surprising number' of French direct investments in the United States before 1914.[23] It is known that there was considerable French business activity in Tsarist Russia.[24] There were even quite a number of American-style French multinationals in operation even before the First World War, including Michelin, St Gobain and Schneider, and their activities expanded in the inter-war years.[25] Moreover, French fdi in this period might be even higher if – as some have suggested, a substantial amount of Belgian and Swiss fdi was in fact French, routed through foreign countries for tax evasion purposes.

Table 1.2   Estimated stock of accumulated fdi by country of origin, 1914–83 (current US$)

	1914 $m	%	1938 $m	%	1960 $bn	%	1973 $bn	%	1983 $bn	%
Western Europe										
Germany	1 500	10.5	350	1.3	0.8	1.2	11.9	5.7	40.3	7.0
France	1 750	12.2	2 500	9.5	4.1	6.2	8.8	4.2	29.9	5.2
Belgium ⎫					1.3	2.0	2.2	1.0	6.7	1.2
Italy ⎪					1.1	1.7	3.2	1.5	9.8	1.7
Netherlands ⎬	1 250	8.7	3 500	13.3	7.0	10.6	15.8	7.5	36.5	6.4
Sweden ⎪					0.4	0.6	3.0	1.4	10.1	1.8
Switzerland ⎭					2.3	3.5	7.2	3.4	19.8	3.5
Sub-Total	4 500	31.4	6 350	24.1	17.0	25.8	52.1	24.7	153.1	26.8
Other										
UK	6 500	45.5	10 500	39.8	10.8	16.3	26.9	12.8	95.4	16.7
USA	2 652	18.5	7 300	27.7	31.9	48.3	101.3	48.1	227.0	39.6
Japan	200	0.1	750	2.8	0.5	0.8	10.3	4.9	32.2	5.6
Other	630	4.5	1450	5.6	5.9	8.8	19.9	9.5	65.1	11.3
Total	14 482	100.0	26 350	100.0	66.1	100.0	210.5	100.0	572.8	100.0

Source
Calculated from Dunning, John H., *Explaining International Production*, London, 1988, Table 3:1, p. 74. This is a revised version of a table first published in Dunning, John H., 'Changes in the level and structure of International Production: The Last One Hundred Years', in Casson, Mark (ed.), *The Growth of International Business*, London, 1983, p. 87. (See Table 1.5 (p. 22) for data for 1967 and 1988.)

From the 1950s, more reliable statistical data begins to be available for many European countries, but national differences in definitions and methodology continue to cause endless problems in comparative exercises on fdi. A few examples will illustrate the scale of the problem. Some countries, like Belgium and Luxembourg, France, Sweden and Spain, do not keep statistics on the aggregate stock of fdi. Stock levels have to be calculated, which is no easy matter. Usually the stock is calculated on the basis of outflow of capital for fdi. This method raises two questions at once: what is 'outflow' and what is 'fdi'? The latter problem is dealt with below. The former can be illustrated by the example of Sweden. In most cases, Swedish fdi is calculated according to the sums of fdi approved by Sveriges Riksbank, the central and state bank. Sveriges Riksbank publishes this data in its annual report. However, the stock of Swedish fdi cannot really be calculated on this basis. In order to obtain freedom of manoeuvre, Swedish multinationals traditionally applied for much more foreign exchange than they really needed. Therefore, the actual outflow of capital for direct investment has to be used. This approach has been used by Krägenau, among others, with the effect that his calculation of the stock of Swedish fdi is considerably lower than Dunning's.[26]

However Krägenau's data is also flawed. The real stock is about 30 per cent higher, though lower than Dunning's, because only the outflow of capital, and not foreign reinvestment, is taken into account. This issue is explored in Chapter 5. This problem exists for all countries whose data are based on unadjusted outflow statistics, of which France is a prominent example. The stock of Swedish and French fdi, therefore, is considerably higher than given in the figures, but we have no reliable estimates on the order of magnitude. Switzerland, Japan and Germany also publish statistics based on outflow of capital, which suggests that their stock of fdi is higher than published estimates, but to a different extent. The Japanese data, which are based on approved outflow and, since 1980, on notification by investors, is particularly dubious.

Germany maintains three different statistical series on fdi. These figures are comparable to each other, which suggests that they are quite reliable and relatively near to the real ones. The first series is based on the outflow of capital, to which an estimate on reinvestment is added. This statistic is published by Deutsche Bundesbank. The second series is a special set of statistics ('K-Statistiken') which is published by the Ministry of Economics. It is rather more precise than that of the Bundesbank, which is published as soon as possible. It is based on the announcements of investors, a procedure which is compulsory for sums above DM 0.5 million. Thirdly, figures on the stock of fdi published in the *Statistical Yearbook* are based on balance sheet assessments. Though they should show the actual value, the German business practice of hiding reserves means that the real value of German fdi is higher than that published.

Detailed statistics based on the balance sheet method are available from the USA, the UK, the Netherlands and Canada, but even here there are differences in approach. All agree that ownership and control are the most prominent characteristics of fdi, but there is disagreement as to how much ownership is needed for control. In the USA and in Canada, an investment is regarded as direct if at least 10 per cent of the equity is owned. British companies need 20 per cent for a direct investment. Germany suggests a level of 25 per cent, while classification of Dutch investment is up to the investor.[27] The upshot is that the published stock data for British and German direct investment, for example, is underestimated if American definitions are used.

There are numerous other statistical pitfalls. Data published in statistical yearbooks are often corrected in later years. Data are constantly distorted by exchange rate factors. Firms often choose the conversion rates they use in their published reports. International comparisons are plagued by exchange rate problems.[28] Direct investment via holding companies seated abroad represents a special difficulty. Statistically their fdi in third countries (and even in the first one!) goes into the stock of their nominal home economy. This is very important for countries such as Switzerland, but even in the case of Germany it can make a real difference.

Given these problems, Table 1.2 is most useful for suggesting movements, the aggregate picture over time of European fdi. It is evident that such investment was substantial in the late 19th and early 20th centuries. By the eve of the First World

War, Western Europe, as a whole, probably accounted for over three-quarters of world fdi, and even excluding Britain it accounted for almost one-third. Thereafter, Western Europe's relative importance declined to a low of around 37 per cent in 1973, a trend which was greatly influenced by both the low level of German fdi after 1914, and by the United Kingdom's replacement by the United States as the world's largest multinational investor after the Second World War. From the early 1970s, however, Western Europe's relative importance as a home economy moved upwards again.

The period from the 1960s, and especially from the mid-1970s, has seen a rapid acceleration of world direct investment. Figure 1.1 shows the growth of stock of selected leading industrial economies.[29] The United States remained by far the most important individual direct investor, although the EC as a whole had reached parity with it by the late 1980s (see above, p. 4). Equally striking was the growth of both British and Japanese foreign direct investment. The British case was extraordinary. From the 1950s slow economic growth, caused by low productivity levels and declining competitiveness, resulted in the relative economic decline of the United Kingdom. Porter, like Chandler, selected it as his 'worst case' of

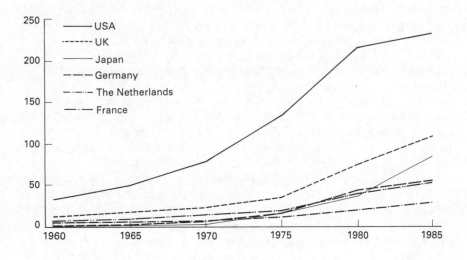

Sources
Dunning, J.H., *Explaining International Production*, London 1988, Table 3:1; Krägenau, H., *Internationale Direktinvestitionen*, vols 1975–87.

Figure 1.1   Growth of stock of fdi of leading industrial economies, 1960–85, US$ billion (current prices)

failure.[30] Yet the United Kingdom was one of the world's most dynamic direct investors, remaining, in the early 1990s, the largest source of inward direct investment into the United States. Clearly, the size of a country's outward direct investment is not an automatic indicator of its national 'competitiveness'.

Figure 1.2 focuses on the six leading continental European direct foreign investors. Perhaps the most striking feature of this graph is that the Netherlands was the leading foreign direct investor until the late 1970s. The Dutch importance was a function of its long-established position as home to some of the world's leading multinationals, including Shell, Unilever and Philips, the first two remarkable examples of Anglo-Dutch collaboration in business. Nevertheless it was striking that Dutch fdi doubled between 1975 and 1985, the same rate of expansion as Germany. Germany's direct investment was, given the size of her economy, notably modest, until it 'took off' after 1975. By 1990 Germany held the largest stock of continental direct investment, ahead of the Netherlands and France.

There were, and remain, wide divergences in the sectoral distribution of the outward direct investment of different continental economies. Before the 1960s, there is almost no aggregate data on this matter, although plenty of anecdotal and qualitative evidence that, for example, Swedish fdi was heavily concentrated in engineering, and German in the chemical and electrical industries. From the 1960s

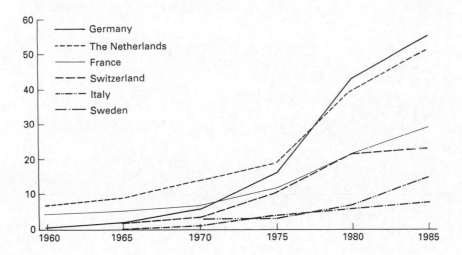

Sources
As Figure 1.1.

Figure 1.2   Growth of stock of fdi of selected continental European economies, 1960–85, US$ billion (current prices)

data starts to be available for some countries which illustrate the national differences more scientifically. For example, the Clegg estimates of outward direct
foreign production (DFP) by Sweden, Germany and the United Kingdom for 1965
confirm that the Swedes were heavily concentrated in mechanical, instrument and
electrical engineering, while the Germans were particularly active in transportation equipment, electrical engineering and chemicals. In contrast, the British pos-

*Table 1.3   The sectoral composition of the stock of outward direct investment of
France, Germany, Netherlands, the UK and the US, c.1975 and
c.1988 (% share)*

	Sectors		
	Primary	Secondary	Tertiary
France			
1975	22.1	38.2	39.7
1988	15.0	36.6	48.3
Germany[1]			
1976	4.5	48.3	47.2
1988	2.8	43.4	53.7
Netherlands			
1975	46.8	38.6	14.6
1987	36.4	24.7	38.8
United Kingdom[2]			
1987	26.9	34.4	38.6
United States[3]			
1975	26.4	45.0	28.6
1989	16.7	40.9	42.3

Notes
1. This analysis is not compatible with data released by the Deutsche Bundesbank, which gives for
    1976 a much higher (60.8) and for 1987 a much lower (34.3) percentage for the secondary sector
    in both cases, viewed from the German investor and viewed from the foreign investment too.
    Deutsche Bundesbank, Stand der Direktinvestitionen Ende 1976, in Monatsberichte, vol. 31,
    April 1979, p. 28; Die Kapitalverflechtung der Unternehmen mit dem Ausland – Stand Ende
    1987 und aktuelle Entwicklung, in Monatsberichte, vol. 41, April 1987, p. 27.
2. Data for primary and secondary sectors are not available for the 1970s.
3. The vertically-integrated petroleum industry is included in the primary sector in 1975. In 1989,
    only the extractive portions of the industry is included in the primary sector, with processing
    included in the secondary sector and marketing and distribution in the tertiary sector.

Source
UNCTC, *Directory of Transnational Corporations*, New York, UNCTC, 1991.

sessed little dfp in engineering or equipment, but nearly one-half in food, drink and tobacco, a sector in which there was almost no Swedish investment.[31]

Table 1.3 explores this issue further by providing a breakdown of their outward fdi by primary, secondary and tertiary sectors for France, Germany and the Netherlands, together with the United Kingdom and the United States, for two benchmark years, 1975 and 1988.

Table 1.3 confirms the sharp differences in the sectoral distribution of the fdi between different European economies, more especially in the extent of their involvement in the primary and tertiary sectors. Germany had, according to all sources, little fdi in the primary sector. In contrast, the Netherlands had almost half of its fdi in that sector in 1975 – a reflection of the importance of Shell in that country – while it was under-represented in the tertiary sector. In the following decade, this pattern was considerably modified, as the Netherlands was affected by worldwide trends such as the growth of services and the policies in many developing countries of taking control over their national resources. French fdi was more balanced between sectors, and quite similar to that of the United States in that respect. All three Western European economies showed a marked decline between 1975 and the late 1980s of the percentage share in the primary sector, some decline in secondary, and a rise in tertiary investment.

To summarize, the statistical data on the long-term historical levels of fdi by most continental European countries remains very deficient. The available estimates suggest that Western Europe (excluding the United Kingdom) has throughout the 20th century accounted for around one-quarter of world fdi, and probably more before the First World War. Including the United Kingdom, Europe was by far the largest home for fdi before the Second World War, and a near-second to the United States in the three post-war decades. The EC's return to parity with the United States at the end of the 1980s can be regarded as, in some senses, a return to a long-run historical trend. The novel feature of the 1980s, perhaps, was the growing integration of the European economies, which had previously displayed considerable divergences. Finally, the importance of fdi from small European states, such as the Netherlands and Switzerland, must be emphasized. In Europe, there has been no clear correlation between the size of a country's GNP and its propensity to engage in fdi.

The continental model

It was Franko, in his 1976 study, who first suggested that a distinctive Continental European 'model' of mne might exist – distinctive from Anglo-Saxon and Japanese varieties. He did see a number of similarities between Continental multinationals and American ones – they were large size, based in similar industries, and had a research and development orientation. However, continental firms appeared to have a much greater export propensity than American firms, greater product diversity in their overseas operations, and they also appeared to avoid the high political profiles of Anglo-Saxon and Japanese multinationals. 'Continental multi-national enterprise', Franko concluded, 'had its own special personality and history'.[32]

It is now widely accepted that the Franko study suffered from major methodological flaws. It was based on the history of the 85 continental European firms included in the Fortune '200' list of the largest companies in the world in 1970. Beginning with these large firms active in 1970, Franko traced their history backwards. The result was that the sample was heavily biased towards large and long-surviving enterprises. This problem, and the fact that the book contains a large number of factual errors, clearly rendered its generalizations unsafe. Some of his observations – such as that European multinational activity typically originated from large firms – have been demonstrated to be quite wrong.

Subsequently, the search for a Continental 'model' continued. Hertner and Jones, writing in 1986,[33] noted the disproportionate roles of some small European economies as homes of multinationals before the Second World War, and ascribed to the view that continental multinationals 'in certain vital respects grew, organised and behaved in different ways than American mnes'. They noted how some continental firms made their first multinational investments at an early stage of their corporate careers, and how banks and governments sometimes appeared to have played a considerable role in the growth of continental multinationals.

Wilkins explored this issue further. A starting point for her analysis, which the work of Porter would support, is the vital influence of the home economy on the pattern of multinational growth. Wilkins argued that the European nations and the United States differed in at least five important respects in the pre-First World War decades when the first multinationals appeared. These were the size of domestic market; cultural and other heterogeneity at home; capital importing status; geographical location; and anti-trust law and traditions.[34]

What, then, do the essays in this volume add to debates on the existence of a continental 'model' of mne? To begin with, it needs to be observed that the data presented here on the chronology of their growth and on the reasons for that growth fit closely with established views on the history of mne .

The work of Dunning and others has made it clear that multinational growth occurred in distinct phases: in the 50 years before the First World War; during the 1920s; and, with an ever-growing dynamic, since the 1960s. All the studies presented here conform broadly with this pattern. There are no cases of substantial fdi from the 1930s to the 1960s, for example. The premature attempts at fdi into the Silesian zinc industry of Vieille Montagne in the 1850s, mentioned in Chapter 10, failed. The existing facilities for transport and communication, which according to Chandler and Wilkins represented a precondition for multinationals, did not allow such management-directed foreign investment at that stage.[35] It seems to be a case parallel to that of Colts with its direct investment in Britain mentioned above (p. 8). However, history always presents exceptions, and the direct investments of Siemens in Russia and Britain in the 1850s were a success. The reason for this was that these investments were run in a traditionally family-based way, by brothers of the founder living where the investment was situated. In general, however, continental multinationals were in line with the pulse of world development.

It is clear, too, that the main economic models of the multinational are fully applicable to the continental experience. The eclectic paradigm and the internalization theory are used by many authors in this volume. The concept of ownership advantages has been particularly utilized in explaining fdi. R. & D. is identified as particularly important for the growth of Swiss, Swedish and German multinationals, and this factor is also evident in the case studies of Pirelli and Gevaert in Chapters 9 and 10, though it seems that R. & D. was of only secondary importance in the Dutch case. Several chapters show in detail how multinationals acquired advantages in the respective countries by internalization. Location factors, too, emerge as decisive. The access to wider markets was an important reason for investment by firms from small states, but in larger ones also. In many cases, this access was a precondition for economies of scale, both in the home country and abroad. Besides the improvement of technology, organizational capabilities were vital. In this point, Swedish, Swiss and German multinationals again show similarities, and there are some French and Dutch cases as well. Multinationals active in machinery, automobiles and chemicals were based not only on advanced technology, but on constant after-sales service. In the case of Pirelli, reconstruction of the internal organization was an important factor in its success. Some German and Swiss multinationals, such as Bertelsmann and Nestlé, had their greatest ownership advantages concentrated in their organizational capabilities. It seems that the same applied to Dutch and German direct investment in insurance. Though more research is needed, evidence from this volume suggests that the development of such organizational capabilities, which are stressed by Chandler as the core issue for international competition, were more important than lowering transaction costs by internalization.[36]

Research and development has been identified as the most important advantage for Swedish, German and Swiss multinationals, though the concept of R. & D. is a very imprecise one. Basic research is different from applied research, which in its turn differs from development. Basic research was carried out especially by very large multinationals in the chemical and electrical sectors. Pirelli and Gaevert provide examples for applied research, while medium-sized machine-building multinationals, such as Grohe from Germany, confined themselves to development in most cases. However, the role of multinationals in the transfer of technology receives little attention in the following chapters and here, as in many issues, there remains more questions than answers.

Many of the following chapters suggest strong continuities in the history of continental mne. In his discussion of German multinationals, Schröter points to the unbroken continuities of core competence in certain sectors of industry, which survived the many traumas which afflicted Germany in the 20th century. There were strong continuities, also, in the geographical destination of German fdi, with the exception of a period in the 1950s and early 1960s, when German firms became briefly interested in production in various Latin American and Asian states. A similar theme of continuity pervades the Swedish case discussed in Chapter 5. Olsson observes that three-quarters of Sweden's total manufacturing abroad today is carried out by Swedish companies that were already multi-nationals three decades ago. Leading European multinational companies of today, such as Pirelli or Unilever, began their multinational careers even before the First World War. Continuity can be observed even in the Norwegian case. Although most Norwegian firms only began multinational expansion in the 1970s and 1980s, those firms had a long standing tradition of competitiveness within Norway.

Yet, major discontinuities can also be observed, and in particular the effects of the two world wars. It is evident that continental multinationals were more considerably affected by the world wars than their American or even British equivalents. The pattern of German international business activity, especially its very low level from the First World War to the 1960s, can only be understood by reference to the double sequestration of German fdis in 1918 and 1945, to the general German economic conditions of the 1920s stemming from the war, and to the nature of the political regime in power between 1933 and 1945.

The impact of the wars is visible on other European countries as well. Firms based in nations involved in the hostilities had to transfer headquarters abroad and struggle to maintain their firms in one piece. In some instances, even firms from countries on 'the winning side' lost. For example, Chapter 4 describes how the Dutch firm Océ-van der Grinten lost its crucial American patent rights because of the Second World War. Even the firms of the European 'neutrals' were not left untouched by the events of the wars. While the First World War gave a boost to Swiss fdi through providing new opportunities, the Second World War had a more restrictive impact, and Swiss fdi did not begin a strong upwards movement again until the 1960s. However, it is possible that service sector firms based in neutral countries achieved more benefits from the Second World War. Swiss and Swedish banks, for example, were active in recycling gold and other valuables looted from occupied countries by the Nazis.

In a long-term perspective, it is noteworthy that the majority of continental multinationals relied not so much on low price mass products but on quality. As Wilkins notes, the nature of home markets was a critical factor here which made the European and American experience different. Porter has also pointed to the function of the home market and suggested that, for instance, in Switzerland, Sweden and Germany, the home demand for quality products is a strong incentive for firms to manufacture ever higher-quality commodities. In contrast, the relative low incomes, combined with the low standards, of British consumers provides contemporary British-based multinationals with little incentive to produce quality goods.[37]

Many contributors to this book suggest that a broad general education combined with special focus on technical learning have been crucial for the growth of the multinationals of their countries. This has served a two-fold function. It led to high technical standards in demand, while providing not only engineers, but also a supply of blue-collar workers motivated to care for the quality of product they worked with. For the majority of continental multinationals, this advantage was more important than paying low wages. Again, there is a contrast between the Continent and the United Kingdom. Even in the 1980s, only one-quarter of British managers had higher education, with rather more possessing a professional qualification in accountancy, while British firms traditionally offered little training to their workers.[38] This may explain the British obsession with short-term financial goals, and their great difficulty in competing in most industries requiring levels of technical skill or quality, with prominent exceptions such as pharmaceuticals.

Wilkins considered that continental multinationals displayed a greater tendency to collaborate or co-operate than American ones, and that public policy towards cartels was one explanatory factor. Certainly up to 1939, the European multinationals studied here were extensively involved in international cartels. Gevaert and Pirelli, for example, took part in cartelization. This type of co-operation was even more widespread in the electrical and, especially, the chemical industries. However, American and British multinationals were also active in cartels in this era. After 1945, far less cartelization occurred, surviving mainly in service industries such as airlines and telecommunications, where again American firms were also involved in agreements. In most cases, cartels came to be closely monitored by the European states or by the EC.

The late 1980s saw new forms of co-operation, focused not so much on production, but on marketing and R. & D. Most remarkably, not only medium-sized multinationals such as Océ-van der Grinten participated, but the largest continental multinationals took the lead in the process. Nestlé collaborated with Coca Cola, Siemens with IBM, while Daimler-Benz even courted – though probably in vain – the biggest conglomerate in the world, the Mitsubishi group. There were differences between countries in the extent of their participation in international alliances. Some of the most notable cross-border alliances and mergers within Europe involved Swedish firms: examples included Renault and Volvo, Saab and GM of Europe, and Asea-Brown Boveri, a merger of the Swedish firm with Brown Boveri & Cie of Switzerland. Conversely, Italian firms, as mentioned at the end of Chapter 9, appeared slow to forge such alliances. Again there was nothing uniquely continental about these developments, which formed part of worldwide attempts to gain competitive advantage through strategic alliances and coalitions, a trend in which Japanese and American multinationals were also very active participants.[39]

Nevertheless, the history of continental multinationals does reveal a tendency to inter-firm and inter-industry links which is distinctive from the Anglo-Saxon experience. The pre-1914 strategy of German electrotechnical producers in creating *'Unternehmergeschäft'*, discussed in Chapter 7, provides one important illustration. Again, half of the largest 20 Swedish multinational manufacturing firms in the mid-1980s were part of Sweden's largest industrial group owned by the Wallenberg family. In Sweden, as well as Germany and Switzerland, banks played an important role in fdi, although this role was usually passive rather than active, and the chapters on other countries do not highlight banks as being of special importance.

Like Japanese multinationals, and unlike Anglo-American ones, it seems that, historically, continental multinationals have expanded abroad through greenfield investment rather than acquisition. As always, exceptions can be noted. The two Dutch predecessor firms to Unilever, for example, grew internationally in the opening decades of the 20th century by a series of cross-border acquisitions. Nevertheless, most continental European countries have possessed less active capital markets than those of the United States and the United Kingdom. As a result, their firms had less experience of acquisitions and disposals via the capital markets, and very much less experience of the kind of hostile takeover bids seen in Britain and America since the 1960s. Continental firms were also much less interested than Anglo-American ones in purely financially-driven takeovers, generally preferring to make an international acquisition only if there was an industrial logic to the case.

Undoubtedly, since the 1960s, this tradition has been modified. Like Japanese multinationals, continental companies have become more willing to acquire foreign firms, although the generalization about industrial logic taking precedence over financial engineering probably still stands. Chapter 5 describes the rapid international growth of Electrolux through foreign acquisitions during the 1980s, and German and other continental enterprises have also been far more active in foreign acquisition in the last decade. This period also saw the arrival of the first 'hostile', or contested, takeover bids, of which the struggle between Banque Indosuez and Carlo De Benedetti for Société Générale de Belgique was one of the first. The failed Pirelli takeover of Continental, mentioned in Chapter 9, was another illustration. In the late 1980s and early 1990s continental firms played a prominent role in restructuring parts of the European food industry through a series of large-scale acquisitions, some of them hostile.[40] Nevertheless, Table 1.4 suggests that there are still differences between European countries in their interest in foreign acquisitions.

Too much weight cannot be given to data for a single year, especially as single large acquisitions can make a substantial difference. Nevertheless, any ranking of foreign acquisitions by European companies over the 1980s is likely to have featured the United Kingdom at the top and Germany near the bottom. As Schröter notes, German firms were well-satisfied with the competitive 'diamond' of their home economy, and not convinced that foreign 'diamonds' could provide them with the resources to maintain the quality of production to which they were committed. In contrast, many British companies in the 1980s were deeply unhappy about the quality of their 'diamond', and sought to escape from it by buying foreign companies, hoping thereby to acquire some competitive advantage.[41]

It is noteworthy that the direct influence of governments receives little attention by our authors. It is well-known that tariffs provided a major stimulus to fdi from the late 19th century, but in contrast from the Second World War it was the decline of protectionism through GATT and the EC which provided the greater incentive to multinational expansion. It seems unlikely that the home government influence on multinationals was very great. Sweden and France, among others, had ex-

Table 1.4   Ratio of domestic investment to foreign acquisitions, 1988

Country	Domestic Investment[1] US$m	Foreign Acquisitions US$m	Ratio
UK	128 969	44 530	2.9
Switzerland	38 970	8 907	4.4
Sweden	30 978	2 134	14.5
France	176 525	11 162	15.8
Belgium	21 280	827	25.7
Norway	23 704	720	32.9
Netherlands	43 098	1 276	33.8
Germany	231 096	2 752	84.0

Note
1.   Calculated from gross domestic fixed capital formation, ignoring foreign investment undertaken through existing foreign operations and R. & D. expenditure.

Source
KPMG Peat Marwick McLintock, *Deal Watch*, 1989.

change controls for decades after the Second World War, but this was no hindrance to fdi, as demand for foreign exchange by this purpose was met by state banks in those countries.

There are, then, some distinctive features of continental multinationals which suggest that a continental 'model' is discernable, although only in the most general of senses. Moreover, the search for such a model must not obscure the considerable differences between continental countries in their propensity to engage in fdi, and in the industries in which it occurred. These differences are intriguing, but difficult to explain. Why were some small European economies, for example, much more active in multinational investment than others? Why was France less active as a direct investor than the size of its economy would suggest?

The different national propensities to engage in fdi are clear from the historical record discussed earlier in this chapter. One means to demonstrate the point statistically is to relate the stock of outward fdi to a country's gross domestic product (GDP). Table 1.5 does this for the two benchmark years of 1967 and 1988, using data on stock levels which is directly comparable to that given in Table 1.2.

Table 1.5 highlights the importance of outward direct investment to the Dutch, Swiss and Swedish economies. In 1967 the stock of Dutch direct investment represented an extraordinary one-third of that country's GDP. While the Dutch ratio grew only marginally thereafter, the rapid growth in importance over the 20-year period of Swiss and Swedish fdi is evident. Of the larger European economies, the growing importance of fdi in relation to GDP is striking in the cases of

Table 1.5   Stock of outward fdi of selected countries compared to GDP, 1967 and 1988

	1967		1988	
	Stock ($bn)	% of GDP	Stock ($bn)	% of GDP
Western Europe[1]				
Germany	3.0	1.6	103.4	8.6
France	6.0	7.0	56.2	5.9
Italy	2.1	2.8	39.9	4.8
Netherlands	11.0	33.1	77.5	34.0
Sweden	1.7	5.7	26.2	16.4
Switzerland	2.5	10.0	44.1	23.9
Other				
UK	15.8	14.5	183.6	26.1
USA	56.6	7.1	345.4	7.1
Japan	1.5	0.9	110.8	3.9
Total[2]	112.3	4.0	1140.5	6.7

Notes
1.   Separate data for Belgium is not available in this source.
2.   This is total world outward direct investment. The percentage is calculated against world GDP.

Source
Calculated from Dunning, John H., 'International Direct Investment Patterns in the 1990s' (mimeo, 1991).

Germany and the United Kingdom, while France was unusual in experiencing the reverse trend.

Various answers have been suggested to explain variations between countries in their enthusiasm for fdi. There is an obvious historical link between the possession of an overseas empire and large fdi. The Netherlands and Britain are striking examples. Conversely, it is argued in Chapter 6 that Norway's lack of a colonial heritage was an influence on that country's late development as a multinational investor. However, both Switzerland and Sweden lacked colonial experience. Capital exporting status was important too, though Sweden in the late-19th century was a capital-importing economy, as was the United States. A country's position as a capital exporter may have influenced the type of fdi undertaken. For example, some large continental capital exporters before 1914, such as the Netherlands and Switzerland, possessed a considerable number of British-style free-standing companies. Chapter 4 discusses the Dutch versions of such firms.

*Table 1.6   Distribution of Europe's 500 largest companies by country, 1990
(ranked according to sales)*

Country	Total number of companies among 500	(Thereof: manufacturing companies)	Number per million inhabitants
Denmark	4	(–)	0.78
Norway	4	(1)	0.96
Belgium	11	(5)	1.11
Spain	12	(–)	0.31
Finland	14	(9)	2.84
Netherlands	21	(7)	1.43
Italy	24	(9)	0.42
Switzerland	32	(9)	4.83
Sweden	33	(19)	3.93
France	72	(27)	1.29
Germany	103	(42)	1.68
UK	130	(41)	2.28

Source
Based on *Growth and Integration in a Nordic Perspective*, Helsinki, 1990, p. 56.

It is evident, also, that concentration levels within home economies, and especially, the relative importance of large companies within the economy influenced the propensity to engage in fdi. Table 1.6 examines the distribution of Europe's 500 largest companies by principal country in 1990.

It was the European countries whose economies were highly concentrated, such as the UK, Switzerland and Sweden, that were prominent in direct investment, while those in which the role of small and medium-sized companies was important have been less active internationally. These traditional structures are changing to some extent as the European economies converge. The industrial structure of the Finnish economy, for example, assumed a greater similarity to the Swedish in the 1980s, as Table 1.6 indicates, and this has been accompanied by very rapid internationalization, much faster than Denmark and Norway.[42]

As emphasised above (pp. 13–15), the sectors of industry out of which fdi emerged varied widely between continental countries, at least before the 1980s, and even today. While Dutch investment was heavily engaged in raw materials, German and Swedish were not. In Switzerland and the Netherlands food represented an important part of fdi, but not at all in Belgium, Sweden, Norway and Germany. Reputed national specialities did not influence their multinational patterns. While French and Italian food is famous, there were no competitors to Burger King or

MacDonald's from these countries. In contrast, a significant share of British fdi was located in the food industry despite the notorious nature of the British cuisine. The toy and musical industries of Germany were the biggest in the world before the Second World War, but they made few attempts to become multinational. In toys, it was Lego of Denmark which become the leading European multinational, while in musical instruments Yamaha of Japan or Steinway of the United States are prominent. It may have been difficult for an established small and medium-sized industry from the Continent to create multinational activities.

This raises the more general question of the relationship between multinationals and its home economy. While there are differences between each nation's favourite investment sectors, another feature was noticeable in all states. In the period when fdi became substantial before 1914, only a small proportion of it was associated with the 'leading' sector in each economy. The list includes metallurgical and forest products in Sweden, in Norway also shipping, heavy and railways connected industries in Belgium and Germany, agriculture, trade and banking in the Netherlands, heavy industry and textiles in France, and textiles in Italy and Switzerland. In these countries, the bulk of fdi emerged from sectors, which before 1914, sometimes even before 1945, were second rank. This points towards a mechanism in which such new economic sectors, after having competed successfully with the old-established ones for funds, workers, political influence, and so on, were more prepared to invest abroad than their older counterparts. Of course the 'new industries' of the 'second industrialization' (notably chemicals and electrotechnicals) played an important role in this mechanism, as the cases of Germany and Switzerland in particular show. But Sweden, with its multinationals in machinery, Norway, the case of Pirelli, or the whole automobile sector, provide evidence beyond the 'new industries'. Unilever, too, had little in common with Dutch agriculture. As always, this generalization cannot be pushed too far. Before 1914, much Swiss direct investment was in textiles and the food sectors, while in Belgium there was international activity in heavy industry: all leading sectors during the industrialization of their respective countries. However, few of these multinationals survived after the First World War, the largest exception being Nestlé.

The following chapters suggest that competition was an important element for the growth of multinationals in the long run. Competition, first on the home market, later at home and abroad, led to international advantages. This was the case in the French automobile industry as well as in Swedish machine building. With the exception of Pirelli, we find these patterns in the chemical industry, electrotechnics, the transport sector, etc. Royal Dutch, Unilever, Asea, LM Ericsson, Gevaert and many more had during their first years strong local, and later international, competitors. This regularity suggests that Porter's approach, to look for *clustered* competitive industries in order to explain national advantages, can be used to illustrate not only national enterprise, as he did, but multinational firms as well.

However, it has already been argued that Porter gave too little attention to mne, and his book represents, in many ways, a traditional approach to economic problems, because it is based on the nation state. In many cases, continental multinationals have progressed beyond that stage. The largest industrial companies (those with global sales of more than US$ 1 billion in 1989) now produce about one-third of their output from outside their home countries, but multinationals from the smaller European economies have much higher ratios. By 1975 Dutch multinationals already employed 75 per cent of their workforce abroad. In the long run, this situation has very important repercussions, because home country advantages become less significant for such firms and their national identity becomes blurred. Multinationals can, by establishing different parts of their value-added activities in different countries, access a range of other national 'diamonds'. By the 1980s important headquarters functions such as R. & D. were being geographically dispersed within many multinationals, and no longer confined to their home countries. Some of the largest continental multinationals, again especially from the smaller nations, located at least one-third of their R. & D. abroad. Examples included Nestlé, SKF and Philips. New organizational structures evolved as a result. The earlier mother–daughter relationships between parent company and foreign subsidiaries were replaced with looser structures with decision-making taking place in a number of centres in a number of countries.[43]

In the light of such developments, it is not surprising that the authors of the chapters in this book on multinationals from small European nations all suggest that the national approach to the question of multinationals based in those countries had reached its limits by the 1980s. Unilever, Asea-Brown Boveri, and other large companies appear to represent a new kind of multinational enterprise, which will emerge more and more on the Continent. They are transnational or, rather, European firms. Yet would the most highly-skilled jobs within such a multinational, and decision-making over crucial and sensitive issues, really come to be distributed without regard to the home economy of the corporation?[44] Arguably, the 1990s will see the national identities of European-based global corporations become increasingly distinct, or at least replaced by a wider European identity, but in 1993 the case is not yet proven.

Notes

1. For the former view, see Dunning, J.H., *American Investments in British Manufacturing Industry*, London, 1958. For the critical view, see Servan-Schreiber, J.J., *The American Challenge*, New York, 1968; Vernon, Raymond, *Storm over the Multinationals*, Cambridge, Mass, 1977.
2. Franko, Lawrence G., 'Global Corporate Competition: Is The Large American Firm an Endangered Species?', *Business Horizons*, November-December 1991; 'Why the American Challenge Ran out of Steam', *Financial Times*, 24 January 1992.
3. Franko, Lawrence G., *The European Multinationals*, London, 1976.
4. Stopford, J.M. 'The Origins of British-based Multinational Manufacturing Enterprises', *Business History Review*, 1974, XLVIII, 3, pp. 303–45; Nicholas, S., 'British Multinational Investment before 1939', *Journal of European Economic History*, 1982, II, 3, pp. 605–30; Nicholas, S. 'Agency Contracts, Institutional Modes, and the Transition to Foreign Direct Investment by British Manufacturing Multinationals before 1939', *Journal of Economic History*, 1983, 43, pp. 675–86; Jones, G., 'The Expansion of British Multinational Manufacturing 1890-1939', in A.

Okochi and T. Inoue (eds), *Overseas Business Activities*, Tokyo, 1984, pp. 125–53; Jones, G. (ed.), *British Multinationals: Origins, Management and Performance*, Aldershot, 1986.

5. For recent excellent interpretative surveys of the theoretical literature, see Cantwell, John, 'A Survey of Theories of International Production', and Hennart, Jean-François, 'The Transaction Cost Theory of The Multinational Enterprise', both in Christos N. Pitelis and Roger Sugden (eds) *The Nature of the Transnational Firm*, London, 1991. Dunnings eclectic paradigm has been explored in many of his publications. He offers a survey and assessment in 'The eclectic paradigm of international production: a personal perspective', in Pitelis and Sugden, *The Nature of the Transnational Firm*.

6. Casson, M.C., *The Firm and The Market*, Oxford, 1987.

7. Hennart, idem note 5, pp. 85–7.

8. Cantwell, idem note 5, pp. 47–8.

9. Hennart, Jean-François, 'Is Internalization Theory a General Theory of the MNE? The Case of "Free-Standing" Firms' (mimeo, 1991).

10. Chandler, A.D., *Strategy and Structure*, Cambridge, Mass, 1962; *The Visible Hand*, Cambridge, Mass, 1977.

11. Chandler, A.D., *Scale and Scope*, Cambridge, Mass, 1990.

12. *Ibid.*, pp. 496–8.

13. Porter, Michael, *The Competitive Advantage of Nations*, London, 1990.

14. Dunning, John H., 'Dunning on Porter: Reshaping the Diamond of Competitive Advantage' (mimeo, 1990).

15. Dunning, J.H., 'The Eclectic Paradigm of International Production', in Pitelis and Sugden, idem note 5, p. 133.

16. Wilkins, Mira, *The Emergence of Multinational Enterprise*, Cambridge, Mass, 1970.

17. Stopford, idem note 4.

18. Jones, (ed.), *British Multinationals*, idem note 4.

19. Svedberg, P., 'The Portfolio – Direct Composition of Private Foreign Investment in 1914 Revisited', *Economic Journal*, 1978, LXXCX, pp. 763–77; Dunning, J.H., *Explaining International Production*, London, 1988, p. 74. See Table 1.2 in this chapter.

20. Wilkins, Mira, 'Defining a Firm: History and Theory', in Peter Hertner and Geoffrey Jones (eds), *Multinationals: Theory and History*, Aldershot, 1986; Wilkins, Mira 'The Free-Standing Company, 1870–1914: An Important Type of British Foreign Direct Investment', *Economic History Review*, 1988, XLI, 12, pp. 259–85.

21. An excellent introduction to the literature on early continental multinationals is Wilkins, Mira, 'European and North American Multinationals, 1870–1914: Comparisons and Contrasts', in R.P.T. Davenport-Hines and Geoffrey Jones (eds), *The End of Insularity*, London, 1988, pp. 20–8. There is also an exhaustive study of continental multinational investment in the United States in Wilkins, Mira, *The History of Foreign Investment in the United States to 1914*, Cambridge, Mass, 1989. There is a large case study literature of individual firms and countries. This can be approached in various edited volumes, including Hertner and Jones, idem note 20; Teichova, Alice, Lévy-Leboyer, Maurice and Nussbaum, Helga (eds), *Multinational Enterprise in Historical Perspective*, Cambridge, 1986; and Teichova, Alice, Lévy-Leboyer, Maurice and Nussbaum, Helga (eds), *Historical Studies in International Corporate Business*, Cambridge, 1989. There is a survey of research on American, British, French, and German multinational history by, respectively, Mira Wilkins, Geoffrey Jones, Jean Pierre Daviet and Peter Hertner in 'La Storia delle Imprese Multinazionali', *Passato e Presente*, 1987, 13, pp. 15–33.

22. Wilkins, Mira, 'European and North American Multinationals', idem note 21, p. 38, note 23. See also pp. 13–14.

23. Wilkins, Mira, *History*, idem note 21, pp. 167–9.

24. See, for example, Crisp, Olga, *Studies in the Russian Economy before 1914*, London, 1976; Girault, R., *Emprunts russes et Investissements français en Russie, 1887–1914*, Paris, 1973; McKay, John, 'The House of Rothschild (Paris) as a Multinational Industrial Enterprise: 1875–1914', in Alice Teichova *et al.*, *Multinational Enterprise*, idem note 21.

25. See, for example, Beaud, C., 'The Interests of the Union Européenne in Central Europe', and Bussière, Eric, 'The Interests of the Banque de l'Union Parisienne in Czechoslovakia, Hungary and the Balkans, 1919–30', in Alice Teichova and P.L. Cottrell, (eds), *International Business and Central Europe, 1918–1939*, Leicester, 1983. There is a valuable discussion of Rhône-Poulenc's inter-war acquisition of May & Baker, the British speciality chemical firm, in Slinn, Judy, *A History of May & Baker 1834–1984*, Cambridge, 1984, pp. 97 ff.

26. Krägenau, H., *Internationale Direktinvestitionen*, vols 1976–85.
27. In fact, the same applies ultimately to Germany also. The 25 per cent level is suggested as a rule, but the investor decides how his operation should be counted.
28. The calculations below utilize the rates given in Schwarzer, O., and Schneider, J., 'Europäische Wechselkurse seit 1913', in W. Fischer (ed.), *Handbuch der Europäischen Wirtschafts-und Sozialgeschichte*, Stuttgart, 1987, pp. 1048–93.
29. The data for Figures 1.1 and 1.2 comes from Krägenau. This data has two main advantages. His statistics provide data for end-year of decades as well as five-years intervals. And, most important, he presents in his volumes the exact and ultimate sources for each of the tables, together with a short introduction on methodology. Furthermore, all data is in local currency, which gives an impression of a nation's economy and its fdi unaffected by exchange rates. However, Dunning's data is used when Krägenau presented no figures. All figures include intra-EC foreign direct investment.
30. Porter, idem note 13, pp. 482–507.
31. Clegg, Jeremy, *Multinational Enterprise and World Competition*, London, 1987, pp. 59–60. Direct foreign production is the value of output generated by foreign direct investment.
32. Franko, idem note 3, p. 21.
33. Hertner, Peter and Jones, Geoffrey, 'Multinationals: Theory and History', in Hertner and Jones, idem note 20, pp. 7–11.
34. Wilkins, 'European and North American Multinationals' idem note 21; Wilkins, Mira, 'The History of European Multinationals: A New Look', *The Journal of European Economic History*, 1986, 15.
35. Chandler, A., 'Technological and Organizational Underpinnings of Modern Industrial Multinational Enterprise: the Dynamics of Competitive Advantage', in Teichova, *et al.*, *Multinational Enterprise*, idem note 21, p. 31; Wilkins, 'European and North American Multinationals', idem note 21, p. 9.
36. Chandler, idem note 35, p. 52.
37. Porter, idem note 13, pp. 321–4, 345–8, 371–3, 499–501.
38. Handy, Charles, *et al.*, *Making Managers*, London, 1988, chapter 6; Barsoux, Jean-Louis and Lawrence, Peter, *The Challenge of British Management*, London, 1990, chapter 4.
39. Porter, Michael E. (ed.), *Competition in Global Industries*, Boston, Mass, 1986, chapters 10 and 11; Dunning, John H., *Explaining International Production*, London, 1988, chapter 13.
40. Examples included, in 1988, Nestlé's acquisition of Rowntree (UK) and Buitoni (Italy); in 1989, the acquisition by BSN (France) of Smiths Crisps, Walkers Crisps, Jacobs (all UK) and Saiwa (Italy) and the acquisition by Südzucker (Germany) of Raffinerie Tirlemont (Belgium); and in 1990, the acquisition by Freia (Norway) of Marabou (Sweden).
41. Hamill, Jim, 'British Acquisitions in the United States', *National Westminster Bank Quarterly Review*, August 1988.
42. *Growth and Integration in a Nordic Perspective*, Helsinki, 1990, pp. 53–4.
43. For examples of the geographical dispersion of research within Swedish multinationals, see Håkanson, Lars, 'International decentralization of R & D – the organizational challenges', in Christopher A. Bartlett, *et al.*, (eds), *Managing the Global Firm*, London, 1990. Also Dunning, John H., 'International Direct Investment Patterns in the 1990s' (mimeo, 1991).
44. For a view that the national identities of multinationals will remain important, see Franko, 'Global Corporate Competition' idem note 2. For the view that the national 'ownership' of multinationals is not of great significance in the contemporary world, see Reich, Robert B., 'Who is US?', *Harvard Business Review*, January–February 1990.

2 Continuity and change: German multinationals since 1850

Harm G. Schröter

Germany belongs to the handful of economies which pioneered foreign direct investment (fdi) in the nineteenth century.[1] As early as 1855, Siemens manufactured in Russia and three years later in the United Kingdom, thus counting as one of the world's first multinational enterprises (mne). In the early 1990s, Germany is the largest home economy for mnes on the European Continent, and the fourth largest in the world, after the USA, the United Kingdom and Japan. However, Germany's prominence in international business was far from continuous. The country twice lost nearly all its fdi because of the two World Wars. However, despite such dramatic disruptions, there were remarkable similarities in both the geographical and industrial distribution of German fdi over a very long period. It is this mixture of continuity and change in the history of German fdi which makes its historical development so interesting, and a challenge to explain. In this chapter it is argued the concept of core competences, explored in Michael Porter's *Competitive Advantage of Nations,* needs to be utilized in any full explanation of German fdi over the long run, as well as more conventional theories of mne, such as Dunning's eclectic paradigm of international production.

In the following pages an overview is offered of German fdi and German mnes from the mid-nineteenth century until the present day. Reliable statistical data is available only from about 1960 onwards, which means that the history of the first 100 years of German fdi must be reconstructed from case studies and other anecdotal material. Exact data on how much was invested in a certain year by which branch of industry in a given country is at hand for the last 30 years only.[2]

Possibly the distinctive patterns of German fdi as well as mnes relies on the fact that Germany experienced industrialization later than the United Kingdom and the USA. This may have worked as an incentive to develop especially those branches that were connected with the second industrialization: electrotechnical, chemicals and machine building. According to Alfred D. Chandler, the precondition for success in the new industries was the development of core competitive advantages, especially 'organizational capabilities'.[3] Even in the 1990s the German economy remains based, to a great extent, on these branches. It is exactly here that the majority of Michael Porter's clusters are to be found, in which the nation's

28

competitive advantages are concentrated.[4] Furthermore, these are the sectors out of which the majority of fdi and the biggest mnes emerged – again representing continuity over the last 100 years. Last but not least, the concept of sectors gives us an idea why German fdi was historically relatively underdeveloped compared with that of the UK or the US.

German fdi before 1914

A considerable body of case study material on the early history of German multinationals has been published by Peter Hertner.[5] He stressed the chemical and the electrotechnical industries. The latter one was special, as it developed financial institutions to promote sales and assets abroad. For example, the biggest German fdi before the First World War was a holding company for electrical assets in South America (Deutsch-Ueberseeische Elektricitaets-Gesellschaft) with assets of US$ 73 million in 1914. Financial institutions such as Deutsche Bank, and insurance companies such as Allianz and Victoria, also undertook direct investment abroad. Especially after the turn of the century, even small and medium sized firms were engaged in fdi, mostly in nearby markets. For example, Dürkopp, a medium-sized firm producing sewing machines and bicycles and later automobiles, acquired two enterprises in Austria and one in France. Most German fdi was concentrated in Europe, but there was also a substantial portion in the United States.[6]

German fdi relied heavily on ownership advantages. Intensive R. & D. entailed sophistication in technology, safeguarded by patents and trade marks, which was exploited best by fdi. However, internalization was a path for growth particularly of the electrical industry. In a comparison with other nations, Mira Wilkins emphasized German salesmanship abroad.[7] It is shown by Peter Hertner in Chapter 7 of this book how ownership advantages and internalization were exploited in the strategies of the German electrical industry. However, there are many parallels in the chemical and other industries as well.

Before 1870 only a few instances of fdi can be identified, but, subsequently, direct investment accelerated. In 1914 German foreign investment (both portfolio and fdi) amounted to US$ 7.3 billion.[8] Dunning has estimated fdi at US$ 1.5 billion,[9] while other sources suggest it was considerably higher, around US$ 2.6 billion.[10] In that year, 153 producing units abroad from the chemical industry alone were traced.[11] More exact figures are given for the United States, which had attracted more German fdi than any other country. Mira Wilkins calculated that German fdi in the US amounted at the eve of the First World War to $ 300 million.[12] This capital was invested in 336 single enterprises, which were engaged in production (48 per cent), trade (29 per cent), transport (17 per cent) and other activities like banking, insurance, holdings, etc. (12 per cent).[13] It is clear that Germany was a major player in the world's fdi in 1914, representing at least 10.5 per cent of the total amount.[14]

German fdi 1914–1945

The First World War caused a deep cut into German fdi, as nearly all assets abroad were sequestrated. If German fdi stood at US $ 2.6 billion in 1914, it had been reduced by 85 per cent to US $ 0.4 billion by the end of 1922.[15] Of the 153 producing fdi of the chemical industry in 1914, only 24 were left in 1920. These were situated mostly in the Central European countries, which had not fought against Germany.[16] Unfortunately, those countries possessed stagnating and in most cases backward economies in this period.

Compared to the pre-First World War decades, German fdi played a smaller role in the interwar years. Dunning estimated German fdi in 1938 to be US $ 350 million only.[17] This represents a dramatic decline from his – or any other – estimate for 1914. The reasons for this decline are manifold. There was only a cautious resumption of German fdi in the interwar period, as businesses – having lost major assets – were reluctant to re-invest. Indeed, during the period of inflation between 1919 and 1924, there were widespread fears of foreign takeovers of companies inside Germany.[18] Economic realities imposed further limitations on fdi. In many industries, capacity was greater than demand and German enterprises were extremely short of capital. As a result, they tried to regain their share of the world market by exports, while engaging – as the work of Chandler has demonstrated – in various forms of business co-operation, notably cartelization.[19]

However, exports rarely provided the sort of long-term market stability which fdi produced. Hertner discusses in Chapter 7 of this book how electrotechnical firms responded to this problem on the Italian market. German firms faced a desire for security in foreign economic relations on the one hand, and an inability or unwillingness to invest abroad on the other. To a considerable extent, they attempted to resolve this problem by adopting substitutes for fdi. After some years, they succeeded in supporting their exports by international cartelization and by special long-term contracts.[20] On the whole, this strategy turned out to be quite successful in those particular markets in which Germany enjoyed considerable competitive advantages, but it failed in those markets where it counted as just a junior player.

Nevertheless, despite the involvement of German firms in cartels and long-term contracts, there was also a drive to re-establish fdi. Unfortunately, little research has been done on German fdi in the inter-war period. Alice Teichova and Peter Hertner have explored German business strategies in southeast Europe and in Italy respectively.[21] As a result, we now know more of German fdi in these areas than of investments in, for example, the Netherlands or the United Kingdom. Nevertheless, a rough overview of developments can be sketched out.

IG Farben, the huge German chemical company formed by a merger of eight firms in 1925,[22] was very reluctant to invest money in any foreign country, but right from its beginning it felt that in the United States it could not manage without fdi. Before the First World War there was relatively little production by German dyestuff enterprises in the USA, the most important assets were patents, trade marks and, last but not least, sales organizations. All this was taken over by the Federal government and sold to indigenous firms. Grasselli Chemical Co. acquired assets related to dyestuffs, and Sterling Products those related to pharmaceuticals. After the war, Bayer immediately approached these two firms, offering technical aid and a sales agreement. The American firms being in need of this technical help agreed.[23] Out of these first steps, IG Farben's fdi emerged quickly: General Aniline Works (1925, for dyestuffs), Winthrop (1926, for pharmaceuticals) and Agfa Ansco (1928, for photo products). Though they all sold IG Farben products as well, their main occupation lay in production. The relationship between these fdi and American competitors was on the whole characterized as friendly or even very good co-operation.[24]

The German chemical industry in the USA served as an exception in the interwar period. Only in that country was a substantial amount of reinvestment carried out. While before the war France, Britain and the USA each had about 30 German fdis producing chemical goods, the two European countries had three and four respectively in 1930, compared to 11 in the USA. On the whole, German fdi in the chemical industry was reduced by 50 per cent in 1930 compared to 1913.[25]

Not only the chemical industry, but all firms concentrated their fdi on Central Europe, and on those nations which had remained neutral during the war. Mannesmann with its production of tubes in interwar Czechoslovakia provides one example. Another was the attempt of Krupp, Vereinigte Stahlwerke and other steel producing firms to acquire Scandinavian iron ore mines, though with no great success, as the Germans were short of capital and special legislation in Norway and Sweden regulated foreign ownership of land.

The Continentale Linoleum Union, Zurich can serve as an example of the fdis of which little is known as they were not located in the major sectors and competitive clusters of the German economy. Like many other enterprises, the Deutsche Linoleum-Werke in Berlin had founded this firm as a holding company in Switzerland, in order to save turnover tax and to gain increased political security. The Berlin firm controlled factories in Sweden, Norway, Latvia, Holland (two), Belgium, Switzerland, Italy and Germany via the Swiss holding company. It is debatable whether this venture should be regarded as a German or a Swiss multinational, as the majority of shares of the Deutsche Linoleum-Werke were in the hands of the Swiss holding company. However the Germans owners of the Berlin firm which had founded the Zurich enterprise kept the majority of the equity of the Swiss holding company and, above all, decision-making remained in Berlin.[26]

Orenstein & Koppel, a machine builder, is another example of German fdi from medium-sized industry. In 1913 it produced in Pittsburgh (USA), Paris, Zurich, Vienna, Amsterdam, Johannesburg (South Africa), St Petersburg (Russia) and Madrid. After the First World War, only sites in the following towns were left: Zurich, Vienna, Amsterdam and Madrid. Others in Hungary, Czechoslovakia, Romania, Yugoslavia, Poland and Johannesburg were built anew or reacquired during the inter-war period.

Some restricting obligations of the peace treaty of Versailles in 1919, which ended the First World War, caused German firms to invest abroad in order to engage in military technical development. MAN acquired Landsverk in Sweden to build what was called 'special trucks' (tanks), while Krupp bought the majority of Bofors, the most famous Swedish armament firm for the same purpose. But all these steps, like other investments in Holland and Spain for the development of submarines etc., were not important economically. Their main task was R. & D., and when in the 1930s this could be done inside Germany at less cost, the specific fdi was sold as its purpose had run out.

During the Nazi period there was very little new investment abroad. All foreign exchange earned had to be handed over to the central bank and all plans for new fdi had to be approved officially. Several applications of private enterprises are known to have been turned down due to the lack of foreign exchange.[27] Only a few exceptions, like that of the joint venture of ICI and IG Farben in Trafford (UK) in the late 1930s, are known.

There was a substantial change during the Second World War. Again each side seized the others' assets. Much German fdi had been prepared for war, that is it was kept via holding companies in neutral countries, but all the legal proceedings and nearly all cloaking[28] turned out to be in vain. On the other hand, new firms were founded or taken over in occupied territories as a step towards building a *Grossraumwirtschaft*, or a large economic area dominated by Germany. The majority of the German acquisitions were of firms owned in central and southeast Europe, the takeovers in the west and the north of the Continent, for example, the French dyestuffs firms and Norsk Hydro by IG Farben, being special cases.[29] In the east many firms were put under the trusteeship of a German enterprise active in the same branch of industry. It was understood that those firms would be handed over to the trustee when the war was over, but because of the special circumstances of the war and the lack of a due legal procedure, these foreign firms cannot be counted as fdi.

There was a marked difference in behaviour between the old established private enterprises and the newly-founded state-owned ones. With the exception of Norsk Hydro, IG Farben was interested only in the dyestuffs sector, in spite of the firm's heavy engagement in other sectors as well. At Siemens it was laid down in an internal meeting that the special situation of the German occupation should not be exploited too much, as in the long run a policy of mutual understanding with firms in all states was preferred to short term acquisitions.[30] Though Siemens and IG Farben did take over several foreign enterprises, there was a significant contrast between them and the behaviour of the state-owned firms. The Hermann Goering-Werke, founded by the Nazis, was extremely greedy and powerful.[31] Such was its influence that it could forcibly acquire Alpine Montan, the Austrian subsidiary of the biggest German steel producer, Vereinigte Stahlwerke.

German fdi since the second World War

The cut into German fdi caused by the Second World War was even deeper than that of the First World War, as virtually nothing was left. Even in the neutral states, such as Switzerland and Sweden, all German assets were seized from the state where the investment was placed. In order to crush German fdi, the United States put pressure on those countries. Most of them gladly accepted this as a pretext.[32] Switzerland tried in vain to resist, as it was more afraid of losing its good reputation as a safe harbour for any capital, than it thought could be gained by expropriation.[33]

From 1952 onwards, the German government allowed fdi as an exception under specific circumstances, which focused on immediate earnings of foreign exchange.[34] Because of the beginning of the boom in the German economy, all restrictions were lifted step by step until 1956. Since then, up to the 1990s there have been no restrictions beyond the duty of a quite detailed registration.[35]

The socialist state, the GDR, founded in 1949 and dissolved in 1990, made very little fdi compared to its capitalist competitor, the FRG. However, several cases of fdi were publicly known. In most instances, these fdis focused on the transport sector, such as shipment facilities in the harbour of Hamburg with river connection into the GDR. Others were discovered only in 1991, two years after the breakdown of the GDR as a political system, because they were kept under cover. Recent research suggests that fdi by the GDR showed one distinctive difference from normal capitalist fdi. In most cases its task was not only to earn foreign exchange, but followed political purposes at the same time.[36] But as fdi of the GDR was small and no research has been undertaken, the following discussion of German fdi after the Second World War is confined to West German cases only.

During the 1950s, German industry focused on expansion mainly inside the country, and relied on exports to penetrate foreign markets. However, even at this stage German firms tried to re-establish close links with former partners abroad, including former affiliates, which had passed into the ownership of other companies. It seems that, similar to the situation after the First World War, in the majority of cases these contacts were appreciated. Out of them joint ventures grew, and later majority or total ownership was taken, in a process which lasted about until the early 1970s.[37]

However, certain German companies suffered long-term or permanent damage from the Second World War. For example, Bayer still cannot use its registered trade mark, the Bayer-cross, in the United States, and it was only in 1986 that the company recovered the right to use its own name in the world's largest market.[38] The Bayer-cross, together with Bayer brand Aspirin, had been acquired by Sterling Drug, which held the trade mark in the United States. Though Bayer USA had a turnover of $6 billion in 1990,[39] the company was better known by the name of its largest subsidiary, Miles Inc., or through its Alka-Seltzer brand.

The strong export propensity of German industry was maintained in the postwar period. Recent research has recalculated the levels of German exports and production abroad, and demonstrated that up until the late 1980s production was less than exports.[40] In comparison, by 1971 the turnover of US fdi was nearly four times greater than US exports, and the turnover of UK and Swiss fdi was more than twice their respective mother countries' exports.[41] Nevertheless, German fdi not

Table 2.1   Stock of German fdi, 1914–90 (current US $ million)

Year	Stock
1914	2 600
1938	350
1950	0
1955	100
1960	758
1965	2 074
1970	5 784
1975	16 027
1980	43 105
1985	55 354
1990	129 100

Sources
Deutsche Bundesbank, *Monatsberichte*; Dunning, J.H, *Explaining International Production*, London, 1988, Table 3.1, p. 74; Krägenau, H., *Internationale Direktinvestitionen*, 1975, 1977, 1982,1987; Schröter, H., 'Aussenwirtschaft im Boom: Direktinvestitionen bundesdeutscher Unternehmen im Ausland 1950–1975', in H. Kaelble (ed.), *Der Boom 1948–1973*, Berlin 1992, p 90, Table 2; Schröter, V., *Die deutsche Industrie auf dem Weltmarkt 1929 bis 1933*, Frankfurt, 1984, p. 118 ff.; *Die Zeit*, 16 August 1991.

only grew, but it grew at a faster rate than German exports. As a result, it will be only a matter of time before German exports will be smaller than production by German-owned fdi. Table 2.1, which is in line with the Dunning estimates,[42] shows the build up of the stock of German fdi after its near-obliteration after the Second World War.

Table 2.1 shows no even flow of fdi. While in the period from 1975–80, US$ 27 billion was added, the next five-year period showed an augmentation of only half that sum. Again the next five years experienced a boost of fdi, as US$ 72 billion was invested. But seen from the German investing company, these ups and downs did not exist. German firms made their accounts and their fdi in Deutsche Mark (DM) and not in US dollars. If the data in Table 2.1 are expressed in DM, we see the even and stable upswing shown in Figure 2.1. Expressed in DM, the German economy showed no signs of becoming tired of fdi during the period 1950 to 1990. The low growth rates between 1980 and 1985, when calculated on a US dollar basis, merely reflected periods of a strong dollar.[43]

As shown in Chapter 1, the stock of Dutch fdi remained larger than that of Germany until the 1970s, but the following decade brought an important change. Between 1985 and 1990 German fdi rose two and a half times. Though Dutch fdi

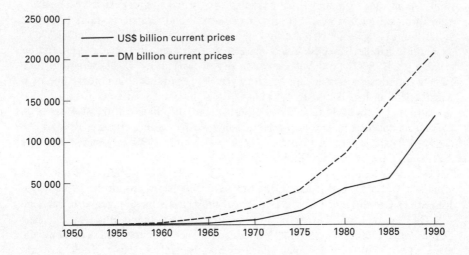

Sources
Krägenau, H., *Internationale Direktinvestitionen*, vols 1975–1987; Statistical Yearbooks of Germany.

Figure 2.1   Stock of German fdi, 1950–90 (in US$ billion and DM billion)

was also dynamic, if calculated in US dollars,[44] its aggregate amount was clearly overtaken by Germany.[45]

Within this overall picture, there were differences between sectors in their propensity to engage in fdi, although once more different statistics suggest different pictures. As indicated in the previous chapter (see Table 1.3 and notes thereon), the data generated by the Deutsche Bundesbank suggests that the secondary sector accounted for around 60 per cent of German fdi in the mid-1970s, or considerably more than its 50 or so per cent share of GNP, although its share fell considerably thereafter. The UNCTC data suggests that the secondary sector already accounted for less than a half of German fdi in the mid-1970s. Both data sources agree, however, that German fdi in the primary sector has been, and remains, small.

Clusters of competitive sectors and fdi

Within industry, some sectors were leaders in fdi. These sectors were heavily export-orientated, and competed on the world market. In the case of Germany, competitive advantages are closely connected with both exports and fdi. According to Michael Porter, writing about the contemporary period, 'perhaps the most dominant cluster (of competitive advantage) is in the chemical field, where German firms are leaders in a vast array of chemical and related products'.[46] It was exactly from this sector that the first substantial fdi came after the Second World War. For example, Hoechst Industries Ltd was founded in Canada as a holding company in 1952, the first year in which any fdi was allowed, as a stepping stone for the American continent. In the same year Bayer founded Quimicas Unidas in Mexico, and in Brazil it bought back its former subsidiary Alliança Commerciale de Anilinas.[47] From that time onwards until today the chemical industry has been the most important industrial foreign direct investor from Germany. In 1961[48] it stood for 18.0 per cent, in 1975 for 19.1 per cent and in 1990, as is shown in Table 2.2, for 15.6 per cent of all German fdi.[49]

Germany's leading companies in chemicals, BASF (often refered to as 'Badische'), Bayer, and Hoechst, re-emerged at the beginning of the 1950s when IG Farben was dissolved by the Allies. All these firms have engaged in massive fdi. They not only sell, but produce more abroad than at home. But, as in the case of the Netherlands or Switzerland,[50] many small and medium-sized firms show the same pattern. For Germany, companies such as Henkel, Schering, Beiersdorf and others provide more examples in the chemical industry. For instance, 60.4 per cent of Beiersdorf's turnover was sold abroad in 1990, while two-thirds of its workforce of 18 980 was employed outside Germany.[51]

Table 2.2   Stock of German fdi by industrial sector, 1990 (current US $ billion)

Sector	Stock	%
Trade	25.3	19.6
Banking and insurance	23.2	18.0
Chemical industry	20.1	15.6
Holding companies	9.2	7.1
Electrical industry	8.9	6.9
Automobiles	7.9	6.1
Machine building	5.0	3.9
Housing	3.3	2.5
Mining	2.9	2.2
Other industries	11.9	9.2
Other sectors	11.4	8.9
Total	129.1	100.0

Source
Calculated from *Die Zeit*, 16 August 1991.

'German firms lack national competitive advantage in service industries of almost all types.'[52] This statement from Michael Porter carries considerable truth, but there are exceptions. During the 1950s and 1960s banks and insurance companies were not very active in fdi, but since then this situation has changed. Allianz, an insurance company, became the largest in Europe and collected US $ 6.4 billion of premiums in 1985. It now possesses a substantial amount of fdi, including Allianz of America Inc. and Riunione Adriatica di Sicurita, the second biggest insurance company in Italy. However, the pioneer role in fdi was performed by Victoria, a competitor. This company grew big when it applied in Germany the British innovation of small life insurance contracts sold on a mass market. Before 1914, it founded several foreign subsidiaries, mainly in Central and East Europe. Victoria was a slow but steady mover. It rebuilt its fdi twice, after the two World Wars. Meanwhile, since 1990 German insurance companies have been attracted to new opportunities in Eastern Europe. One example of this new trend was the new investment of Aachen und Münchener in the Fireman's Union of Czechoslovakia.[53]

German multinational banking has been better researched than multinational insurance. The first major fdi in banking was made by the Oppenheim Bank, when it founded the Internationale Bank in Luxembourg as a free-standing company in 1856.[54] However Deutsche Bank has historically been the most prominent German multinational bank. It was founded in 1870 with the purpose of aiding German industry abroad. Before 1914, Deutsche Bank had substantial fdi, but very little in the inter-war period and for a long time after the Second World War, as explained by Tilly in Chapter 8 of this book. In the 1980s, however, Deutsche Bank invested abroad as part of a comprehensive strategy of aggressive expansion.[55] Acquisitions in Italy and in Spain were followed by the takeover of the British merchant bank Morgan Grenfell, a major strategic step, which made Deutsche Bank the largest asset managing bank in the EC.[56] This acquisition was the result of Deutsche Bank's determination to acquire new types of expertise which it lacked. As Hilmar Kopper of the managing board of Deutsche Bank explained: 'The international merchant banker thinks, speaks and acts anglosaxon. For us we have to accept this culture, integrate it as a multinational element, let it unfold itself and use it'.[57]

For most of the 1970s and 1980s, fdi by German banks and insurance companies was more reactive than proactive. The purpose was not so much to offer their services to foreign customers as to serve their domestic customers abroad. For this purpose, the insurance company Victoria in 1979 founded a joint venture called International Network of Insurance, which aimed to insure all assets of companies, including their fdi, worldwide.[58] But in the early 1990s, there were signs of more aggressive business strategies. Deutsche Bank, for example, was active in the Pacific Rim and Japan, and tried actively to encourage German firms to undertake fdi in this dynamic region.[59]

Table 2.2 shows that a significant proportion of the stock of German fdi in 1990 took the form of holding companies. Switzerland and Luxembourg, in particular, have been used as a base for German holding companies, and this partly explains the importance of these countries as recipients of German fdi, as shown in Table

2.3, below. However, the business activities of these holding companies are so diverse that further analysis is not practical.

The unimportance of mining in German fdi is striking, especially as it includes oil. Historically German enterprise has been weak in the oil sector, although before the First World War the Deutsche Bank owned oilfields in Romania and distribution facilities throughout Europe. These were lost after the war, and subsequently foreign multinationals exercised a predominant influence on the German domestic market. After the Second World War the oil industry was thought to be of strategic importance, and German firms active in it received special aid from the government. Fdi in the petroleum sector reached 5.9 per cent of the German total in 1975. However government policy changed when the United Kingdom started to export oil, as dependence on politically unreliable sources was not felt so strongly any more. As subsidies diminished, so did fdi from this sector. The German petroleum enterprises, such as Veba, Wintershall and DEA, all have substantial non-oil interests or are otherwise part of a bigger firm. DEA, for example, is a subsidiary of Rheinisch-Westfälische Elektrizitätswerke (RWE). Coal and potash mining firms, in spite of their large size, have also undertaken little fdi, although this might now be changing. In 1991 RWE made a large investment in coal mining in the USA.

The second biggest industrial investor listed in Table 2.2 is the electrical industry, which includes electronics and telecommunication. Surprisingly, Michael Porter did not find a cluster which forms competitive advantages here, but this is implausible. The sector is now headed by Bosch and Siemens, the latter being the biggest European company in this field.[60] Before the First World War German competence in this field was undisputed, as at that time Siemens and AEG counted as two of the four biggest firms in this field in the world, and 46 per cent of world exports were in German hands. Chandler has portrayed the German electrotechnical industry as one of the fields where organizational capabilities were created and international advantages emerged.[61] The companies invested abroad heavily.[62] Though there are no exact figures, this sector almost certainly headed the German list of fdi before the First World War. After 1918, most foreign assets were lost and relatively little reinvestment was carried out. This situation changed once more after the Second World War. In 1961 this sector accounted for 13.7 per cent of total fdi, and in 1975 10.5 per cent. The 6.9 per cent share in 1990 shown in Table 2.2 reflects the substantial growth in fdi from the tertiary sector rather than a decline in the absolute importance of the international investments of German electrical industry. In 1990 Siemens, for example, was a global corporation with some 210 plants outside Germany.[63]

The next largest sector of industrial fdi in 1990 was automobiles. The German transport sector was identified by Porter as a cluster with international competitive advantages,[64] but as neither shipbuilding nor the aviation industry were especially big or internationally advanced, it is evident that the real competitive strength was in automobiles. This industry has a peculiar history. While the chemical and the electrotechnical firms have maintained their advantages since they acquired them in the late 19th century, the automobile industry's experience was different. Daimler-Benz (Mercedes) was a first-mover in the world industry, while the Diesel engine was also invented in Germany, yet the international performance of the German automobile industry was not outstanding before the 1950s, and there was little multinational activity. Subsequently, however, international competitive advantages developed alongside a mass market at home. From the early 1950s onwards, Volkswagen and Daimler-Benz invested abroad, while BMW and MAN, a truck maker, followed later. In 1961, 7.5 per cent and in 1975, 6.7 per cent of German fdi came from the automobile sector, which seems to be relatively stable in its share of fdi.

In recent years, the strategies of Daimler-Benz and Volkswagen have developed differently. The former invested heavily in electronics and aeronautics. AEG (electronics) and most of the whole German aircraft industry was acquired, though there was little investment abroad in these sectors by Daimler-Benz. The strategic intent was to forge the company into an enterprise for traffic and technology. Volkswagen preferred a more traditional route, acquiring Audi in Germany and Seat in Spain, before taking over the workforce which had built the Trabant car in East Germany.[65] The Czech car manufacturer Skoda was also purchased. The German company argued that East Europe would become, in the near future, a substantial market, especially for small cars, and that Skoda's brand name and distribution network would be major assets. With its policy of concentration on scale effects, Volkswagen raised its share of the West European car market from 11.1 per cent in 1975 (third place) to become the market leader with 15.4 per cent in 1990.[66]

Germany retains a tradition of being proud of its machine building industry, which in some sectors is justified. There are very many small and medium-sized firms in this industry, while only two big ones exist (MAN and Mannesmann). Its attitude toward fdi has been as dispersed as the industry itself. While some firms have invested heavily, others have concentrated on an export strategy. Counted together, however, there is a substantial amount of fdi from machine building. Its share of all German fdi amounted in 1961 to 6.2 per cent and in 1975 to 7.4 per cent, but it diminished substantially in 1990. During the 1980s the industry lost much of its competitive edge because it was slow to adopt modern electronics. Though this has been reversed, the industry has recovered only part of the lost ground.

Not only in the machine building sector but from all others, many medium-sized firms have established themselves as mnes since the 1970s. The case of Friedrich Grohe AG illustrates this. Grohe, founded in 1936, established itself during the 1980s as Europe's largest tap, mixer and shower manufacturer and the world's number one in exports of these goods.[67] However, for an mne the company was still medium sized with a total turnover of US $ 0.4 billion in 1990 and a workforce of 3 415 employees. In spite of this, Grohe in that year operated ten wholly-owned subsidiaries abroad, including companies in the USA, Japan and in the UK, and it co-operated with 56 distributors worldwide.

Table 2.2 mentions 'other sectors'. In spite of Porter's remark on German services, this sector includes big mnes in this industry. During the 1980s, Otto Versand of Hamburg became the world's largest mail order company after heavy investments in the USA.[68] Another company, Bertelsmann AG, was also one of the biggest media concerns, after it had acquired Bantam Books, New York, in 1977.[69] The takeover of Doubleday & Co. and the music division of Radio Corporation of America (RCA) (both in 1986) confirmed the leading role of Bertelsmann. The company, founded as a publishing house in 1835, was revived after the Second World War, as it had been closed by the Nazis. It started its fdi from 1962 onwards. However, the two enterprises mentioned do not contrast with Porter's verdict on German services, as the core competitiveness of these two extremely successful companies was concentrated in their organizational capabilities. [70]

What is missing in the number of sectors engaged in fdi are, besides extractive industries, new growth industries such as microelectronics. Probably it is not just fdi that is lacking in Germany in these fields, but core competences of clusters of firms which have developed competitive advantages.[71] However, not all new growth industries are missing in fdi. In biotechnology, for instance, little research and even less production is carried out in Germany, due to tight environmental laws. The picture of Germany lagging behind in this industry is right, but it does not apply to German mnes. For instance, all of the three big chemical firms, BASF, Bayer and Hoechst concentrated their R. & D. and the production facilities abroad, especially in the USA.[72] In cases like this one, Porter's approach is misleading, as the activities of these companies statistically count into the US list of achievements only.

Geographical destination of German fdi

The destination of German fdi traditionally focused from the beginning on industrialized states, and to a certain degree on those which were in the process of industrialization, such as certain states in Latin America. Very little was placed in developing countries, which lacked a substantial home market or a large number of inhabitants. As there was very little fdi in raw materials and in agriculture, deposits, arable land, climate and similar advantages were not decisive influences on destination.

During the first period of rebuilding after the Second World War, however, the strategy was different. Rolf Sammet, chairman of the board of Hoechst, explained in 1970: 'for the German chemical industry it is vital, to widen its field of activities abroad. It should foster the industrial development of young industrial states, to enlist them as trading partners of tomorrow'.[73] This meant fdi in industrializing countries, a strategy which was widespread at that time. By allocating fdi there, direct confrontation with competitors in their home market was circumvented – for some time. Additionally, a stronghold in important markets of the future could be obtained. In pursuit of such policy, considerable fdi was placed in large or populous states, such as Argentina, Brazil, India and Iran. In 1961, 38.3 per cent of all fdi was situated in developing countries. Though, from a German mental perspective, being situated far away, Brazil alone had attracted more than three times as much of German fdi as neighbouring France.[74]

However, the assumptions proved to be wrong, as the development of the newcomers slowed down. This caused a redirection of German fdi towards Europe, as shown in Table 2.3. Within a decade, the share of developing countries

Table 2.3   Geographical destination of German fdi, 1961–90 (% of total stock)

State	1961[1]	1972[1]	1980	1990
EC	14.0	35.5	33.9	40.9
France	5.3	9.9	10.3	8.5
UK	1.2	2.6	3.9	6.2
The Netherlands	2.3	5.0	5.6	5.6
Spain	2.6	6.0	3.6	5.1
Belgium[2]	2.8	10.9	3.7	4.8
Italy	3.5	3.7	3.0	4.6
Luxembourg[2]	n.a.	n.a.	6.0	3.9
Others in EC	0.0	3.4	1.4	2.2
Switzerland	12.1	14.1	5.5	4.1
Austria	3.6	4.6	3.6	3.5
USA	8.7	8.1	21.6	27.1
Brazil	16.6	6.8	6.7	4.6
Canada	11.9	8.0	2.7	2.7
Japan	n.a.	0.5	1.2	1.9
All others	29.3	16.4	21.2	15.2
Total (%)	100.0	100.0	100.0	100.0
Total (US$ billion)	0.961	8,312	43,105	129,100

Notes
1.   Figures for 1960 and 1970 are not available.
2.   For 1961 and 1972 Luxembourg's figure is included in the Belgian one.

Source
Calculated from: Deutsche Bundesbank, *Beilage zu Statistische Beihefte zu den Monatsberichten der Deutschen Bundesbank, Reihe 3: Zahlungsbilanzstatistik*, no. 3, March 1987, p. 21; *Die Zeit*, 16 August 1991; Schröter, H., 'Aussenwirtschaft im Boom: Direktinvestitionen bundesdeutscher Unternehmen im Ausland 1950–1975', in H. Kaelble (ed.), *Der Boom 1948–1973*, Berlin, 1992, p. 99, Table 7.

was halved to 20.8 per cent, while that of Europe jumped from 38.5 per cent in 1961 to 60.5 per cent in 1972.[75] This figure was down again to 43.4 per cent in 1985.[76] Whether the upswing to the 1990 figures[77] is a reflection of a movement in preparation of the single European home market or not, can only be guessed. But this guess seems to be a good one; if we have a look at the figures for EC member states, they read for 1985, 30.7 per cent and for 1990, 40.9 per cent. Within these five years a considerable concentration on EC states was implemented. Their share grew by 10.2 points while that of non-member states was reduced from 12.7 per cent to about 8–9 per cent.

During the early 1990s, large-scale fdi in the former socialist states in the East seems unlikely, in spite of political encouragement from the respective governments. Many issues remain to be dealt with, including the implementation of Western style administration and justice, the improvement of infrastructure, and last but not least estimates of the purchasing power of the population.

From a German point of view the United States has remained a desirable country for fdi.[78] It is attractive as a vast market, if one where competition is strong. Many German firms have sought a place in the American market, sometimes discovering it was as easy to make losses as to earn profits. In 1961 the US share of German fdi was 8.7 per cent, and in 1975, 10.1 per cent. It seems that from the second half of the 1970s German firms felt competitive enough to invest in the USA on a more substantial scale. By 1990 27.1 per cent of German fdi was located there.

Japan has never been a large recipient of German fdi, as Table 2.3 makes evident. Most German firms shared the general Western perception, at least until recently, that Japan was exceptionally hard to penetrate as a market. In the 1980s this perception was modified, and some large German multinationals have become more active in Japan. Bayer, for example, has not only started production there, but in 1985 also founded a centre for R. & D. Nevertheless even in 1990 German fdi in Japan was noticeably small compared to that of the United States, or even Switzerland.

The marked German aversion to joint ventures should be noted in this context. German firms have sought to own the majority of shares, or at least of votes, of their fdi – and 100 per cent is thought to be best of all. Joint ventures with an ownership of less than 50 per cent are in most cases seen as a co-operation, which will not last for more than a couple of years, or, as a stepping stone to buy additional equity. Joint ventures have tended to be chosen in periods of rapid fdi and of a booming home economy, which causes financial stress. Examples include the decade before the First World War and during the 1950s and 1960s. The traditions of German business culture help to explain this syndrome. It is considered that property shared by many causes difficulties and hampers decision making. This is the lesson taught by family ownership, which is still very widespread, for example, Merck of Darmstadt, a medium-sized multinational active in producing pharmaceuticals.[79] German firms generally only maintain joint ventures over the long term in special circumstances. For instance, Volkswagen and Ford merged their activities in Brazil on a fifty:fifty basis, after both firms faced heavy difficulties there, and received no dividends from their investments for many years. Even in this case, however, Volkswagen claims to be the leading factor in the management of the Brazilian joint venture.

Reasons for German fdi

Compared to nations like the United States, the United Kingdom or Switzerland, Germany's fdi still is underdeveloped, while at the same time her exports are oversized. Mercedes-Benz and BMW do not manufacture their best models abroad. This raises the question of why exports are not replaced by more production abroad. The example of the German car industry suggests one answer. It is the emphasis on the quality of production, which many German companies think they cannot obtain in foreign countries.

Such arguments rest on certain location factors, mostly related to the German labour force, and especially the high level of education and training. Teachers at all levels are traditionally well paid which attracts able persons for the job. The system of apprenticeship turns out people who are proud of their qualification and eager to keep it up to date. Engineers are highly valued in society and co-operation between trade unions and employers is equally important. Modern Germany has strikes, but not wildcat ones. As both sides of industry are highly organized, collective bargaining has to go through a series of procedures before a strike is declared. Both employers and trade unions co-operate in encouraging employees to undertake training.

Some companies have embarked on a policy of implementing the German practice of co-operation in industrial relations to their plants abroad. Bayer, for instance, established a 'European forum', in which representatives of employees and employers from Bayer subsidiaries in six European nations meet. The purpose of the forum is to promote 'a confidential co-operation within the European companies of the concern'.[80]

Two more factors are stressed by Porter. They are the demand in the German market for quality products and local competition in its context of suppliers and industrial customers. Among others, Porter presented the printing industry as one example of competitive clusters, as nearly all major firms worldwide are situated in the southern parts of Germany (and in Switzerland).[81] Competition in a situation where the competitor is visibly at hand turned out to be a strong incentive for competitiveness, not only in this example.[82] Many of these reasons are factors against investing abroad, and they sound similar to those of Japan. Nevertheless these factors do not work uniformly in all industries. In contrast to the printing industry, for example, the need to ensure product quality led the electrical and chemical industries to establish centres abroad for technical advice and repair shops, and from this production emerged.

As with other nations, a range of factors explain why German firms engage in fdi. Again we have little hard data. However, the results of an inquiry, made in the mid-1970s, are suggestive.[83] The decisive motives were expansionist ones, with strategic fdi in growing markets identified as the most important. A second group of reasons focused on desires to safeguard existing markets. In contrast, government policies, such as taxes, fiscal matters, special incentives or pressure seemed to play only a minor role. Both expectations of higher profits than at home, and hopes of gaining access to lower production costs abroad, were not revealed as very important.[84]

The results of the inquiry were influenced by the fact that only large mnes were questioned. But the stress on long-term strategic fdi, which may take into account some years of low returns, is a common feature of German mne, as well as of the Swiss one.[85] The following quotation from Siemens's report in 1990 for the company's activities abroad is representative: 'Our policy of "long breath" has turned out to be the right way'.[86] This policy of slow, but steady growth obviously has its advantages, not only for the company but for its employees as well. But there are also costs. German firms are slow-moving and cautious in their foreign acquisition strategies. In the US, Daimler-Benz was looking for several years for a company to buy, before it finally acquired Freightliner. The American company was offered for sale. No hostile takeover bid was involved.[87] Interestingly, this approach to mergers and acquisitions is also again similar to that of the Swiss and Japanese.[88]

Conclusion

Before the First World War, Germany was a major home economy for fdi. The consequences of the two world wars meant that it took more than 50 years to reacquire a position similar to that held in 1914. When Germany resumed its role as a large source of fdi, its firms favoured the same regions as they had in 1914 – Europe and the USA.

There was a striking continuity in the sectors of German business which invested abroad, reflecting continuity of core competence in these activities. The chemical and the electrotechnical industries were always at the forefront of German multinational investment. The record of German banking and insurance was less continuous. Only in recent years have German enterprises in these sectors recaptured their former pre-First World War importance in fdi. In contrast, the post-war period has seen new entrants to German fdi, notably from automobiles.

German fdi occurred through a number of factors, including ownership-specific and internalization incentive advantages, and, as the attraction of markets is included in this category, location-specific ones.[89] Proprietary technology, derived from a deep-rooted commitment to technical improvement, if not to R. & D., led to patents and trade marks. Internalization incentives were important factors, especially for large firms. The wish to be present in important markets was an obvious influence. During the 1950s fdi was placed in developing countries, when the substantial growth of those markets was predicted, but in the 1960s, when it became clear that growth prospects were higher in Europe, new fdi was placed there. In the 1980s the USA was chosen, not only because of the vast market, but in order to be near to the type of customer, which had very often acted as a trendsetter.

In many cases the need of the German seller to protect the quality of the product worked as a strong incentive for internalization by fdi. Other location specific advantages were found as well. Some host governments had a strong preference for local production of special goods, such as pharmaceuticals or telecommunication equipment. German firms sometimes invested abroad to acquire, as in the case of Deutsche Bank's acquisition of Morgan Grenfell, particular types of expertise.

On the whole, it was location specific factors oriented on the sales market rather than the factor market, that played the most important role in explaining German fdi. German decision-making was based on a long-term strategic approach, which aimed to internalize business in major markets.

Notes

1. In this context, a fdi represents a foreign subsidiary owned by the mother company. A multinational enterprise (mne) owns one or more fdi (for details see Chapter 1).
2. The best material for the last 30 years is compiled in Deutsche Bundesbank, *Monatsberichte*, and Krägenau, H., *Internationale Direktinvestitionen*.
3. Chandler, A.D., *Scale and Scope*, Cambridge, Mass., 1990, pp. 596ff.
4. Porter, M., *The Competitive Advantage of Nations*, London, 1990, pp. 355–82.
5. P. Hertner, 'German Multinational Enterprise before 1914: Some Case Studies', in G. Jones and P. Hertner (eds.), *Multinationals: Theory and History*, Aldershot, 1986, pp. 113–34; *Il capitale tedesco in Italia dall' Unità alla Prima Guerra Mondiale, Banche miste e sviluppo economico italiano*, Bologna, 1984; 'Vom Wandel einer Unternehmensstrategie, Die deutsche Elektroindustrie in Italien vor dem Ersten Weltkrieg und in der Zwischenkriegszeit', in H. Schröter and C. Wurm (eds), *Politik, Wirtschaft und internationale Beziehungen, Studien zu ihrem Verhältnis in der Zeit zwischen den beiden Weltkriegen*, Mainz, 1991, pp. 139ff.
6. Wilkins, M., *The History of Foreign Investment in the United States to 1914*, Cambridge, Mass., 1989,
7. Wilkins, M., 'The History of European Multinationals: A New Look', *Journal of European Economic History*, winter 1986, **15**, (3), pp. 499ff. Her views are underlined by consumer oriented fdi such as Kathreiner's in malt coffee or Stollwerk in chocolate (see idem note 5, 'German Multinational Enterprise').
8. Idem note 6, p. 156.
9. Dunning, J.H., *Explaining International Production*, London, 1988, Table 3.1, p. 74.
10. Schröter, V., *Die deutsche Industrie auf dem Weltmarkt 1929 bis 1933*, Frankfurt, 1984, pp. 114–36. We think the higher figures given by Verena Schröter are more reliable than Dunning's, as they are based on extensive research on contemporary German sources. Mira Wilkins thought Dunning's figure for 1914 to be too low (Wilkins, Mira, 'European and North American Multinationals, 1870–1914: Comparisons and Contrasts', *Business History*, **30**, p 38, note 23.)
11. Schröter, H., 'Die Auslandsinvestitionen der deutschen chemischen Industrie', *Zeitschrift für Unternehmensgeschichte*, 1990, p. 4.
12. Idem note 6, p. 169.
13. The remaining 6 per cent could not be identified. Kabisch, T., *Deutsches Kapital in den USA*, Stuttgart, 1982, pp. 209ff.
14. Idem note 9, p. 74.
15. Both figures calculated in the same (pre-war gold) currency: Schröter, idem note 10, p. 118.
16. See list, idem note 11, p. 4.
17. Idem note 9, p. 74.

18. As Gerald Feldman has shown, these fears were much overstressed. Feldman G. 'Foreign Penetration of German Enterprises after the First World War: the Problem of Ueberfremdung', in A. Teichova *et al.* (eds), *Historical Studies in International Corporate Business*, Cambridge, 1989, pp. 87–110.

19. Idem note 3, pp. 587ff.

20. See Schröter, H. 'Risk and Control in Multinational Enterprise: German Businesses in Scandinavia, 1918–1939', *Business History Review*, Autumn 1988, **62**, 420–43; Schröter, H. 'A Typical Factor of German International Market Strategy: Agreements between the US and German Electrotechnical Industries up to 1939', in A. Teichova *et al.* (eds), *Multinational Enterprise in Historical Perspective*, Cambridge, 1986, pp. 160–70

21. For Hertner, see the list of literature in Jones and Hertner, idem note 5; for Teichova, see Teichova A. and Cottrell, P.L. (eds), *International Business and Central Europe, 1918–1939*, Leicester, 1983 with contributions on Mannesmann (by Teichova), IG Farben (by Schröter), Siemens (by Schröter) and German fdi in Poland (by Tomaszewski).

22. These eight firms were: AGFA, BASF, Bayer, Cassella, Farbwerke Weiler ter Meer, Griesheim Elektron, Hoechst and Kalle.

23. Schröter, V. 'Participation in Market Control through Foreign Investment: IG Farbenindustrie AG in the United States: 1920–1938', in Teichova *et al.*, idem note 20, pp. 171–84.

24. Quoted in Schröter, idem note 23, p. 181.

25. In number of producing units abroad, as values are unavailable. (See Table 2:1, idem note 11, p. 4.)

26. There are several other examples in which German companies placed a holding company into Switzerland, in most cases for reasons of security or (turnover-) tax evasion. For instance, IG Farben founded a holding company in Basle for most of its fdi. (See Chapter 3 in this volume.)

27. Schröter, H., *Aussenpolitik und Wirtschaftsinteresse, Skandinavien im aussenwirtschaftlichen Kalkül Deutschlands und Großbritanniens 1918–1939*, Frankfurt, 1983, 289ff.

28. Examples are given by G. Aalders and C. Wiebes, 'Stockholms Enskilda Bank, German Bosch and IG Farben. A Short History of Cloaking', *Scandinavian Economic History Review*, 1985, **33**, 25–50.

29. But of course all enterprises in the occupied territories, whoever the owner was, were redirected to the efforts of the German war machine.

30. Minute of Diercks for C.F. von Siemens and others, 10 October 1940 (Siemens Archiv Akte 4/Lf690).

31. Overy, R. J., 'Göring's Multi-national Empire', in Teichova and Cottrell, idem note 21, pp. 269–98.

32. For Sweden's case: Nordlund, S., *Skördetid eller maktpolitisk anpassning? De tyska företagen: Sverige efter andra världskriget*, Umeå, 1988.

33. Lenzinger, Hans W., *Die deutschen Vermögenswerte in der Schweiz und ihre statistische Erfassung aufgrund des Abkommens von Washington vom 25.5.1946 und des Ablösungsabkommens vom 26.8.1952*, Winterthur, 1960.

34. Seifert, H., *Die deutschen Direktinvestitionen*, Köln, 1967; Schröter, H., 'Aussenwirtschaft im Boom: Direktinvestitionen bundesdeutscher Unternehmen im Ausland 1950–1975', in H. Kaelble (ed.), *Der Boom 1948–1973*, Opladen, 1992, pp. 82–106.

35. These registers form a relative diversified basis of statistics on German fdi.

36. Research has been done mainly by economists and lawyers in order to detect hidden fdi owned by the former state party SED and its members or by the secret service of the GDR. For instance, in November 1991 the Spanish firm Camet SA was detected to have been a joint venture of a West German company (März, Rosenheim) since 1982 and the so-called Bereich Kommerzielle Koordinierung, which was a special part of the secret service. The aim of Camet was not only to earn money, but to 'gather information about political and economic activities of the class-enemy in its respective territory'. (Cited from a memorandum of the (GDR) ministry of state security after *Frankfurter Allgemeine Zeitung*, No. 269/47D, 19 November 1991, pp. 1ff.)

37. Schröter, H., 'Die Auslandsinvestitionen der deutschen chemischen Industrie 1930–1965' (forthcoming).

38. After an agreement with Sterling Drug, which still owns the rights of the Bayer-cross (Verg, E., *Meilensteine*, Leverkusen, 1988, p 489.)

39. *Financial Times*, 25 September 1991, p. 21.

40. Oesterheld, W. and Wortmann, M., 'Trends der bundesdeutschen Direktinvestitionen', in *Informationen über Multinationale Konzerne*, 1989, (4), p. 22.
41. Calculated from: United Nations, *Multinational Corporations in World Development*, New York, 1973, p. 159, tab. 19.
42. Idem note 9, p. 74.
43. In 1980, US$1 = DM 1.96. In 1985, US$1 = DM 2.67 (Schwarzer, O. and Schneider, J., 'Europäischen Wechselkurse seit 1913', in W. Fischer (ed.), *Handbuch der Europäischen Wirtschafts- und Sozialgeschichte*, Stuttgart, 1987, vol. 6, pp. 1048 ff.).
44. Calculated from 'Standen van de directe investeringen van Nederland in het biutenland en van het buitenland in Nederland in 1984–1989,' De Nederlandsche Bank ed., *Kwartaalbericht* 1991/1, June 1991, p. 55.
45. See Chapter 4 of this book, especially Figure 4.1.
46. Idem note 4, p. 358.
47. Verg, idem note 38, p. 325.
48. Figures for 1961 are used as there are no detailed data published before that year.
49. But in other years the percentage was lower, though still the highest of all sectors (1965: 14.6 per cent; 1973: 13.1 per cent); figures taken from Schröter, 'Aussenwirtschaft', idem note 34, Table 5; for 1975, calculated from Krägenau, *Direktinvestitionen, 1973–1975*, idem note 2, p. 64, Table C.1.4.
50. See the contributions in this book.
51. *Frankfurter Allgemeine Zeitung*, 19 November 1991, p. 19.
52. Idem note 4, p. 367.
53. At the same time, International Hellas SA in Greece was taken over by Aachen und Münchener Beteiligungs AG, *Frankfurter Allgemeine Zeitung*, 19 November 1991, p. 19.
54 Treue, W., 'Die Gründung der internationalen Bank in Luxemburg vor 125 Jahren', in *Bankhistorisches Archiv*, No. 1, 1981, pp. 3–15.
55 Especially the pursuit of the 'Allfinanz-Konzept', which means that Deutsche Bank now offers all services of any financial significance. This is more than the known German universal-banking concept, as it includes insurance and building societies, etc. Other steps have been the extremely quick, broad and massive investment in the new German Länder in East Germany, which caused embarrassment at competitors' headquarters.
56. Deutsche Bank, *Bericht über die Hauptversammlung 1990*, p. 13.
57. Deutsche Bank, *Bericht 1990*, p. 13.
58. Together with US, British and Japanese competitors (Schröter, H., Victoria, in *International Directory of Company Histories*, Vol. III, London, 1991, p. 400).
59. In 1991 Deutsche Bank was active in 15 countries of the Pacific region, with 60 offices, employing a workforce of 3000 *(Frankfurter Allgemeine Zeitung*, No. 271, 22 November 1991, p. 24).
60. In 1990 with a turnover of US$39.4 billion Siemens was no. 9 on the list of all European industrial enterprises, followed in its field by Philips of Holland (no. 13 on the list, turnover of US$ 30.6 billion). (Calculated from 'Die 100 größten europäischen Industrie-Unternehmen', in *Die Zeit*, 23 August 1991.)
61. Idem note 3, pp. 464ff., 538ff.
62. Idem note 5, 'Unternehmensstrategie'.
63. Siemens, *Bericht über das Geschäftsjahr 1990*, pp. 29ff.
64. Idem note 4, p. 367. Curiously, Porter omitted Volkswagen in his study.
65. Within several months, Volkswagen constructed complete new buildings. The old buildings where the Trabant car was manufactured were completely run down. For example, the conveyor had broken and the workers manually pushed the Trabant on the assembly line from one work station to the next.
66. *Financial Times*, 29 August 1991.
67. Prospectus of Grohe in *Frankfurter Allgemeine Zeitung*, no. 276, 28 November 1991, pp. I–III; *Financial Times*, 28 November 1991, p. 16.
68. Otto Versand was founded in 1949. It had a turnover of US $ 10 billion in 1990, being active among other countries in the US (Spiegel), France (3 Suisses), the UK (Grattan) and Japan (Otto Sumisho).
69. *150 Jahre Bertelsmann*, Gütersloh, 1985.
70. Both companies are good examples that the Chandlerian approach works, not only with industry but with other sectors as well (idem note 3).

71. Future development is not yet clear. For example, Siemens in the early 1990s invested huge sums in order to become competitive with Japanese firms in microchips. Though bio-industry is not very well developed, research is carried out in Germany. More important, German chemical firms have invested in bio-industry abroad, as German legislation in this field is very tight. Inside a multinational firm knowhow can relatively easily be channelled into the mother firm's country. These are only two examples, which make any prediction of Germany's future development unsafe. See Wortmann, M., 'Multinationals and the Internationalization of R&D: New Developments in German Companies', *Research Policy*, (19), 1990, 175–83.
72. In the United States, Bayer, for instance, owns Molecular Diagnostics Inc. and Molecular Therapeutics Inc., both situated in New Haven at Miles Pharmaceuticals (a subsidiary of Bayer) in order to co-operate with Yale University.
73. Sammet, R., 'Die Rolle der deutschen Chemie in der Weltwirtschaft', *Wirtschaftsdienst*, 1970, **1**, 96.
74. In 1961, the shares of all German fdi were Brazil, 16.6 per cent; France, 5.3 per cent; The Netherlands, 2.3 per cent; UK, 1.4 per cent (Schröter, 'Aussenwirtschaft', idem note 34, p. 99, Table 7).
75. Idem note 34, p. 99, Table 7.
76. Calculated from Krägenau, *Internationale Direktinvestitionen*, 1987, p. 252, Table C.1.12.
77. From Table 2.3 a share for Europe of 57.0 per cent can be calculated.
78. This, too, has a long standing tradition, as Mira Wilkins has shown in her overview on European Multinationals (idem note 7, p. 499).
79. The US enterprise of Merck was a fdi of German Merck before the First World War. It was not rebought and it became much bigger than its offspring. This has happened with other firms as well, such as Röhm & Haas.
80. The establishment of the forum was provoked by the formation of the single European home market. The forum included representatives from Belgium, France, Germany, Italy, Spain and the UK (Bayer, *Aktionärsbrief '91*, Zwischenbericht 1, Halbjahr, 1991, p. 7).
81. Idem note 4, p. 180.
82. This situation is to be found in many competitive sectors in Germany. For example, Mercedes trucks are challenged by MANs, its cars by BMWs etc. Similar situations are to be found in other nations, too. All of the three big Swiss chemical firms are situated in Basle, competing with each other. In Sweden, Volvo's cars and trucks compete with Saab's and Scania's etc.
83. The inquiry was made for 119 cases of fdi, all from leading industrial mnes, engaged mainly in the sectors of cars and trucks, chemicals and electrotechnics. Jungnickel, R., *Einfluß multinationaler Unternehmen auf Aussenwirtschaft und Brachenstruktur der Bundesrepublik Deutschland*, Hamburg, 1977.
84. An overview on the rather bulky inquiry is presented in Schröter, 'Aussenwirtschaft', idem note 34.
85. See Chapter 3.
86. Siemens, *Geschäftsbericht '90*, p. 31. It is interesting that just the same results for fdi reasons have been found in an evaluation on mne from small nations before 1914. (See Schröter, H., *Multinationale Unternehmen aus kleinen Staaten bis 1914*, pp. 81–112, forthcoming.)
87. A major exception to this tradition was the hostile takeover of the British Plessey company by Siemens in 1988/89. It was the first of its kind in Siemens's history and it would have not been attempted without the co-operation of British General Electric Company. But even in this case, Siemens made a step which is seen to be crucial in German eyes. It got in touch with Plessey's workforce and when it got the impression that decisive parts of the workforce were willing to co-operate with Siemens, it took over Plessey. In Germany, it is a common conviction, not only by trade unions but also by management, that co-operation with the workforce is a key element for both economic success and security.
88. For example, see Kester, W. C., *Japanese Takeovers*, Boston, 1991.
89. Defined as in Dunning's eclectic paradigm: Dunning, J. H., 'Explaining the International Direct Investment Position of Countries: Towards a Dynamic or Developmental Approach', in J. Black and J. H. Dunning (eds), *International Capital Movements*, London, 1982, pp. 84–121.

3 Swiss multinational enterprise in historical perspective

Harm G. Schröter

Switzerland is, on a per capita basis, one of the world's most active foreign direct investors. However, it also raises in an acute form more general and perplexing questions concerning the nationality of multinational enterprises (mnes). This chapter provides not only a survey of the historical development of Swiss mnes, but also explores these more general issues raised by the Swiss experience.

The history of foreign direct investment (fdi) by Swiss enterprise goes back more than 150 years. Switzerland industrialized early. The cotton industry, which exported most of its products, was especially prominent. From the 1830s the textile industry invested abroad.[1] Switzerland was one of the few nations which pioneered multinational enterprise not only with two or three firms, but with dozens. Undisputed, also, is the importance of fdi for the Swiss economy. As a small nation, it has been strongly orientated to foreign markets, both as an exporter and as a direct investor. In 1860 the country was first, and in 1913 second, on the world's list of nation's exports calculated per inhabitant.[2] In the early 1970s, Switzerland was well ahead even of the United Kingdom, if the importance of exports is related with the importance of fdi.[3]

In the 1980s the first investigation on Swiss fdi after the Second World War[4] was started by Silvio Borner and Felix Wehrle. Their work, based on an empirical enquiry, was focused on the possibilities of Swiss survival on the world market. In this context, Swiss fdi was seen as a necessity: 'In the economic reality of today and tomorrow the alternative of "export or fdi" becomes rare, but more and more increasing is "fdi or definite loss of foreign markets"',[5] a view which was put forward by one industrialist already in 1934.[6] According to Borner, the promotion of Swiss fdi emerged, on the one hand, out of the economic necessity to invest abroad, and, on the other, out of the ability of Swiss firms to apply their core competences in foreign markets as well.

Borner suggested that these core competences, which provide competitive advantages, are enterprise-specific ones, while the national level provided a framework of 'real attractivity' for the Swiss economy as a whole.[7] 'Technological and managerial know-how has very little to do with national endowments... Competitiveness is, therefore, *no meaningful attribute of a nation state*.'[8] In this sense,

49

Borner, in explaining Swiss competitiveness and Swiss fdi by emphasizing the single enterprise versus the nation approach, provided an alternative hypothesis to that of Porter in *The Competitive Advantage of Nations*.[9]

For Switzerland, representing a small and open economy, mne, fdi and Swiss national economic advantages are one of the most important topics of policy and public discussion. They form a problem of inextricable complexity. In the Swiss case, therefore, fdi has to be discussed in the context of national advantages on which mne is based. Porter's approach to explain international competitiveness is used in this context as an example of a nation-based one.

However, in 1991 Borner and Porter published a book together on the international competitive advantages of Swiss industry, in which Borner moderated his views.[10] He also accepted for Switzerland, the existence of a system of mutual interdependent factors, which Porter calls the national 'diamond'.[11] However, Borner suggested that, in the case of Switzerland, these factors are not entirely Swiss ones, a view which challenges a nation-based approach. The discussion is by no means academic, as it focuses on the question: To what extent are Swiss mnes Swiss? Indeed, should the largest of Swiss mnes, Nestlé and ABB, which in 1990 employed 95 per cent of their workforce abroad, still be called Swiss companies or, as it has been suggested, rather 'supernational' or 'stateless'[12] mnes? For the case of ABB, this question is even more open than that of Nestlé, as ABB was formed by a merger of the Swedish ASEA and the Swiss BBC. [13]

In the case of Germany, as shown in Chapter 2, Porter's paradigm, focusing on recent advantages, can be also directly related to the historical development of mnes. In the following discussion we will try to identify, with the help of Porter's clusters of related industries, Swiss mnes in history. The most competitive industries of a nation are centered inside these clusters, and usually enjoy a considerable longevity. We will combine the existing scattered information on the history of Swiss fdi, and then look for continuity or change in confrontation with such clusters of today.

In the case of Switzerland, clusters of competitive industries have been identified in a surprisingly wide variety of sectors. Industries related to health care and to textiles, chemicals, processed food and metal products, machine tools and, last but not least, general business services (banking etc.) have been listed. [14]

Swiss mne in history

Switzerland has a very long tradition of fdi, and its importance for the nation's economy is undisputed. In spite of these facts very little research has been done on the subject and there is less information on Swiss fdi than for all the other leading home economies. Most is known about the period before the First World War, but from that time until the 1970s there are few data.

The first fdi was in the textiles sector. For the 1980s, too, Porter identified industries related to textiles as forming a competitive cluster. This suggests that

Switzerland managed to keep and renew competitive advantages in this sector for more than 150 years. However, development was not static, and there was much change in the course of time. It is important to see how the centre of gravity moved inside the cluster of textiles-related industries.

At the turn of the 18th century, fdi emerged out of the silk ribbon industry of Basel.[15] Some years later it was the cotton industry which headed Swiss fdi. The formation of the German customs union in 1834 caused many Swiss firms to fear for their exports. Therefore they decided to erect plants in southern Germany. However, this was not a great step in either geographical or cultural terms. The new factories were built just over the border, in a region whose inhabitants were linguistically (and in most other ways) identical to the Swiss. After 1860 many cotton firms invested in Italy, mainly because of the cheap labour offered there.[16] By using Dunning's paradigm, location specific advantages were sought by Swiss fdi in both states. While in Germany access to the market was decisive, in Italy the wages made the lowering of production costs possible. The geographical destination of Swiss fdi up to 1914 is shown in Table 3.1.

Table 3.1   Geographical destination of Swiss fdi, 1870–1914 (%)

Destination	1870	1900	1914
Germany	88	49	40
France	0	14	17
Italy	4	11	11
USA	0	12	8
Russia	0	4	7
UK	0	4	5
Austria	8	4	4
Others	0	2	8
Total	100	100	100

Source
Schröter, H., 'Etablierungs- und Verteilungsmuster der schweizerischen Auslandsproduktion von 1870 bis 1914', in P. Bairoch and M. Körner (eds), *Die Schweiz in der Weltwirtschaft*, Zurich, 1990, p. 396, Table 2.

Up to a period ending in the 1860s, the characteristics of fdi were maintained in the majority of cases only for a few years and mne was not developed. After some time, connections to Switzerland receded. The investment became independent and there was no longer managerial control from Switzerland. Capital connections usually ceased later, together with family links.[17] This process, by which out of a fdi an emigration of industry emerged, was widespread until the 1860/1870s. After that decade only a few examples of this phenomenon are to be found and instead more and more Swiss firms invested abroad, not only in one but in several nations, and became mnes by this process. The years around 1870 can be traced as the pioneer period not only for Swiss mne, but for continental ones, as has been argued in Chapter 1.[18]

Table 3.2   Number of Swiss industrial fdis, 1870–1914

	1870	1880	1890	1900	1905	1910	1914
Swiss mnes	23	30	51	98	112	127	160
Foreign affiliates	25	37	64	144	161	207	265

Source
See Table 3.1.

In 1870, 25 foreign manufacturing affiliates have been traced,[19] most of them from the textile sector. Though their number doubled by 1914, the importance of Swiss textile production sank from before the turn of the century. That was reflected by the relative decline of fdi from this sector, while that from other sectors, notably from food and drink, raw materials, chemicals and machinery expanded. The inter-war period was characterized by stagnation. Due to a change in fashion, specialities of Swiss mnes in the textile sector, such as silk, embroideries and products of straw, were not sought after so much any more. Some decades later, since the 1960s, industries related to textile cluster took up fdi again. But this time the focus was on special machinery for the textile industry, a branch which had a tradition as long as the textile industry itself. Up to that time it had concentrated on exports only. During the whole period of more than 150 years core competence in textile-related industries was sustained within the cluster.

However, inside this cluster the focus of competitive advantage moved together with fdi activities from one industry to the other, crossing the dividing lines of traditional sectors of the textile industry and machine building. It is Porter's approach which binds the textile related industries together. The traditional line of argument was different. It suggested that first the cotton, and later the silk industry, lost core competitive advantages, while special sectors of textile machine-building maintained it for more than 100 years. Porter and Borner stressed the effects of direct and indirect connections between these industries – and there are examples for such linkages in ownership, local concentration of industries, consumer demand and others in both historical and recent times.[20]

It could be maintained that such linkages were weak and, above all, not national Swiss ones. History provides much evidence for such a view, for instance the application of machines for embroideries by Sastig, the largest Swiss enterprise by capital before the First World War. Though the invention was (mainly) a Swiss one, the machines, ordered for Sastig's plants in Switzerland and in the US, were built in Saxony, Germany. Indeed, the structure of demand for textile machinery in the Dutch or German market would not differ very much from the Swiss market from the pre-First World War period until today.[21] The recent factor market for the machine-building industry is also by no means purely Swiss. A third of its workforce is of foreign origin. As in the case of the chemical industry, the home market for the Swiss machine-building industry includes Germany. For Switzerland, Borner and Porter presented this as a variation to Porter's theory.[22]

Other clusters of related industries with competitive advantages can be traced back into history as well. In the cluster of 'processed metal products', represented by multinational firms such as Alusuisse-Lonza, von Roll, Georg Fischer and more, substantial fdi can be found from 1890 onwards.[23]

In continuity from before the First World War, the clusters of processed food and chemicals are of extreme importance. Both are dominated by only a handful of mnes. And in both cases, the majority of activities, measured not only by turnover, but also by production and perhaps even R. & D., is situated abroad. Especially these two clusters, because of the dominance of mnes, cannot be understood using a nation-based approach, and an enterprise-oriented one is far more productive.

We miss in Porter's list of recent clusters such ones formed by industries related to electrotechnics and machine building. For instance BBC (Brown, Boveri & Cie, now ABB) kept its name on the world's top list of producers of high performance electrical machines for generation and transformation continously for about a century; the same applied to Sulzer in machine building. Not only these firms mentioned became mnes before 1914, but many others in these sectors as well.[24] The gap on the list was closed, however, in the book jointly written by Borner and Porter. There Porter's approach to identify competitive sectors with the help of oversized exports as an indicator was combined with more traditional ones. The combination brought forward clusters of real strength of Swiss economy, which includes machine building among others.

The First World War gave a great boost to Swiss fdi (see Table 3.3). Though Switzerland faced considerable problems in obtaining enough food, fuel and raw materials, Swiss firms with foreign relations, above all mnes, expanded. Considerable sums were earned by trading with both belligerent sides, while the neutral status was strictly kept. As in the Netherlands,[25] many enterprises increased both their share capitals and their fdi, mainly in neutral and (anti-German) *entente* states.

During the inter-war period, Swiss fdi on the whole did not grow as quickly as before the First World War. Furthermore, important sectoral variations took place. While there was a sharp decline in the textile industry, which caused many mnes in this field to sell or close down fdi, firms in the chemical, the electrotechnical and food industries continued with direct investment, while new Swiss firms also ventured abroad. In 1936 Nestlé even founded a holding company in Panama, Unilac, for its business in the Western Hemisphere, which turned out to be of great advantage during the Second World War.

At that time the company had experience of more than 50 years of multinational activities. In 1880, Nestlé or rather Anglo-Swiss Condensed Milk, a company which merged with Nestlé in 1905, already operated four plants abroad.[26] In 1902, in a strategic retreat, it sold all its plants in the USA to Borden, a competitor.[27] In 1911 the company branched out by taking directing influence in the Swiss chocolate producing mne Peter, Cailler, Kohler, Chocolats Suisses SA.[28]

During the inter-war period Nestlé grew steadily, after a deep crisis in 1921/22. The world economic crisis, beginning in 1929, caused a fragmentation into national markets sheltered by high tariffs. Therefore, Nestlé took up production in more states than ever before. By 1938 it operated 105 foreign plants.[29] The above mentioned foundation of the Unilac holding company was a major strategic step, not only during the Second World War. Well into the 1960s, that company was central for operations in the dollar zone, which together with the sterling zone and Europe covered the major geographical areas of Nestlé's strategic activities. After the war, Swiss competitors were acquired, notably Maggi in 1947 and Ursina-Franck in 1971. Abroad, the most important acquisitions were the takeover of Crosse & Blackwell (UK) in 1960, Libby (USA) in 1971, and Rowntree (UK) in 1988.[30] In 1990 Nestlé was still concentrated on Europe, where it sold 49 per cent of its products, while North America came in second place with 24 per cent.[31]

While Nestlé represents the largest of all Swiss mnes since the First World War, it is important to consider small and medium-sized Swiss mne. Before 1914, three-quarters of Swiss fdi was placed in neighbouring countries, especially in Germany and France.[32] Most of this investment came from medium-sized firms. Though there are no comprehensive studies on the subject, an overview of company histories suggests that this pattern was retained during the inter-war period.

The case of Terra-Film AG can provide one example. This German company was bought in 1930 by Eugen Sconti, a financier of Zurich.[33] The firm was of medium size, but it held the rights to distribute United Artists Corporation's films in Germany. During the 1930s, Terra had much success in the production of several right-wing films in co-operation with the Nazi Ministry of Propaganda. In spite of this, the company's finances were not sufficient enough for larger film projects. Therefore it was sold in 1937.

Another example is represented by the investments of Villiger, a cigar maker. Villiger's first fdi in Germany dated back to 1910.[34] During the 1930s a German competitor was bought and the number of producing units raised, finally, to eight. But most of these, except those at Tiengen and Munich, were very small. During the Second World War, as all other neutral fdi, this one had little to fear from the Nazis in power in and outside Germany. But after 1945 all establishments were closed, because there was no longer any market. Later, in 1949, the factory at

Tiengen, near the Swiss border, resumed production, and it continues to turn out Swiss cheroot today.

Many more examples of Swiss medium-sized mne could be given for the period before and after the Second World War.

The performance of Swiss fdi during the Second World War was different from that of the First World War. Switzerland was surrounded by only one of the belligerent sides and cut off from the world market. Though the nation fared better than all its neighbours, opportunities for trade and fdi differed greatly from those experienced in the First World War. On the whole Swiss fdi could be kept but not augmented extensively.

The overall cautious attitude by Swiss firms towards fdi during the inter-war period was maintained well into the 1960s. Since that decade, however, massive and sustained fdi has emerged. Investment has come from the same branches as before the Second World War, as well as from new ones. However, the textile industry has not recaptured its pre-First World War position. A significant change was represented by fdi from many branches of the machine-building sector. Firms in this sector expanded rapidly, not only by concentration inside the country,[35] but by fdi.

Swiss mne after 1980

Swiss laws and traditions on confidentiality in business affairs have led to an extraordinary dearth of statistical data on Swiss fdi. Of course its importance was obvious; years ago a special expression was minted for Swiss fdi – 'the sixth Switzerland'[36] – but official figures on the amount were released only after 1985. The latest (and best) book on the economic history of Switzerland hardly mentions fdi at all.[37] In 1984, Silvio Borner submitted the result of a heavily-funded national research programme on Swiss fdi without giving an estimate as to its total amount.[38] But besides the lack of data, another good reason for doing so was the fact that Switzerland is a home for many foreign-owned holding companies (see below).

We are left, therefore, with estimates rather than hard data. For many years, estimates of fdi relied on various sources, of which those of the Schweizerische Bankgesellschaft (Swiss Bank Corporation), one of the leading banks, were the most prominent. The situation is reflected in Table 3.3 with its contradictory figures. It can be taken as an example for the many methodological questions related to the assembly of fdi figures, and not only in Switzerland. Any of the figures in Table 3.3, are to be understood as absolute minimum ones. As not everything is included (for instance reinvestment is excluded), and the Swiss habit of extensively writing down assets has to be taken into account, we may modestly estimate the market value of Swiss fdi to be about 100 per cent higher than published. On the other hand, figures on Swiss investment include fdi by foreign-owned holding companies, which again raises the question of nationality.

Table 3.3   Estimates of the amount of Swiss fdi, 1914–89 (US $ billion, current prices)

Year	A	B	C	D	E	F
1914	n.a.	n.a.	n.a.	n.a.	0.07	0.07
1919	n.a.	n.a.	n.a.	n.a.	0.12	0.12
1960	n.a.	2.32	n.a.	n.a.	2.00	n.a.
1965	n.a.	4.05	n.a.	1.88	n.a.	1.88
1966	2.10	n.a.	n.a.	n.a.	n.a.	2.10
1970	7.82	8.10	5.79	3.63	8.62	3.63
1975	20.88	20.88	16.11	10.42	19.37	10.42
1980	n.a.	n.a.	33.24	21.53	n.a.	21.53
1985	n.a.	n.a.	n.a.	23.17	n.a.	23.17
1989	n.a.	n.a.	n.a.	n.a.	48.47	48.47

Sources
A   Krägenau, H., *Internationale Direktinvestitionen*, 1975, p. 203; *ibid.*, 1977, p. 131.
B   *Ibid.*, 1982, p. 308.
C   The biggest 25 firms only; *ibid.*, 1982, p. 308.
D   *Ibid.*, 1987, p. 516.
E   For the year 1914: Schröter, *H., Multinationale Unternehmen aus kleinen Staaten bis 1914*, forthcoming, p. 152. 1919: Himmel, E., *Industrielle Kapitalanlagen der Schweiz im Ausland*, Langensalza, 1922, Tab. 'Rekapitulation'. 1960 and 1970: Dunning, J.H., 'Changes in the Level and Structure of International Production: The Last One Hundred Years', in M. Casson (ed.), *The Growth of International Business*, London, 1983, p. 87 (as the figure for 1970 is lacking, that for 1971 is presented). 1975: Niehans, J., 'Benefits of Multinational Firms for a Small Parent Economy: The Case of Switzerland', in T. Agmon and C. P. Kindleberger (eds.), *Multinationals from Small Countries*, Cambridge/Mass., London, 1977, p. 5 (as the figure for 1975 is lacking, that for 1974 is presented). 1985: see D. 1989: calculated by the author from *Swiss Statistical Yearbook*.
F   Presentation of what the author thinks are the most reliable figures. No figure is presented for 1960 as both estimates given are too high.

Table 3.3 indicates that Swiss fdi was substantial, and grew over time, but it is evident that more exact quantification is as yet impossible.

The author gives his view of the most reliable estimates of the amount of industrial fdi in column F. It consists mainly of the figures of calculations D and E. John Dunning's[39] figures for 1960 and 1971 (taken for 1970 in calculating E) seem to be a little bit too high, as well as Krägenau's (calculations A to C). While Dunning's figures cannot be checked, as he gives no special information on his sources, Krägenau's rely on estimates of the Schweizerische Bankgesellschaft. Niehans, too, got his figure for 1974 (taken for 1975 in calculation E) from a Swiss bank, the Union Bank of Switzerland. As it is to be taken from Table 3.3 (calculation A to D), the bank figures were several times heavily revised downwards. But again we stress that, what we present as best data, calculation F, is based on or near to official figures, which have to be increased in order to obtain real market value (but this is true for most European data on fdi). In terms of market value, it is perhaps no surprise that the best figures are those of the banks, the early ones of Schweizerische Bankgesellschaft and the Union – which means that all figures from 1970 onwards have to be doubled.

If we now accept the figures in column F, we see a picture of considerable growth. Dunning's calculation for the years 1960 to 1978 showed not only a sharp upswing but a doubling of the Swiss share of the world's fdi from 3.0 to 7.1 per cent.[40] Another calculation presents a share of about 8 per cent for 1975/76.[41] However, Dunning's more recent calculations suggest a stable 3.5 per cent of world's fdi for Switzerland from 1960 to 1983.[42] These are remarkable figures, as other established fdi-nations lost considerable shares during that period.[43]

On the other hand, a small part of the rising figures of Swiss fdi have to be deducted, as they did not evolve from the Swiss national economy. Switzerland has always been a safe haven for other people's money. For that reason, holding companies of foreign mnes were founded there, which are included in the Swiss statistics. The foreign use of Swiss holding companies has a long standing tradition. Before the First World War, considerable sums of French capital were invested via Switzerland (as well as via Belgium) for tax evasion purposes. In the inter-war period, German, east and southeast European enterprises founded Swiss holding companies, for the same, and for safety, reasons. From the 1960s onwards, this process increased substantially. In 1989 the list of the 50 biggest firms registered in Switzerland included several holding companies, owned from abroad, including Marc Rich, Pirelli, Michelin, Merck, Kühne & Nagel, etc. The same list of enterprises showed that the majority of their workforce was employed abroad and not inside Switzerland.[44]

In their investigation on Swiss fdi, Borner and Wehrle took account of such foreign holding companies by excluding them from their lists. While holding companies can relatively easily be shifted from one state to the other,[45] the authors wanted to investigate the prospects for the Swiss national economy. The large amount of Swiss fdi was taken for granted by them and used as a stepping stone for further investigation. One of the most important results presented was the diversification of Swiss fdi into 'new investment forms':[46] Swiss firms, not merely mnes but small and medium-sized ones as well, not only distributed and produced abroad, but increasingly searched for contracts on licensing, subcontracting, consulting, industrial co-operation (co-production), joint ventures and other combinations.[47] Through this strategy, the core skills of firms could be exploited more effectively than by traditional fdi.[48]

In 1989, Nestlé signed a joint venture with General Mills to form CPW (Cereal Partners Worldwide) under which CPW promoted and sold cereals all over the world, except the USA and Canada. A year later, Nestlé founded a joint venture with Coca Cola. By this agreement, drinks based on coffee and tea were offered worldwide (except in Japan) via Coca Cola's distribution network. Of strategic importance is that, in both cases, all products covered are to be sold under the brand name of Nestlé.[49]

These strategies are, however, by no means 'new' for Swiss mnes, for they were widely used from the early 1890s onwards.[50] Two examples can illustrate this. From the 1920s, well into the 1960s, Ciba, Sandoz and Geigy, three major chemical enterprises, jointly operated production facilities in the USA, the UK, Italy and elsewhere. In 1977 Sandoz, together with the French enterprise Rhône-Poulenc, formed a joint venture in the field of hospital supplies.[51]

As in the case of other nations, Swiss mnes tended to resort to such strategies in conditions of stress, such as relative economic insecurity, rapid expansion and so on. Such patterns, surely, are not uniquely Swiss. In the history of mne of several nations, they were generally applied, especially in boom periods of rapid expansion, while those of consolidation showed a tendency to either incorporate such contracted relations into the firm, or to terminate the contracts.[52]

Two sectors, in which Swiss products have a worldwide reputation, have yet to be discussed in our survey of Swiss fdi: banking and clocks. The reason is that, at the beginning of the 1990s, both sectors were still concentrated on Switzerland. Some fdi related to clocks has been carried out, especially since the industry's recovery from the Japanese onslaught on the world market in the 1970s, but the old-established Swiss specialities in the expensive spectrum of the market are still produced inside the country. This is not surprising, given that the mark 'made in Switzerland' is a major intangible asset in the clock industry, so much so that thousands of watches manufactured in Asia have this illegally stamped on their faces.

The same applies to the financial sector. For reasons of Swiss liquidity, the international expertise, and its liberal system of justice, Switzerland was made a home for mnes, which focused on financing utilities in the field of the electrical industry, as shown in Chapter 7 by Hertner in this book.[53] A certain category of foreigners has long been interested in a bank account in Switzerland, but not in an account at a Swiss bank abroad. Though this is now of diminishing importance, it has in the past provided no incentive for fdi. Swiss banking, therefore, represents rather a paradox. Though up to the Second World War, Swiss banks had less than a dozen branches abroad, their foreign business was relatively large. Some 26 and 13 per cent of their investment were placed in foreign countries in 1906 and 1950 respectively.[54] This tradition continues and it can be exemplified by the Swiss Reinsurance Company, one of the largest of such firms in the world. In the 1980s, it collected less than 10 per cent of its premiums inside Switzerland, but it had only a handful of fdi.

The traditional strategy of Swiss banks was not too surprising. Before the developments of the Euromarkets in the 1960s, much international banking could be conducted without extensive multinational branching.[55] American banks also had very limited direct representation abroad. Since the 1960s, however, a multinational presence – at least in major world financial centres – has become essential for a competitive commercial bank. Swiss banks have modified their strategy, though at a very cautious pace. They have increased the number of their foreign branches and, in the 1980s, made a series of large acquisitions in the financial sectors of the UK, the United States and Germany.

This is a reflection of a strong movement of Swiss financial institutions to become more 'normal' (if normality is defined by the majority of structures of comparable developed nations). For political and economic reasons, Swiss banks cannot offer 'special services', such as numbered accounts and so on, to the same extent as they used to do. The move of competitors towards global banking and the creation of a single market inside the EC, among other reasons, have also influenced this movement. Therefore we can expect in the future much more fdi to come from Swiss financial services.

From 1980 onwards, Borner and Wehrle predicted for Swiss fdi a period of 'in the best case modest growth'.[56] As Table 3.3 shows, this was clearly an error.[57] The following decade turned out to be the peak period of Swiss fdi. In 1980 Swiss fdi had already reached an outstanding amount. In that year, the largest 50 mnes produced 2.1 times more abroad than at home,[58] while they employed a workforce of 535 270 abroad and only 233 120 inside Switzerland.[59] In 1989, however, the 50 largest mnes doubled their employment abroad to 1 167 845, while the corresponding figure for Switzerland remained at the same level.[60] If the total of Swiss employment, abroad and at home, was taken into account, in 1980 about 16 per cent of the workforce of Swiss firms was employed abroad, while in 1989 this percentage had risen to 36[61] – an outstanding amount even for small nations.

At the background of this massive investment abroad, Swiss mnes, in contrast to their Swedish or Finnish competitors, did not need a special preparation for the single European market to come into force from 1993. Swiss discussion connected with the single European market was not focused on Swiss fdi, but on the political role of Switzerland and on transport problems in a reshaped European economy.

As in other matters, the geographical destination of Swiss fdi shows strong continuity over time, though data limitations are severe in this area. As in the case of Germany, Swiss fdi was concentrated on Europe and the USA.[62] However the trend to spread its fdi over an increasing number of states, as shown in Table 3.1, prevailed in Swiss mnes. But hard data after 1914 are not at hand until the very recent period. In 1980, SFr. 6.1 billion, or 16.1 per cent of Swiss fdi, were invested in developing countries. No data are available for a more detailed breakdown by countries.[63]

As in other nations, too, the reasons for Swiss firms to invest abroad were many. A survey for the pre-1914 period suggests that reasons related to the factor market, representing 29.3 per cent, were slightly more important than those related to the sales market (26.6 per cent) and government intervention (25.0 per cent). Reasons based on strategic considerations representing a percentage of 18.0 were only fourth rank.[64] Within the factor market, most of the reasons were related to backward integration for access to raw material and energy,[65] while in the sales market they were focused on expected market growth in the host country.[66] Government intervention reflected mainly tariffs, and, to a minor degree only, patent legislation, preferences for local production for state orders, and so on.[67] Finally, strategic reasons focused on diversification of location of production and presence in certain national markets.[68]

In 1934 a survey on reasons for Swiss fdi of the silk industry was published by Schwarzenbach, one of the leading industrialists active in this sector.[69] He stressed that Swiss silk companies would have preferred not to invest in foreign countries, but felt compelled to do so, mainly because of tariffs abroad and high wages at home.

A general survey for the 1970s brought forward only variations of these historical reasons, though without suggesting their respective importance to each other.[70] Except the erection of legal barriers for further employment of foreigners inside Switzerland at the end of the 1960s, no issue was entirely new on the list compared to the surveys of 1914 and 1934, but the weight of some of the reasons for fdi had been displaced. Though in 1914 Swiss production costs were already high, compared for instance with Italy, they were much higher in the 1970s. This certainly prompted fdi, as did a strong Swiss franc. More emphasis, too, was on the acquisition of technology by fdi. Strong finances in all aspects, such as self-financing, heavy depreciation and so on, were suggested as a general precondition for the success of Swiss fdi.[71]

The reasons for Swiss competitiveness are very similar to German and Swedish ones. Swiss products have traditionally been quality products,[72] based on R. & D. and technical expertise. Industrial relations have been even more stable, and investment policy even more long-sighted than in Germany. While the standards for general and technical education are similar to Germany, the relations between banks and industry have been even more close. In this respect, Sweden seems a close comparison. In contrast to the German case, the reason for the large dimension of Swiss and Swedish fdi was evidently related to the narrowness of the national market. The multilingual Swiss population provided, in some respects, an outward-looking national culture whose language skills provided one basis for successful operations in foreign markets.

Conclusion

Switzerland was one of the first countries to develop mnes. In 1914 a total number of 265 fdi from industry alone has been traced (see Table 3.2). Switzerland has kept this tradition of being a leading fdi-nation until today. It can be said that Swiss fdi per head has been ranked among the top three of all countries for more than 100 years without interruption. Swiss fdi has been characterized by great continuity. The same firms, branches, geographical destinations, and forms of fdi are to be found repeatedly. If we apply Porter's concept of clusters of related industries and not of industrial branches used in statistics etc., we find extreme continuity. Where the branch concept shows shifts, for example, from fdi by the textile industry to those by machine building, Porter's approach plays these movements down, as it counts them into one cluster of textile-related industries.

For Switzerland, fdi is of extreme importance. In 1989 one-third of the total workforce of Swiss firms was employed abroad. The extent and importance of Swiss fdi raises questions about its national identity. The same question is put forward by certain clusters of competitive industries – their factor and their sales markets cannot be called national Swiss ones any more. Historically, Swiss mne has undoubtedly been rooted in the Swiss economy, which provided core competences and competitiveness. However, recent trends reveal that the Swiss character of Swiss mnes is declining. Large Swiss mnes have simply outgrown their home country's ability to provide them with national competitive advantage.

Swiss fdi and Swiss mnes are characterized by three striking features: continuity, scale and scope. All three are developed to an extreme extent. Continuity is obvious over a period of more than 100 years. The scale shows remarkable dynamism, keeping the amount of Swiss fdi in the top world list for more than 100 years. For the scope, finally, we may cite Porter: 'For a nation of only six million people, the range of industries in which Switzerland has a position is extraordinary'.[73] And again this has been true for more than 100 years.

Notes

1. Albert Masnata pointed out to roots going back to the Napoleonic Wars. Masnata, A., *L'emigration des industries suisses*, Lausanne, 1924, pp. 12 ff.
2. Bairoch, P., 'European Foreign Trade in the XIX Century: The Development of the Value and Volume of Exports', *Journal of European Economic History*, Spring 1973, **2**, (1), p. 18.
3. In 1971, production of fdi divided by the home country's exports was 2.4 for Switzerland, 2.1 for the UK, and 4.0 for the USA. (Krägenau, H., *Internationale Direktinvestitionen*, 1975, p. 43.)
4. The other ones, those of Masnata (idem note 1) and of Himmel, were published in the early 1920s (Himmel, E., *Industrielle Kapitalanlagen der Schweiz im Ausland*, Langensalza, 1922). Niehans's contribution was never intended as investigation (Niehans, J., 'Benefits of Multinational Firms for a Small Parent Economy: The Case of Switzerland', in T. Agmon, and C. P. Kindleberger, (eds.), *Multinationals from Small Countries*, Cambridge /Mass, 1977, pp. 1–39).
5. Borner, S. and Wehrle, F., *Die Sechste Schweiz*, Zurich, 1984, p. 213.
6. 'There are perhaps people, who, from a point of view of Swiss national economy, deplore the emigration (fdi), on the other hand it is totally excluded, that only a part of export could have been saved for Swiss industry.' Schwarzenbach, A., 'Die Schweizerische Seidenindustrie', *Zeitschrift für schweizerische Statistik und Volkswirtschaft*, 1934, **70**, p. 36.
7. Borner, S., Brunetti, A. and Straubhaar, T., *Schweiz AG, Von Sonderfall zum Sanierungsfall?*, Zurich, 1990, p. 102.
8. Borner, S., *Internationalization of Industry, An Assessment in the Light of a Small Open Economy (Switzerland)*, Berlin, 1985, p. 75.
9. Porter, M., *The Competitive Advantage of Nations*, London, 1990.
10. Borner, S., Porter, M., Weder, R., Enright, M., *Internationale Wettbewerbsvorteile. Ein strategisches Konzept für die Schweiz*, Frankfurt, New York, 1991.
11. See Chapter 1, p. 7.
12. Idem note 10, p 24.
13 See Chapter 5, p. 124.
14. Idem note 9, p. 317.
15. Idem note 1, p. 12.

16. Wavre, P.- A., 'Swiss Investments in Italy from the XVIIIth to the XXth Century', *Journal of European Economic History*, spring 1988, **17**, (1), pp. 85ff.
17. Many of such cases are to be taken from Bonnant's study: Bonnant, G., 'Les colonies suisses d'Italie à la fin du XIX siècle', *Schweizerische Zeitschrift für Geschichte*, 1976, **26**, pp. 134ff.
18. Mira Wilkins, too, identified the 1870s as the beginning era of European mnes. ('European and North American Multinationals, 1870–1914: Comparisons and Contrasts', *Business History* 1988, No 1, pp. 8–45). In her major study, *The History of Foreign Investment in the United States to 1914*, Cambridge, Mass., 1989, she stressed these years as dividing ones as well for inward fdi into the US by forming two periods only, 1607–1874, and 1875–1914.
19. Schröter, H., 'Etablierungs- und Verteilungsmuster der schweizerischen Auslandsproduktion von 1870 bis 1914', in P. Bairoch and M. Körner (eds.), *Die Schweiz in der Weltwirtschaft (15.-20. Jh.)*, Zurich, 1990, p. 395.
20. Swiss competence in the textile machine industry goes back to Honegger's inventions in the first half of the 19th century. Honegger started both textiles and textile machine-building industry. The same applies to Rieter 50 years later. Rieter became a mne only after the Second World War. Sastig grew to be the biggest Swiss mne in terms of share capital in 1914 after it had combined the marketing of embroideries and embroidery machines.
21. For instance, the embroidery machines for Sastig were built in Saxony (Germany).
22. Idem note 10, p. 108. In some matters, like this one, Porter's views on Switzerland presented in one of the chapters of his general book (*The Competitive Advantage of Nations*, 1990) have been changed during his co-operation with Borner on this special book on Switzerland.
23. Schröter, H., *Multinationale Unternehmen aus kleinen Staaten bis 1914*, forthcoming, pp. 42ff.
24. Ibid., pp. 31ff., pp. 178ff.
25. See Chapter 4. However, in contrast, Swedish firms, which had expanded heavily during 1914–17, were hit so hard during 1918-23 that they lost nearly all advantages acquired previously. This, together with the expropriation of their vast fdi in Russia, placed Swedish mne on the loser's side after the First World War.
26. Three in England and one in Germany: Heer, J., *Weltgeschehen 1866–1966, Ein Jahrhundert Nestlé*, Rivaz, 1966, pp. 63ff. There is an English edition: *World Events 1866–1966, The First Hundred Years of Nestlé*, Rivaz, 1966.
27. Wilkins, *History of Foreign Investment*, idem note 18, pp. 332ff.
28. Idem note 26, p. 119.
29. Idem note 26, p. 190.
30. Other acquisitions mentioned were Locatelli (1961), Findus (1962), Stouffer (1973), L'Oréal (1974), Alcon (1977), Chambourcy (1988), Hill Brothers Coffee (1985), Carnation (1985), Herta (1986), and Buitoni-Perugina (1988): Nestlé, *Annual Report for 1990*, p. 31.
31. Latin America and Asia each accounted for 11 per cent. In 1990 the largest single markets were the USA (22 per cent), France (13 per cent), Germany (11 per cent) and the UK (8 per cent), while Switzerland stood for 2 per cent only. Ibid., p. 9.
32. Idem note 19, p. 400, Table 4.
33. See Kramer, T. and Siegrist, D., *Terra, Ein Schweizer Filmkonzern im Dritten Reich*, Zurich, 1991.
34. Gesellschaft für Unternehmensgeschichte, *Villiger, Ein Schweizer Tabakunternehmen in Deutschland*, unpublished mss (Cologne, 1991).
35. For instance, Sulzer today keeps its stake in nearly all major Swiss machine-building firms.
36. In German this expression sounds very good ('die sechste Schweiz'). The 'other Switzerlands' are: 1, 2, 3 and 4 – the French, German, Italian and Romansch speaking people; 5 – all Swiss people in foreign countries (in 1980, 350 000 or 6 per cent of all Swiss people); 6 – Swiss enterprises abroad.
37. Bergier, J.-F., *Wirtschaftsgeschichte der Schweiz*, Zurich, 1990.
38. Idem note 5.
39. Dunning, J.H., *Explaining International Production*, London, 1988, p. 74, Table 3.1; Dunning, J.H., 'Changes in the Level and Structure of International Production: the Last One Hundred Years', in M. Casson (ed.), *The Growth of International Business*, London, 1983, p. 87.
40. Dunning, 'Changes in the Level and Structure', idem note 39, p. 87.
41. Calculated from Krägenau, *Internationale Direktinvestitionen*, 1977, p. 12.
42. Dunning, *Explaining International Production*, idem note 34, p. 74, Table 3.1.

43. Idem note 34. USA: 1960 48.3 per cent, 1983 39.6 per cent; UK: 1960 16.3 per cent, 1983 16.7 per cent.
44. *SZH-Liste* 1990 (Schweizerische Handels-Zeitung (ed.), Die größten Industrie- und Handelsunternehmen, Banken und Versicherungen in der Schweiz.
45. This is illustrated by the following example. The German coffee concern Jacobs bought the Swiss chocolate firm, Suchard, and instantly moved its headquarters to Switzerland. Jacobs-Suchard became Swiss. But in 1990 the Jacobs family sold out to Philip Morris of the United States, which kept Jacobs-Suchard as their holding company in Switzerland.
46. Idem note 5, p. 180.
47. This was not only diagnosed, but suggested for a future strategy to keep up the competitive advantages of Swiss mnes. Idem note 5, pp. 180ff.
48. Again stressed in Borner, Brunetti, Straubhaar, idem note 7, p. 36.
49. Nestlé, *Annual Report*, 1990.
50. Idem note 23, pp. 144ff.
51. Riedl-Ehrenberg, R., *Alfred Kern, Edouard Sandoz, Gründer der Sandoz AG, Basel*, Zurich, 1986, p. 89.
52. These patterns are shown by Germany, the Netherlands, Sweden and Switzerland. Schröter, H., *Multinationale Unternehmen*, p. 142ff; idem note 19, pp. 403ff.; Schröter, H., 'Changes in the Managerial Structure and Strategy on Foreign Markets, 1870–1914. Case Studies on Medium Sized Firms from The Netherlands, Sweden, Switzerland and Germany', in H.-J. Siegenthaler (ed.), *Studies in Small and Medium Sized Enterprise* (forthcoming).
53. More aspects are to be found in Hertner, P., 'Les sociétés financières suisses et le développement de l'industrie électrique jusqu'à la Première Guerre Mondiale', in F. Cardot (ed.), *1880–1980. Un siécle d' électricité dans le Monde*, Paris, 1987, pp. 341–55.
54. Cassis, Y., 'Swiss International Banking, 1890-1950', in G. Jones, (ed.), *Banks as Multinationals*, London, 1990, pp. 160–72.
55. Ibid., p. 168.
56. The year of 1980 will enter the history of Swiss industrial foreign activities as a turning point.' Both quotations from Borner and Wehrle, idem note 5, p. 152.
57. A possible source of error in Borner and Wehrle's book is their distinct distaste of business history, as they cannot imagine any contribution to knowledge from this side: 'We can spare the history of fdi here, as the American copper-mines in Chile, or the banana plantations in Central America in the hands of American firms at the turn of the century obviously have little in common with today's investments of IBM in Europe or Ciba-Geigy's in Japan.' Borner and Wehrle, idem note 5, p. 78.
58. Calculated from Wehle, F., *Veränderungen der Weltwirtschaftlichen Rahmenbedingungen und die Internationalisierung der Schweizer Industrie*, Basle, 1983, p. 64.
59. Brauchlin, E.A., 'Role and Structure of Swiss Multinationals', in K. Macharzinat and W.H. Staehle (eds.), *European Approaches to Industrial Management*, Berlin, 1986, p. 69, Table 2.
60. *SHZ-Liste* 1990 (Schweizerische Handels-Zeitung ed.), Die grössten Industrie- und Handelsunternehmen, Banken und Versicherungen in der Schweiz, Table – 'Die 50 grössten Arbeitgeber im Ausland'.
61. Calculated from: *Swiss Statistical Yearbook*; Brauchlin, idem note 59, p. 69; *SHZ-Liste* 1990, Table – 'Die 50 grössten Arbeitgeber im Ausland'.
62. Wilkins, *History of Foreign Investment*, idem note 18.
63. Krägenau, H., *Internationale Direktinvestitionen*, 1987, p. 512.
64. Schröter, *Multinationale* idem note 23, p. 102, Table 4.7. For Swiss mnes before 1914, 444 single reasons have been extracted from various sources.
65. Ibid., p. 379, Table CH-22.
66. Ibid., p. 379, Table CH-21.
67. The percentages within the rubric 'government intervention' were: tariffs 89 per cent; patent legislation 8 per cent, preferences for indigenous production for state orders 6 per cent, taxes etc. 8 per cent. Total number of reasons in this rubric were 111 (Ibid., p. 378, Table CH-20).
68. Ibid., p. 381, Table CH-23. The remaining small percentage reflected purely personal reasons, such as a better climate for the health of the patron.
69. Idem note 6, pp. 30–53.
70. List in Brauchlin, idem note 59, pp. 72.

71. Fürer, A., 'Die Bedeutung von Verlagerungen aus volkswirtschaftlicher und politischer Sicht', *Industrielle Organisation, 1972*, **41**, (2), 90.
72. This does not hold true for all sectors and all periods. The Swiss silk industry, for instance, at its time of peak development before the First World War, concentrated on a medium quality, which was not in direct competition with the famous French industry of Lyon.
73. Idem note 9, p. 317.

4 Outward bound. The rise of Dutch multinationals[1]

Ben P.A. Gales and Keetie E. Sluyterman

The Dutch have a comparatively strong position in foreign direct investment (fdi), a position held ever since the First World War. Table 4.1 gives an impression of the development in both fdi and total private investment abroad by the Dutch.[2] At the turn of the century, direct investment across the borders by Dutch companies accounted for about 20 per cent of all private investment, if investment in the colonies is classified as fdi. The percentage increased to 40 in 1914. The Netherlands then occupied a fifth position after the UK, USA, France and Germany in the world's stock of accumulated fdi. In 1938, the Dutch ranked third with a share of 10 per cent. The Dutch Indies were of major importance, but Dutch investment was noticeable in some other countries as well. In 1938, the Netherlands was the third largest direct investor in the USA, after the UK and Canada. All direct

Table 4.1   Estimated stock of accumulated Dutch foreign investment and Dutch fdi, 1900–85 (US $m)

	Total foreign private investment	Foreign direct investment			
		Total	Dutch East Indies	USA	Dutch share in world's stock of fdi (% of total)
1900	1 600	330	305	8	–
1914	2 050	925	690	135	6
1938	4 860	2 700	1 620	380	10
1947	2 865	1 550	750	–	–
1960	–	7 000	–	–	11
1973	–	15 900	–	2 232	8
1985	103 735	54 350	–	22 187	6 (1983)

investment accounted for more than one-half of total private investment abroad in that year. In 1947, the stock of fdi was 40 per cent less than it had been before the war, mainly due to disinvestment in the colonies. During the following decades, direct investment abroad increased faster than national income. Its share in total private investment in foreign countries fluctuated around 55 per cent. In 1960 and 1973, the Netherlands occupied a third position in the world's stock after the USA and UK; a decade later, its rank was third or fourth.[3] Recent estimates give the Dutch a joint fourth position with the Germans, after the USA, Britain and Japan.[4] Relative to national income or wealth, Dutch fdi would figure even more prominently.

Studying the history of multinationals, many authors restrict themselves to backtracking the development of the now large and important multinationals. In this way, all the firms which never expanded, but nevertheless operated on an international scale, are neglected. Of course, large multinationals have been of paramount importance in the Netherlands. In the 1930s, two companies were responsible for 95 per cent of all Dutch fdi in the US: 70 per cent was invested by Shell Union, 25 per cent by Algemeene Kunstzijde Unie (AKU).[5] In the 1980s, the ten largest multinationals accounted for 75 per cent of the accumulated stock of Dutch foreign investment.[6] However, if one wants to know more about entrepreneurial behaviour, as we do, the smaller firms are equally interesting as the acknowledged multinationals. In this chapter we will pay some attention to small firms with foreign subsidiaries without neglecting the large multinationals. With the literature at our disposal, we cannot do more than search for the motives behind the international activities of firms and look for the countries most favoured. By analysing the motives, we hope to gain a better understanding of the strong position of the Netherlands in fdi.

Free-standing enterprises and the Royal Dutch Shell, 1870–1914

'Internationalism is a cardinal feature of business life in the Netherlands', according to a present-day, foreign observer P. Lawrence.[7] The same might have been said by an observer a century ago. The international character of business life then was due to trade, the export of private capital and the exploitation of colonies. From 1880 onwards, a few hundred 'free-standing companies' were founded to grow and market the primary products of the Dutch East Indies. Sugar companies, but also coffee, tobacco, rubber plantations, and tin and oil companies were founded with capital from Holland. Some quickly failed or were taken over. A few are still in business as the Deli Maatschappij, the Handelsvereeniging Amsterdam and, of course, the Royal Dutch/Shell.[8]

Mira Wilkins drew attention to the phenomenon of the free-standing enterprise and its great contribution to fdi in the last decades of the 19th century. A free-standing enterprise operates mainly in a foreign country, while the board of directors and a secretary remain at home. Many British free-standing enterprises operated in the USA.[9] The Dutch used the same kind of firm to invest abroad. The majority of the Dutch free-standing companies worked in the Dutch Indies. This economic institution is well suited to the exploitation of mineral or natural resources. Occasionally, such firms operated outside the colonies. Several oil companies were active in Romania, one oil company, Petroleum Maatschappij Salt Creek, tried its luck in the USA in 1907 and the Nederlandsch-Surinaamsche Goudmaatschappij tried to find gold in Surinam.

Are free-standing companies investing in the Dutch Indies to be counted as direct investment? These firms were certainly the product of overseas investment, with all the problems attached to carrying on a business in an unknown territory, in a completely different climate and amongst people with different customs. Managing these companies from the Netherlands required a special approach and involved many risks. The history of the Oliefabrieken Insulinde gives an illuminating illustration of the great problems involved in managing from a distance.[10] Can a free-standing enterprise be considered a multinational enterprise (mne)? Without operations in the home country the qualification is debatable. The phenomenon is, nevertheless, interesting as an early stage of multinational business life. The growth of the Royal Dutch/Shell can be seen as a process of concentration among several of such free-standing enterprises.

The existence of petroleum in the Indonesian archipelago was known from the earliest times.[11] Since the 1860s, individuals tried regularly to create an industry. Concession hunters were well known in the 1880s and limited amounts of venture capital for prospecting were available in the Dutch East Indies. For exploitation and refining, however, larger amounts of capital were needed and could be found abroad. The Royal Dutch attracted Dutch capital. Firms dominated by capital of foreign origin needed more effort to enter the colonies than Dutch companies, but it was not impossible. Samuel's Shell Transport and Trading Company co-operated with a Dutch exploring company and acquired concessions in the late 1890s. Samuel was unable to do the same in British India. Production of the Royal Dutch took place in the Indies and the product was also destined for markets in the East. The first plans visualized sales and transport subordinated to production. The central sales office was initially located in the Indies, later Singapore. It was the unexpected result of Deterding's recall that this office was established in the Hague.

During the first decade of the 20th century, the Royal Dutch became the dominating producer in the Indies by taking over other 'free-standing' oil companies founded in the preceding decades. Sales contracts and other contacts between companies independent of the US Standard Oil Company changed gradually into loose co-operation and ended in the amalgamation of the Royal Dutch and Shell in 1907 on a 60–40 per cent basis. The Dutch part was to concentrate upon exploration, exploitation and refining; transport and commercial aspects would be managed from the British headquarters. This division remained largely intact over the years. However, Deterding, the head of the Royal Dutch and general manager of the new combination, set up office in London and strategic decisions were usually taken in Britain.

Before the amalgamation, the Royal Dutch had opened its first European production unit, a simple refinery, in Rotterdam in 1902 and a second one in Germany a year later. Deficiencies in the supply of petrol by the Standard provided independent producers with an opportunity to penetrate the European market. Though its original statutes tied the Royal Dutch to the Dutch Indies, its management was interested in other producing areas. The company became involved in the production of oil in Romania through a subsidiary. Russia followed and, on the eve of the First World War, the United States, Mexico and Egypt. In the early 1920s, most oil still came from the Dutch Indies, but a few years later, the United States contributed most to production. During the same decade, the Royal Dutch slowly expanded into other activities. The company became a producer of chemicals as well. Together with Hoogovens, which supplied gas from its blast-furnaces, a factory for chemical fertilizers was formed.

Compared to these risky and large international transactions, the activities of the first manufacturing companies with mainly production units just across the Dutch border were of minor importance. For some individual firms, activities abroad were of more significance. The first modern multinational entrepreneur was the founding father of the Dutch potato flour industry, which emerged around 1850. Between 1864 and 1889, W.A. Scholten established nine factories in the potato growing rural areas of North Germany, Poland, Russia and Austria. He closed some of these soon because they were insufficiently profitable, but his company retained a presence abroad. Scholten was one of the Dutch who ventured into the Galician oilfield in the 1870s, but without luck. Two margarine companies, Van den Berg and Jurgens, exported most of their margarine long before they tried to conquer the Dutch market. Rising tariffs motivated them to start production abroad. They invested close to home – Germany, Belgium and England. Van Berkel's Patent was more daring with a plant in the USA as early as 1909. The chocolate manufacturer Bensdorp & Co. had a factory in Vienna. The last two are examples of smaller manufacturing firms which had foreign subsidiaries.[12]

Banks and life insurance companies abroad

A large part of the service sector produces locally for local demand. Within services, insurance is often seen as an outstanding example of a national industry, life and health insurance in particular being overwhelmingly the province of domestic companies. Banking has a more international image. Dutch banking was international, but less multinational than one would expect. Life insurance was national, but more multinational around 1900 than often realized. We will touch on the history of banking cursorily as a contrast to the development in insurance.

Traditionally, Dutch private equity investment was large. Some Dutch bankers were major intermediaries in international government finance.[13] During the 19th century, Dutch banking houses acquired 'special competence' in American railroads and formed investment companies which sold their own securities to the public.[14]

Occasionally, representatives of the Dutch investors participated in the daily management of railway companies to safeguard their capital. From the beginning of the 20th century, these firms handled industrial stock as well. Multinational banking, banks opening branch offices or acquiring banks abroad, was nevertheless of minor importance in the Netherlands before 1914. There were two exceptions, the Banque de Paris et des Pays-Bas, in fact a French firm, and the Nederlandsche Handel-Maatschappij (Netherland Trading Society).[15] The latter, initially a trading company with a monopoly on transport and the sale of the government's produce from the Dutch East Indies, had the most extensive network abroad: 17 agencies in the Dutch Indies, another five elsewhere in the Far East and one in Surinam in 1912.[16] The other main, corporate banks were not multinationals or had only a minor presence abroad.[17] The Dutch colonies were not as conducive to the emergence of overseas banking with substantial branch offices as the British. The colonial banks were to a large extent free-standing. These banks concentrated mainly upon the colonial market, which they shared with foreign banks established in the Far East. Their European business, however, grew from the beginning of the 20th century.[18] Credit to plantations established a special niche for estate banks, which combined banking with agricultural activities. It seems that the Dutch offices of both types of banks amounted to less than the headquarters of the independent British overseas banks in London.[19] Outside the colonies, Dutch overseas banking was restricted to South Africa. These African banks were anything but vigorous.

The relatively low Dutch interest rate stimulated the development of overseas mortgage banks.[20] Most were established in two waves after 1880. Specialized banks invested in the Dutch Indies, South Africa, Argentina, but mainly in the United States and Canada. In 1900, these banks had invested US$ 10 million in the United States. Investment increased rapidly after 1910. In 1913, the value of all foreign mortgage bonds was US$ 43 million, of which 27 was invested in the United States.[21] The mortgage bank attracted small investors; some banks did not establish their head office in the financial centre, Amsterdam, but in small towns in rural areas.[22] Wilkins characterizes some of their activities in the United States as formidable.[23] As with the colonial free-standing entreprises it is debatable whether these banks were multinationals. The mortgage banks had no branches abroad, but co-operated with trust companies. The fortunes of the mortgage banks varied widely. Already before the end of the First World War, they had to cope with serious financial difficulties. One bank credited losses to an account 'Arcadia', but neither this nor other remedies could avert the decline of this sector. The value of the foreign mortgage bonds decreased to US$ 9 million in the mid-1930s.[24]

The insurance industry was international and some sectors were remarkably multinational before the First World War.[25] In transport and marine insurance, representatives of foreign companies had a larger market share than Dutch companies since the middle of the 19th century. In these sectors the Dutch specialized in broking within and across borders. Almost half of the premiums of the fire offices came from abroad in 1910. Life insurance was more a domestic business. Still in

1910 one-third of the portfolio of Dutch companies was insured abroad, while foreign companies had a market share of 14 per cent within the Netherlands.[26] Life insurance companies were either national or multinational firms. Systematic data on non-life insurance are scarce, but sectors such as sea or fire insurance and reinsurance resembled international banking: firms conducted business abroad through correspondents or agents, but mostly not through subsidiaries. In this period, the links between different types of insurance were weak. Most companies confined themselves to either life or fire or another branch of casualty insurance. We will concentrate upon life insurance, the most important and best researched sector, as an example of multinational business in services.

The first Dutch life insurance company to go abroad was the Vennootschap Nederland, one in a minor wave of new companies which entered the Dutch market around 1860. Soon it tried to enter the German market, but failed to attract customers there. In 1893, the company tried to sweep the American market. The production of policies was overwhelming, the financial reserves, however, were too small to cope with high growth rates.[27] Canvassing was stopped after four years, but the portfolio was kept till 1924. Other companies made similar efforts to expand across the borders, mainly into Europe. Usually the outcome was the same. Most attempts to internationalize were short-lived trials ending within three or four years. Attempts bore fruit most easily in the colonies. The Belgian market also provided opportunities for a cautious internationalization. Most companies selling insurance in either the Dutch Indies or Belgium operated in only one foreign market. From the 96 life insurance companies in the Netherlands in 1910, 22 had branch offices abroad, the other 74 operated only in the Netherlands.[28] The 22 companies had between them 49 foreign branches, of which 15 were in the colonies. In 1910 three firms were represented in three or more foreign markets, excluding the colonies. A few companies were truly multinational. The Dordrecht was represented in six countries, the Algemeene Maatschappij van Levensverzekering en Lijfrente sold policies in eight different markets. The Verzekeringsmaatschappij Kosmos had substantial interests abroad, but its foreign portfolio was largely concentrated in Germany. Capital assured by these three companies outside the Netherlands and its colonies rose to about 50 per cent during the first decade of the century.

Expansion abroad was a curious mixture of chance and rational considerations. It is hard to see a well thought-out strategy in the pattern both of failures and successes. Somebody received the title of agent and the company awaited the outcome. Often the agent or managing director of the foreign branch had himself taken the initiative to contact the company's management. In the 1890s, increasing competition and regulation made expansion more costly. Companies became convinced that unassuming growth no longer was a real option. A minimal size and an unmistakable presence abroad were required. Companies opened branch offices, created an elaborate sales organization as soon as possible and invested in imposing and very visible property. Despite the rising set-up costs, expansion remained arbitrary. Uncertainty about what to expect was high. Central management found it hard to control effectively the operations in other countries. Good information was scarce and not easy to interpret at some distance. The preferred method of entry was to build up an organization from scratch. Takeovers were not practised; major legal and financial problems stood in the way of success. Links with the capital market were limited and amalgamations had to be financed internally. Even within the Netherlands, amalgamations were rare until the eve of the First World War. The segregation of national markets increased from the 1890s onwards, as supervision by national states became increasingly strict. This made mergers across borders even more difficult.

The major argument to invest abroad put forward by managers was the small size of the country. The Dutch market was described as saturated. In the Netherlands – and in Belgium – insurance companies seemed excessively numerous in comparison with the more extensive markets of the large European countries. Capital insured by Dutch companies per capita had been less than the amount insured by the German companies in the early 1880s, but passed the German level in that decade and might have been 40 per cent higher by the turn of the century. Growth within the Dutch market was astonishing. That very growth generated worries about the future. It could not last and internationalization seemed inevitable. Furthermore, profits in the Netherlands were low, at least since 1900. They were considerably lower than during the 1920s or 1930s.[29] It is not surprising that Dutch managers searched for better markets, even if they were unsure whether or not profits elsewhere were any better.

Did the Dutch companies enjoy a comparative advantage? Mortality, the rate of interest and costs determine the price of life insurance. The first two did not confer any specific advantages to Dutch companies. The costs of doing business abroad were underestimated, economies of scale were of no importance. The Dutch companies created a foreign outlet, but not a flourishing business. The Dordrecht started to evaluate systematically the profitability of the different geographical markets in 1898, almost 25 years after it opened its first office abroad. Except for the colonies and industrial insurance in Belgium, all foreign markets were unprofitable. Accumulated profits in the Netherlands and Dutch Indies till 1914 did not fully match the losses elsewhere. The other multinational, the Algemeene, did not fare better. Already before the war, experts started to comment furtively on the Algemeene as a weak company. In 1915, the managers themselves characterized their company as colossal but not strong. The First World War and its aftermath ended the first wave of internationalization. Disappointed in the results of their expansion abroad, the owners of the Dordrecht sold their company and the new owner parted with most foreign portfolios. The end of the Algemeene and the Kosmos was more disgraceful, as by the beginning of the 1920s both were insolvent. For many years to come, foreign operations in life insurance were almost exclusively confined to the colonial markets.

The rise of Unilever, AKU and Philips, 1914–30

The Netherlands remained neutral during the First World War. The supply of raw material and other resources caused problems, ships got lost. Many firms, however, did very well and came out of the war much stronger. A well supplied capital market and a hard currency enabled Dutch companies to buy foreign firms or to share in their capital. In the 1920s, international combinations were formed through equity-sharing, joint-ventures and mergers. The history of Unilever is well known thanks to the extensive study by Wilson.[30] Interesting in this context is to note that this economic empire did not emerge by internal growth, but was the result of a series of takeovers and mergers. The two internationally operating Dutch margarine companies, Jurgens and Van den Bergh, extended their business by buying going companies inside and outside the country. Investment abroad served to achieve a dominating position in the margarine market and to move into the soap market. Both firms had extensive operations in Europe, including Britain and Ireland, and a small interest in Cameroon, while Jurgens also had minor interests in Nigeria, the Dutch Indies and South America. The two companies had a profit pool agreement since 1908, but this did not work at all. In 1920, the two Dutch margarine firms and the central European companies Schicht AG and Centra AG arranged to exchange shares. The extensive Austrian-Hungarian monarchy had been Schicht's and Centra's home market before 1914, but trade barriers had fragmented their base after the war.

The co-operation remained rather loose, until the two Dutch companies merged in 1927. This merger had an original construction. A dual Anglo-Dutch company was created, the Margarine Unie NV for the continental part of their operations and the Margarine Union Ltd for the British part. This construction was chosen to simplify legal and fiscal problems. The two companies had two boards of managers with the same members and two head offices, one in Rotterdam and one in London. The central European companies were included in the amalgamation the following year as were the Dutch firm Hartogs (meat products) and the French–Dutch combination Calvé-Delft (vegetable oils). Immediately, measures were taken to bring some order and economic rationality in the mass of production units. In the meantime, negotiations were started with the English Lever Co., a soap producer which had begun to manufacture margarine. The outcome is well known. In 1930 the joint Anglo-Dutch company, Unilever Ltd-Unilever NV, was formed. The ingenious legal construction of one company with a dual personality was taken over from the Dutch concern. The new concern had two head offices, the main one in London and an additional one in Rotterdam. The continental part of the company was run mainly by the office in Rotterdam. The British and overseas interests were supervised from London.[31] Just as its location near the mouth of important rivers made the Netherlands the gateway to continental Europe, and especially to the German hinterland, so the Dutch part of the combination gave access to the vast continental markets. It was logical that London would become the main headquarters, all the more so as the Dutch company had already run part of its activities from London. On the Dutch influence on Unilever's management, Fieldhouse remarked: 'Far more international in outlook than most in Britain, speaking English, French and German, where most Englishmen spoke only English, the Dutch obviously made a very large contribution to the success of Unilever as a bilingual international enterprise'.[32]

Besides the Anglo-Dutch multinationals, a German–Dutch combination came into being during the 1920s.[33] In 1911, J.C. Hartogs had set up the Nederlandsche Kunstzijdefabriek (ENKA), a company producing artificial silk (viscose). Earlier, Hartogs had worked a short time with the British viscose company Courtaulds. The second founder of ENKA was F.H. Fentener van Vlissingen, partner in the Steenkolen-Handelsvereeniging (SHV).[34] The large demand for artificial silk during the First World War made the new company a thriving business. Some sort of secret agreement was reached with the German Vereinigte Glanzstoff Fabriken AG (VGF) in 1920. It is unclear whether the two companies agreed to divide markets or exchange research results or both. The literature we used was very vague about ENKA's patent position, which is unfortunate as patents played an important role in this new industry. ENKA worked almost exclusively for foreign markets; little effort was made to create a home market. Increasing tariffs threatened its expansion and motivated the Dutch company to found foreign subsidiaries in Italy, the UK, the USA, France and Germany. The German subsidiary was a joint venture with VGF; the French participation was only short-lived. In Italy two existing factories were bought; in the UK and USA new factories were built. Hartogs clearly liked complicated financial structures. In 1929, the smaller but financially stronger Dutch ENKA bought all shares of VGF.[35] Both companies were united in a new holding company, the Algemeene Kunstzijde Unie (AKU), share capital was multiplied and control was divided equally between the German and Dutch directors.[36] The earlier-mentioned British company, Courtaulds, received four priority shares, the other 44 priority shares were divided equally between the German and Dutch interested parties. The German–Dutch merger was motivated by the wish to diminish competition and strengthen technical ability. Both companies kept their legal and economic independence. In the same year, VGF concluded an agreement with IG Farben regarding the sale of artificial silk in Germany. The Dutch company had succeeded in conquering a place among the large international chemical concerns.

The third well-known Dutch multinational that sprang into life during these years was the electrical engineering company Philips. The three elements most important in the expansion of Philips were the use of other companies' inventions, their own inventiveness in adopting and improving both products and processes, and Philips's willingness to come to an understanding with competitors. Philips started in 1891, a period – lasting until 1911 – in which patents were not protected in the Netherlands. This lack of protection encouraged production and sales at home, but did not help if one wanted to export. According to Heerding, Philips's light bulbs were not cheaper than those of their German competitors. Philips aimed at a quality product, which was the main reason why the company actively promoted research.

Philips joined the German syndicate in carbon filament bulbs in 1902. The German competitors tried to keep Philips out of their home market, but had no qualms in giving the Dutch firm 'the rest of the world'. This was a constantly recurring pattern in international agreements: the first concern of Philips's competitors in Germany, the UK and the USA was to protect their own home market. Philips was left free to roam the world. The firm did very well out of that. Before the First World War, a team of agents was working to promote sales abroad. The first two sales companies were set up in 1912, one in France and one in joint venture in the USA. Its American subsidiary brought Philips in more direct contact with General Electric. Philips violated several patents with its metal wire bulb, but it was not quite clear which and whose patents were violated most. General Electric, however, had bought up most American patents in this field and sued Philips. At the same time, negotiations were started to reach a closer co-operation. In 1920, both companies agreed to exchange patents and know-how, Philips paid a licence fee to General Electric and the latter took a 30 per cent share in Philips. The agreement was reaffirmed in 1929. Due to its own research, Philips now had sufficient to offer to make a free exchange of patents and know-how attractive to the Americans.[37] Of course, Philips was a partner in the Phoebus cartel agreement of 1924, an internationally incandescent lamp cartel.

In the 1920s, Philips became a multinational. The decision to invest abroad was mainly motivated by unstable monetary conditions and high tariffs, but chance played a role as well. The purchase of a Polish factory in 1922 was triggered off by a special, temporary patent advantage. By the end of the decade, Philips owned production units in Belgium, the UK, Germany, Italy, Poland, Spain and Sweden. It had sales organizations in many more countries. Mostly, existing firms and their production units were wholly or partially absorbed. Joint ventures with important competitors formed part of the internationalization. Two Westinghouse daughters (in Austria and Switzerland) were taken over in a joint venture with Osram. With the 'most important' French bulb manufacturer a combined factory was built in 1931.[38] These three examples – Unilever, AKU and Philips – show that already in the 1920s, there was a tangle of interlocking interests across borders, which makes it difficult to speak of purely 'Dutch' multinationals.

Small yet internationally operating firms

It is not easy to trace the internationally operating small manufacturing firms. From 1902 onwards, an annual survey was published of all firms listed at the Stock Exchange in the Netherlands *(Van Oss' effectenboek)*. Small firms, however, seldom used equity capital, let alone applied for an official quotation. For want of anything better we used this source, although we are well aware that many interesting firms were not included. We discovered some more firms from a wide array of business histories. Nevertheless, a lot of firms have no doubt escaped our attention. We found over 20 manufacturing firms of moderate size with at least one

foreign production unit during the inter-war years, excluding the 10 or 20 manufacturing firms possessing only factories in the Dutch East Indies.

To generalize from such a restricted sample is, of course, rather speculative, but
it is the best we can do at the moment.[39] Most foreign interests were acquired during the 1920s; in the 1930s business had to be curtailed. Most firms had three or
four foreign subsidiaries. Sometimes they built a new manufacturing plant, but
usually they preferred to buy or take a share in a firm already operating. If Dutch
firms took a share in equity capital, it is often unclear how large it actually was.
Occasionally, co-operation might take the form of a 'community of interest' between a Dutch and a foreign firm. The case of Hoogovens is interesting because
expansion abroad preceded production. In 1920, four years before Hoogovens
manufactured its own iron, it acquired a substantial part of the shares of a German
iron and steel company. Co-operating with two other shareholders, Hoogovens
initially had a controlling interest. Concentration in the German industry reduced
the influence of the Dutch firm in 1926, but the investment in equity of the
Vereinigte Stahlwerke remained intact and some industrial co-operation endured
till the mid-1930s.[40]

The firms sampled were most often active in three sectors: food, chemicals and
electrical engineering. There is an interesting coincidence with the large Dutch
multinationals: Unilever in the food sector, AKU a combination of chemicals and
textiles and Philips in electrical engineering. Three countries attracted most attention: Germany, Belgium and France. The rest of the foreign production units were
more or less evenly divided between other European countries. Four subsidiaries
were located in the USA and two in Latin America.

The expectation of profits and the preparedness to take risks were the driving
forces behind fdi. Often the aim of investment in nearby countries was to counteract the introduction or raising of tariffs and other protective measures. The threat
of losing a good export position induced investment. The British subsidies on
sugar production stimulated the Dutch CSM to construct several sugar-mills in
Great Britain during the 1920s. As the subsidies ended in 1934, the factories, now
working at a loss, were closed. No doubt, producing near the customer had certain
advantages. While entrepreneurs often pointed to tariff measures as an argument
to start producing locally, market advantages were seldom mentioned. Only indi-
rectly information is given, as in the case of Van Berkel's Patent. Their American
firm developed special slicing machines adapted to the local market. Production
near the customer can be advantageous with perishable products. However, Britain, Germany and Belgium were near enough to export from Holland.

In the period before 1914, we found one clear reference to the formation of a
daughter firm to accede to patent regulations. The overall importance of this
motive is difficult to estimate, because most business histories hardly discuss the
patent position of the firm. Three firms operating in the USA – Van Berkel, Norit
and Organon – had their position on the market strengthened by the possession of
several patents. In combination with Hoffman La Roche, Organon went to the
USA with several patents of its own and a (hard won) licence from the German

company, Schering AG. The possession of foreign patents could provide a solid starting point for further transactions. The Algemeene Norit Maatschappij formed a community of interest with the German Verein für Chemische Industrie in 1927. Together with French and German firms, among others IG Farben, this German–Dutch combination founded the Carbo Union. This cartel agreement was dissolved in 1939. In one instance, the share in a German firm provided access into a cartel agreement outright: the Hollandsche Draad- en Kabelfabriek participated with her German subsidiary in a rubber cartel. Builders or dredging firms had another reason to create foreign affiliates: large building contracts, such as harbour works, were often awarded to national firms. By presenting themselves as a 'national' firm, they enlarged their chance of getting a contract.

Sometimes, progressive stages could be noticed: entrepreneurs started with exports, then built up a sales organization. Their next move was to pack the goods locally or to start an assembly line, and finally they transferred part of the production. These stages are well known and have often been remarked upon. This process, however, was reversible. Several plants opened in the 1920s with much optimism but were closed in the 1930s. For innovative firms possessing patents in foreign countries a similar route with progressive stages can be noticed. The first stage was to simply sell the patents, a second to give licence to a (partly) independent firm or a dependent firm. The final stage was to set up a foreign production unit. The Dutch firm Océ-van der Grinten is a good example of how a firm gradually became a multinational following this route. In Océ-van der Grinten we see an internationally operating firm without any substantial foreign investment.

Licensing as an alternative to fdi

In 1920, when Océ-van der Grinten[41] made its first entry in the copying market with blueprint paper, it was already used to exporting its colouring agents for butter and margarine all over Europe. The firm successfully interested the American firm Charles Bruning in its paper. The USA was too far away to export a product with a limited shelf-life and the two firms, therefore, agreed in 1923 that Bruning would prepare the blueprint paper with the recipes and chemical mixtures of Océ-van der Grinten. At the same time, the Dutch firm was confronted with a better copying process, introduced by the important German firm Kalle & Co. As Kalle patented the new copying process in many countries, Van der Grinten had to enter the world of patents or leave this market altogether. Van der Grinten tried to design around the Kalle patents and came on the market with a process of its own in 1926. However, Kalle started a legal action and a compromise was only reached after several years of litigation. The two firms concluded agreements over patent exchanges and the division of markets, after Van der Grinten had succeeded in reaching interesting and negotiable research results. From this experience the Dutch firm learned the importance of research, patent protection and opposition to patents of competitors. Especially, a small firm, lacking economic power, had to rely on a good patent position.

To exploit its technological advantage abroad, Océ-van der Grinten had the choice between exporting, contracts with licensees, or setting up foreign production units of its own. Several 'location-specific' factors – tariffs, patent law[42] and production near the customer because of the limited shelf-life of the copying paper – provided incentives to create foreign production units. However, small financial reserves made foreign investment difficult. Furthermore, limited marketing experience made such a course risky. In terms of 'ownership advantages', the firm possessed a technological advantage, but lacked a financial or marketing advantage. Under these circumstances, licensing seemed the best choice.

In the inter-war years, an international network of licensees was built up on the basis of the company's good patent position. Having contracted licensees in the USA and Europe, Latin America and the Far and Near East were visited. In small markets a distribution contract sufficed. Van der Grinten's gave exclusive rights to one firm in every country, in this way following the national boundaries of the patent law. With rising nationalistic feelings in the 1930s, linking with indigenous firms proved advantageous. The agreements with licensees provided Océ-van der Grinten with a royalty income, but also with an outlet for profitable chemical mixtures and the firm's special products, because the licensees made the bulk product only. Licensing and exporting went hand in hand. Regularly visiting the licensees, the managers of Van der Grinten learned a lot about the marketing of their products. In this way, the foundations were laid for the transformation into a 'real' multinational in the 1960s. Océ-van der Grinten was probably not the only firm acting in this way.[43] Van Berkel's Patent, Organon and Noury & van der Lande also used their patents to strengthen their position abroad.

Activities abroad during depression and war, 1930–50

In 1929 and 1930, the economic world changed dramatically. Consolidation was more important than expansion. Nearly all companies faced a considerably reduced demand. Production units had to be closed down. Several small multinationals gave up their foreign affiliates or converted production units into sales organizations. The only way to survive seemed to lie in rationalizing the production process. Immediately after the merger, Unilever started to merge its many production units in the UK. At least three factories were closed, which was not well received by the employees. The continental part had already gone through a similar rationalization earlier. Nevertheless, these companies also adjusted their operations to the reduced sales. What consequences the reorganizations had for employment within the Unilever group, Wilson does not say. AKU reduced its workforce in the Netherlands by half between 1929 and 1931. Shell reduced the number of employees between 1928 and 1936 by more than a half. The spectacular growth of Philips also came to an end. The factories in Eindhoven cut the production of light bulbs. Between 1930 and 1934, probably half of the workforce in Eindhoven was dismissed. At the same time, production of light bulbs was transferred to foreign affiliates in response to tougher trade restrictions. In this case, the depression caused an increase in foreign investment.

From the mid-1930s onwards, the economic situation improved. The subsidiaries of the Dutch multinationals in the USA especially began to show good results. On the Continent, however, business remained depressed and hindered by protectionism. The influence of politics on business was felt even more than before.[44] The German drive for autarchy and severe restrictions on the transfer of money hindered the international concerns in their conduct of business. Unilever even had ships built, considering this the best way to employ the profits earned in Germany. The German part of AKU became more independent than was intended at the time of the merger. Organon sold its German subsidiary as the Nazi policy was hateful to them.[45]

The unmistakable signs of an approaching war compelled the multinationals to take preparatory measures to ensure the continuation of their businesses. Philips formed a British and an American Trust to take care of its respective British and American operations. Head offices were formally transferred first to the Hague and later to Curaçao. The Dutch part of Shell also transferred its headquarters to Curaçao and made preparations to transport indispensable technical experts from the Hague to London. The first members of the 'Hague party' arrived in September 1939. The mixed Anglo-Dutch boards of managing directors of the two Unilever holdings were changed into a Dutch board for Unilever NV and a British one for Unilever Ltd. Since 1937 all interests outside the British empire belonged to the Unilever NV. After August 1939, all interests outside Britain came formally under the direction of the Dutch head office. After the occupation of the Netherlands by the Germans, all activities outside occupied Europe were managed from London. Also, smaller firms like Organon and Océ-van der Grinten prepared themselves to secure, as far as possible, a continuation of their international affairs from London or the USA. Afterwards, one of the managers of Organon remarked that all those preparations had been neither superfluous nor sufficient. Where no special constructions were made, Dutch foreign possessions were confiscated as 'alien or enemy property' by governments at war with the Germans. At home, the Dutch multinationals were saddled with a German administrator. The companies could hardly escape being involved in the German war effort. Their counterparts in the allied countries supported the war production, but with considerably more enthusiasm.

After the war, it took some time to sort out all legal problems. Several American subsidiaries had become very independent, as for instance the North American Philips Corporation. After lengthy negotiations, the AKU got back the Enka-daughters in the USA and UK, but the former VGF ventures were lost. The American Office of Alien Property did not return confiscated patent rights to Océ-van der Grinten, even though it was quite clear that Océ had not traded with the enemy. Return of the rights was not 'in the interest of the USA'. The Dutch multinationals lost their investment in the Eastern European countries.[46] The relations with the Dutch Indies had changed dramatically, as the Dutch learned gradually. Before the war, more than 8 per cent of national wealth had been invested in colonial estate companies and industries. After the transfer of sovereignty to the Indonesian government in 1947, Dutch business continued its activities, but on a much lower level. The final break came with the nationalization of Dutch property in 1957. The owners of plantations were hit hardest. The internationally-operating companies sold their activities or substituted personnel of foreign nationality for their Dutch employees.[47]

Foreign direct investment 1950–90: a statistical overview

The inward and outward flows of direct investment since 1945 are presented in Figure 4.1.[48] Outward direct investment nearly always exceeds inward investment.[49] During the 1950s, the outward stream steadily increased relative to the inward one. The sudden rise in 1958 and 1959 is remarkable. Direct investment boomed, but the peak was the result of two successive emissions of shares by Shell, one to finance the acquisition of the Canadian Eagle Oil Company.[50] The trend was reversed during the 1960s and by the end of the decade there was a net inflow. From 1971 onwards, the outward stream was larger than the inward one and increasingly so. Some authors suggest that the development of fdi was anti-

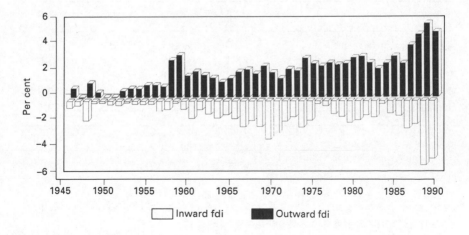

Sources
Van Nieuwkerk and Sparling, R.P., *De betalingsbalans van Nederland: methoden, begrippen en gegeuens (1946–85)*, Deventer 1987, pp. 104–11; De Nederlandsche Bank, *Jaarverslag* 1980–90.

Figure 4.1   Dutch inward and outward fdi, 1945–90

Table 4.2   *Stock of Dutch fdi by geographical region, 1975–89 (% of total)*

	1975	1980	1985	1989
EC	52	48	33	41
USA	13	19	41	34
Japan and other developed countries	18	17	13	14
Africa	1	1	2	1
Asia	4	4	4	4
Latin-America	12	11	7	6
without the Antilles	*4*	*4*	*3*	*3*
Total: thousand million guilders	53.6	89.7	132.1	167.3

Sources
Van Nieuwkerk, M. and Sparling, R.P., *De internationale investeringspositie van Nederland*, Deventer 1985, pp. 116–26; 'Standen van de directe investeringen van Nederland in het buitenland en van het buitenland in Nederland in 1984–1989', *De Nederlandsche Bank, Kwartaalberichtd 1991/1*, pp. 55–67.

Table 4.3   *Stock of Dutch fdi by sector, 1975–89 (% of total)*

	1975	1980	1985	1989
Agricultural/fisheries	0.3	0.5	0.1	0.1
Manufacturing and extractive	85.1	80.5	65.4	59.0
of which: oil and chemicals	46.5	51.1	42.1	35.0
Building	1.6	1.3	0.7	0.3
Services	13.0	17.7	33.8	40.6

Sources
Van Nieuwkerk and Sparling; DNB (see Table 4.2).

cyclical.[51] The correlation with the cyclical development, if any, was weak. Furthermore, the structural rise was more important.

Statistical data on the stock of fdi give an impression both of the geographical spread and the structure of investment (Tables 4.2 and 4.3).[52] Most capital was invested in the EC, but its share decreased. On the other hand, the stock of accumulated investment in the USA grew steadily to reach 41 per cent in 1985. During the last few years, streams of investment have changed again. The relatively large flow of investment going to the United States fell from 42 per cent of the total between 1984 and 1987 to 26 per cent between 1988 and 1990; the stock therefore decreased too. The flow of investment remaining within the EC increased from 42 to 48 per cent. The investment going to the neighbouring EC countries rose even quicker. The change was partly due to the growing importance of smaller firms. One would expect that they are more oriented to markets nearby. If the ten largest companies are excluded, 67 per cent of fdi went to the EC during the last few years.[53]

The stock of fdi in less and newly-developed countries decreased from 12 per cent in 1975 to 7 per cent in 1988. A transfer of production to low wages countries is hardly discernible. Africa plays no role at all. The accumulated stock of investment in Asia grew in the 1970s, stagnated in the 1980s, but seems to have picked up lately. Investment in South America decreased. In 1975, 85 per cent of the stock of accumulated investment was in manufacturing and extractive industries, while services accounted for 13 per cent. More than a decade later, the share of services had tripled.

In 1980, almost 80 per cent of the 220 largest companies, including financial institutions, could be classified as multinational. If a strict definition is used – the share of sales produced abroad at least 50 per cent of total – 40 per cent still qualified as such. Though many large Dutch multinationals reduced employment in the Netherlands since the 1970s, employment by all multinationals, inward and outward, rose from 14 per cent of total in private business in 1970 to 21 per cent in 1980. In manufacturing, the percentages were 29 and 48 respectively. In the last year, the share of multinational firms of Dutch origin in manufacturing was 36 per cent.[54] In 1975, the Dutch multinationals employed three times as many people abroad than at home, while in most countries that ratio was considerably below one.[55]

Outward multinationals were concentrated in the chemical industry, especially intermediate products, and electrical engineering. Multinationals in food manufacturing have a long tradition too. Internationalization in the retail trade, Ahold and Vendex International, is a new phenomenon. The geological conditions of the Netherlands gave rise to specialist multinationals in building, especially hydraulics. The international history of some of these firms goes back the 1920s. In the 1970s, Dutch publishers and printers went abroad.[56] What was the policy behind these data? To explore the motives, four multinationals of long standing – Shell, Unilever, Philips, AKU (AKZO) – will be examined,[57] together with one 'second-generation' multinational, Océ-van der Grinten, and the insurance sector.

Old and new multinationals in post-war years

The countries in Western Europe made a speedy recovery after the Second World War. The large post-war demand stimulated the building of many new production units to increase the output of traditional products and to produce entirely new ones. New operations were founded at home and abroad. Shell extended its traditional activities and set up chemical works in Canada, the Netherlands, Britain, France and Germany, besides its large works in the USA.[58] Unilever used the first ten post-war years for recovery and coming to terms with the end of colonialism. From 1959 onwards, an active acquisition policy was followed to diversify and enlarge its market share. Several old Dutch family firms with well-known trade marks joined Unilever in these years. Sales and investment in Europe became relatively more important than those in Africa. The relative position of North and South America remained the same.[59]

Philips chose to divide its production over many regions inside and outside the country. New factories were built near abundant labour markets or near consumers. Due to the import-substituting policies of South American countries, this continent attracted much investment. Sales organizations were supplemented by production units if these products were consumed locally. Many takeovers of smaller companies contributed to the spectacular growth in turnover achieved in the 1960s.[60] AKU diversified its activities and started to produce synthetic yarn and chemical intermediate products, besides viscose. It entered new fields in joint ventures with American companies, which led to new factories in the Netherlands. To speed up the development of new products, results of research were supplemented with licences from both DuPont and ICI. The old interests in Germany, USA, Spain, Italy and Austria were extended to begin with. Subsequently, attention was paid to the developing countries. Factories were opened in joint ventures in Mexico, Columbia and India.[61]

During the prosperous 1960s, new multinationals emerged. One of these was Océ-van der Grinten. Why did this firm decide to abandon partially its so successful strategy of licensing? Immediately after the war, the firm had concentrated on reconstructing the network of licensees along the pre-war lines. Its contacts with the firms in Eastern Europe, however, came to an end. A second period of expansion started in the 1950s. Growing world trade made the old division in national units redundant. Licensees felt restricted by national boundaries and quarrelled among themselves about the servicing of multinational companies. Gradually, the firm began to feel the drawbacks of a licensee network. It had become more and more dependent on the licensees, not only for the royalty income, but also for its outlets of chemical mixtures and special products. Licensee contracts, moreover, could be terminated within a year. As Océ-van der Grinten had looked for licensees in the same branch, most business partners were potential competitors. To lose such a licensee could be disadvantageous to Océ's business. Most licensee firms were small family firms, which increased uncertainty. The death of an owner-manager could greatly endanger the continuity of the firm. Two unexpected deaths in 1961 brought this insecurity home to the managers of Van der Grinten.

In the 1950s, Van der Grinten had built up financial strength thanks to several very prosperous years. In 1958, the firm was transformed into a public company with shares quoted on the Amsterdam Stock Exchange. Van der Grinten now possessed the financial means and the corporate structure to branch out. The developments in the EC provided an extra argument to participate financially in licensee firms. EC cartel regulations proved a threat to their traditional agreements. Furthermore, the common market offered opportunities to make production more efficient by specializing the plants in various countries. In 1964, two wholly-owned subsidiaries were set up in Belgium and Austria to take over the activities of the former licensee firms. The Swedish and French licensees were transformed into subsidiaries by purchasing almost all their shares in 1966. In this way, Van der Grinten became a real multinational enterprise.[62]

Economies of scale and organizational changes

Though potential increases in efficiency were used as an argument to establish or participate in foreign production units, in fact no use was made of the latent possibilities in the 1960s. The experience of Océ-van der Grinten seems to be in line with those of other firms. Unlike American firms, Dutch multinationals based their organizations largely on national boundaries, probably because they had experienced the force of nationalistic feelings in the past. The separate national identities of the daughters were stressed. The adaptation of Dutch business to local circumstances and its low profile abroad puzzled foreign observers, as did the predilection for 'self-conscious organizational complexity'.[63] Organizational changes within Royal Dutch/Shell in 1959 reaffirmed the national structure, giving the headquarters in London and the Hague largely advisory competence. Unilever had a clear policy of falling in with local customs, accepting local participation and local management, if necessary. Philips's policy was more or less the same.

Since the mid-1960s, the costs of accommodating to national circumstances and of operating on a 'local-for-local' basis became visible. Increased American and, later, Japanese competition made European entrepreneurs aware that they might produce more efficiently in larger units overstepping national boundaries. If they were not yet aware of these advantages, organization consultants of American origin like the McKinsey Company told them. The allocation of resources within a company was supposed to be more efficient than market transactions.[64]

Unilever changed its organization fundamentally in 1965. The continental organization was brought in line with the British one. Product units took precedence over national organizations. Philips had a matrix structure after 1948, with equally important product and national lines of authority. In the mid-1960s, plans were made to give more authority to the product lines, and some efficiency measures were taken, but the power of the national organizations remained unbroken. The new policy was partially opposed to another policy: the promotion of professional products. Strong subsidiaries with a 'national identity' were advantageous to increase sales of these products.[65] Diversifying the product range and increasing the size of production units were the core of AKU's management strategy. AKU diversified by merging with KZO, itself a merger of Organon and a salt mining company of origin, into AKZO in 1969. In the same year, the Dutch AKU activities, textiles, were integrated with the German part of AKU, the Glanzstoff company. Ever since the war, both parts of AKU had developed independently. AKZO's plans to restructure its textile activities in Europe in 1972 met with such fierce opposition that this scheme was given up for the time being.[66] Radical changes in the production in the Netherlands did not really happen until the mid-1970s. In this, the Dutch were no exception. According to Franko, reallocation of production did not seem to be a major preoccupation for most continental firms prior to 1971.[67]

In the 1970s, the flow of Dutch fdi was largely motivated by efficiency measures and the search for low wage countries.[68] Philips set up production units in South East Asia in the second half of the decade. AKZO, however, remained in Europe. The AKU (ENKA)-part of the business did not follow other textile firms. The recurring losses in the textiles called forth sweeping measures implemented from 1975 onwards. Unilever invested more in Europe than in other countries. In fact, its European operations became more important during the 1970s. The share of employment within the Netherlands, relative to the Unilever's total, was rather small – 4 to 5 per cent. In absolute numbers, employment by Unilever in the Netherlands diminished due to centralization of production. Shell increased the Dutch share of total employment; exploitation of oil and gas in the North Sea made the company more European.[69] After the second oil crisis in 1979 many Dutch firms ran into trouble. Diversified firms appeared most weak, notwithstanding their policy to spread risks. Exposed to fierce competition, both the multinational enterprises and the large export-oriented companies became less profitable than the smaller firms oriented to the home market. Part of the problem was caused by higher capital intensity of the larger companies and reduced flexibility.[70] Units were closed and employment reduced.

Changing motives. The example of Océ-van der Grinten

From the mid-1960s till the mid-1970s, the main effort of the Océ-van der Grinten managers was directed towards expanding turnover. New markets and new products were added to the existing activities. Not only former licensees but also other firms with promising products were bought. Océ-van der Grinten even decided to buy licences in order to enter the market of electrographic copying. In 1970 the most ambitious target was to reach a market share of 5 per cent in 1975, which meant a doubling of the annual turnover in five years. To reach this aim a merger with a large firm or with several smaller firms seemed advisable. This goal was achieved, somewhat later than planned, when the English Ozalid Company was taken over in 1977. Before the Second World War the Ozalid Company was a subsidiary of the German firm Kalle & Co.

In the mid-1970s, the organizational structure of Océ-van der Grinten changed, like those of several other multinationals before. Here, too, we see the consultants of McKinsey at work. The centre of decision-making was transferred from the companies in the countries to business units. The centralization of the production, already foreseen as a possibility in the beginning of the 1960s, was realized in the 1970s. Inefficient production units were stopped. Nearly all production was concentrated in Venlo (The Netherlands), France and Britain. There was no transfer of production to low wage countries. Océ-van der Grinten has always made extensive use of subcontractors. It might have been logical to find subcontractors in low wage countries, but this was not the case. European subcontractors delivered 90 per cent of all components. By the end of the 1970s, both the export activities and the contacts between Océ and the independent working licensees and distributors were intensified. There were still many independent licensees and distributors and their numbers were growing. The old formula kept its value in small, new or uncertain markets. In the 1980s, more attention was paid to product innovation and profitability. More researchers were employed to shift the main attention from copying systems to office automation. In 1987, the firm decided to keep itself to the 'core business': communication, the transfer of information on paper. Recently, more attention has been paid to the possibilities of 'strategic alliances'.[71] There is a willingness to co-operate with other parties in certain specified markets in order to participate in new developments.

Like other Dutch firms, Océ-van der Grinten showed a marked interest in the USA, which represented 40 per cent of its prospective market. An interesting example of a change of fortune is the relationship between Océ-van der Grinten and the American firm Bruning. In 1923, Bruning was the first foreign firm to buy copying know-how and chemicals from Océ-van der Grinten. At that moment, Bruning was considerably larger than Océ. The long relationship ended in 1961 because Bruning was no longer interested in the know-how of Océ. At the time, the USA seemed far ahead of Europe. Their paths parted, until Océ-van der Grinten bought Bruning in 1991. Even before the political changes in Eastern Europe, Océ did business with the large state organizations in the communist bloc. Now that private enterprises are emerging, Océ has opened showrooms in Moscow and in major cities in Czechoslovakia, Hungary and Poland. Sales and service organizations are set up or improved. Hard currency is still scarce in Eastern European countries, but Océ hopes to profit from their evolution towards westernized economies in the long run. Océ-van der Grinten did not transfer production to the Far East. However, the industrialization of this region generated interesting markets. Here, the firm co-operated with the Dutch trading firm Hagemeyer, an old colonial firm set up in 1900 and active in this region ever since. Océ-van der Grinten is still a predominantly Dutch multinational with 34 per cent of its workforce employed in the Netherlands. Turnover in the Netherlands is only 10 per cent; Europe and the USA count for at least 90 per cent of the workforce and 90 per cent of turnover. Today, Océ-Van der Grinten has subsidiaries in some 25 countries and in some 65 other countries the company still works closely together with licensees and distributors according to the principles set out in the 1930s.[72]

Recent trends in multinational manufacturing[73]

In the 1970s a vigorous runaway-movement to countries with low labour costs was foreseen. Philips's investment in South East Asia conformed to those expectations. The movement did not accelerate in the 1980s, but instead, more attention was paid to the USA. The recent renewed interest in South East Asia is initiated by the desire to be involved in current developments in this region, more than by labour costs. The multinationals are cautiously interested in Eastern Europe: Unilever bought a former affiliate and several other firms in Eastern Germany;[74] Shell is considering investment in these countries as well as in Russia; some small businesses dared to take over factories in Eastern Europe. However, it is still too early to discern a trend.[75]

The foremost strategy since the 1980s was back to core business. Investment and disinvestment inside and outside the country were motivated by the view of what the core of the business is or has to be. Business strategies were based on acquiring the most promising product mix. A coherent picture of well-formulated product links was the basis of the strategy, with a loose assessment of 'synergy-advantages' losing its former appeal. A difference with business policy in earlier years was that the selling of units was just as important as the buying. Profitability was more important than overall growth in sales. Another recent trend was the search for strategic alliances: close co-operation in specific areas to speed up technological progress. Both the identification of core business and strategic alliances resulted in frequent exchanges of ventures. Parts of concerns were disposed of, new activities were bought, or joint ventures were set up. A constant reshuffling of ownership took place: in 1987 AKZO sold its activities in the food sector to Douwe Egberts, a Dutch firm of long standing, with many foreign subsidiaries. Douwe Egberts could not have transacted so large a deal had not the Sara Lee Corporation been its majority shareholder.[76] Disappointment with the supposed efficiency of the internal allocation of resources was noticeable. Top management tried to make internal prices conform better to market prices and there was a tendency to put out more work to subcontractors.[77]

The global outlook of the 1980s bears some comparison with the 1920s. It becomes more and more difficult to speak of a Dutch multinational. The question arises: What typifies a concern more – the countries in which its operations are located or the ownership of the shares? Furthermore, the ownership is spread more and more over several countries, which makes it all the more difficult to assign a multinational to a certain country.

Insurance abroad: an old phenomenon returns

Concentration and expansion across the borders characterized the history of both banking and insurance since the 1960s. Some authors claim that financial services did not venture independently abroad, but followed multinationalizing firms in manufacturing.[78] Apart from the chronology, this is inaccurate. Banks expanded abroad before the insurance companies. The share of foreign business increased from 26 per cent of total liabilities in 1965 to 45 per cent in the early 1980s. The share decreased to 33 per cent in 1989.[79] ABN was the most international bank; one of its predecessors was the Nederlandsche Handel-Maatschappij, the most multinational of the large banks of old. In 1983, Dutch banks had many foreign branches relative to the size of the home market.[80] Concentration within the national market, however, has been of more importance than multinational expansion. An intended merger between the AMRO and the Belgian Société Générale was called off and AMRO recently amalgamated with ABN.

The re-emergence of multinational Dutch companies in insurance was a phenomenon of the 1970s and particularly of the 1980s. Of old, a substantial amount of non-life insurance premiums was generated abroad. Largely due to this branch, Nationale Nederlanden received 16 per cent of premium income from abroad in 1963. Non-life grew into a more multinational branch in the 1960s, a process that started in life insurance a decade later. Both branches were combined in the composite offices which emerged in the 1960s. Life insurance, however, was the most important activity. In the mid-1970s, foreign revenue, both life and non-life, of the predecessors of the three largest companies of the 1980s was 22 per cent.[81] The major expansion abroad preceded the merger wave of the mid-1980s, though 'the continued development of international activities' was one of the motives to join forces. The international expansion was largely confined to three large companies, Nationale Nederlanden, AEGON and AMEV. The first company was the fourth largest Dutch company measured in stock market value in 1988, larger than AKZO.[82] By the middle of the 1980s, foreign markets generated around 50 per cent of total revenue of these companies. The smaller companies were reluctant to venture outside the domestic market. The last few years, some have been trying to establish themselves in nearby European markets.[83]

In 1984, 40 out of 63 establishments of Dutch insurers abroad were within the EC.[84] As Table 4.4 shows, expansion was nevertheless mainly directed to the US. In that country, companies searched for interesting niches in the market. Therefore, AEGON and AMEV confined their American activities to life and health insurance. AEGON in particular concentrated upon the American market.[85] At the moment, it is the largest foreign insurer in that country. After the USA, Japan is the largest market with the highest per capita volume of premiums paid. Nationale Nederlanden penetrated the Asian markets and was the first European insurance company to establish a foothold in Japan. Outside a traditional European market such as Belgium, Dutch companies preferred to enter southern European countries such as Spain, Portugal and Greece. Expansion in Europe was motivated by the desire to obtain a place among the large European insurance companies, offering a complete line of products. Two of the three companies were pessimistic about the opportunities to acquire such a position by acquisitions or amalgamations in neighbouring countries. AMEV considered the European markets as less segregated.

Table 4.4 *Revenue per area of the major Dutch insurance companies (% of total)*

	Netherlands	Other European	North America	Other	Reinsurance
Nationale Nederlanden					
1985	48	12	23	10	7
1990	51	11	22	10	6
AEGON					
1985	53	7	40	–	–
1990	57	8	35	–	–
AMEV					
1985	38	12	47	3	0
AG-AMEV/VSB (1990)					
1990	36	36	26	2	0

Source
Annual reports.

This company amalgamated with the AG-group, a large Belgian insurer, in 1990. This merger across borders was the first of its kind in the Netherlands.

In contrast to the years around the turn of the century, 'greenfield entry', starting business from scratch was an exception. Companies considered acquisitions a less costly alternative to reach a local market share of 1 or 2 per cent, which was considered a minimum.[86] The long period of strain, high initial losses, and uncertainty of success in the long run made starting from scratch costly. Usually, Dutch companies were only interested in full control. To operate under one's own name was considered an important advantage and minority participation or joint ventures were avoided. These methods of entry were only considered when they resulted in full integration or when legal restrictions or market structure excluded any other alternative. Predominantly, foreign expansion consisted of the three major Dutch companies acquiring middle-sized companies abroad. Management was not interested in a mere transfer of ownership. The costs of goodwill were often high and the economies due to inclusion in a larger organization would not compensate for these.[87] The new owner should add value by organizational changes, the introduction of specialized know-how and integration within larger units in the host country. Entry within the fragmented, but rapidly growing Spanish insurance market provides instructive examples. AEGON acquired a subsidiary in 1980 and concentrated initially on the transfer of know-how in automation and management techniques. From 1986 onwards, other companies were bought and integrated in order to profit from scale economies. Nationale Nederlanden, however, considered this approach less congenial in this country and decided to build up a company on its own.

Two kind of arguments have been brought forward for foreign expansion: the small size and saturation of the Dutch market and the expected gains of foreign operations due to economies of scale and the better spread of the larger risks.[88] The very same arguments were brought forward in the middle of the 1970s and even in the middle of the 1950s.[89] Dutch insurance density was already high in 1960. The rank order of the Netherlands has been remarkably stable. In terms of per capita premiums it was the third country within the EC, both in life and non-life insurance. However, insurance density in the USA, the country the companies preferred to enter, was higher and remained higher. Though premium volume grew faster than national income, income elasticity of demand was relatively low in the Netherlands during the 1960s and 1970s. During the 1980s, however, growth of insurance premiums as percentage of domestic product was more pronounced in the Netherlands than in many other countries. Elasticity was higher in the Netherlands than in the USA.[90] The Dutch market was small, but was not unfavourable.

The life insurance companies were not pushed out of the Dutch market. In contrast to companies at the beginning of the 20th century, the present companies made a good profit. In fact, the insurance industry in the Netherlands was more profitable than in most other European countries, a position maintained since the middle of the 1970s.[91] The Dutch market was competitive and the insurers provided their services at relatively low cost, a good basis to exploit opportunities elsewhere.[92] In an interesting attempt to model the effects of regulation and the gains of integration, Price Waterhouse calculated a possible price fall of less than one per cent in Dutch insurance, due to European integration. Elsewhere, unexploited opportunities existed for low cost producers. In the fragmented Spanish insurance market, prices could fall by almost one-third.[93]

Expansion abroad aimed at reaching a market share sufficiently large on a European scale to stay in business as insurers supplying a full range of products. Managers continually mentioned gains of economies of scale. It is difficult to prove that such economies of scale do exist in insurance.[94] The most important economies stimulating internationalization were probably not connected with the volume of transactions in insurance, but with the increasing integration and concentration of capital markets worldwide. The share of investment income in total revenue has been increasing; investment portfolios were managed at headquarters and required scarce human capital. Entry to capital markets all over the world, round the clock trading, the spread of investment risks and more efficient management of investment portfolios were considered major advantages of multinational enterprises in insurance. Expansion abroad was furthered and chanelled by other factors as well. Insurance is a skill intensive industry. Decreasing information and transaction costs led to concentration upon comparative advantages in skills across borders.[95] The development of the exchange rate increased the relative attractiveness of the USA. The internal market of the USA is fragmented and the insurance industry is not concentrated.[96] The recent financial problems in banking and insurance reduced the goodwill of American firms substantially and stimulated a further wave of acquisitions. The disappearing boundaries between banking and insurance in Europe influenced expansion. Internationally-orientated insurance companies are amalgamating with Dutch banks which have focused upon the home market. Nationale Nederlanden, in contrast to its name more than a national Dutch company, joined forces with the Postbank/NMB and together they have formed the Internationale Nederlanden group.

Conclusion

The motives for fdi by Dutch firms changed over time. Tariffs and pressure by governments in host countries were of some importance before the First World War. Barriers increased substantially the attractiveness of investing relative to exporting in the inter-war years, particularly in the 1930s. After the Second World War, protection gradually became less important, though it still is a force to be reckoned with. Once a foreign production unit had been set up in order to avoid tariffs, further investment was often motivated by other considerations such as the gains of an increased market share and diversification of production. During the 1920s and again from the 1960s onwards, fdi was part of a wider wave of mergers, both within and outside the country. The traditional strategy to produce locally for local markets was not abandoned until the late 1970s. During the 1980s, fdi was no longer mainly motivated by the aim to expand business, but more by the desire to increase competitiveness by obtaining specific knowledge, matching products or processes, or special niches in markets. Instead of duplicating activities, investment was meant to supplement activities elsewhere. It is difficult to assess the importance of patent protection in decisions to invest abroad. The role of patents in negotiations and agreements between firms is seldom revealed. Anyhow, other means to exploit advantages of knowledge like licensing provided a good alternative to fdi.

As in Britain, low labour costs were only a secondary reason for Dutch fdi.[97] In the 1930s, domestic wages were high relative to those in the competing countries and this might have encouraged foreign investment as well as tariffs and host government pressure.[98] However, the international involvement of most Dutch companies lessened in the 1930s compared to the late 1920s. The drift to low wage countries was widely discussed in the 1960s. Labour and other costs of Dutch industry rose relative to other European countries and one might expect such a drift to have been more significant in the Netherlands than elsewhere. It occurred, but fdi was still mainly directed to Europe and the USA, not to the low wage countries. Dutch industry, both manufacturing and services, specialized in skill-intensive products. Life insurance companies too were attracted to nations with a high income per capita. The productive use of human capital, organizational efficiency and, perhaps, cautious investment were the main competitive advantages of these companies. In contrast to the wave of expansion before the First

World War, these advantages seem to give present multinationalization in insurance a sound basis.

Did the Dutch have other specific advantages which might explain their fdi? A geographical position bordering the sea, with access to important rivers and amidst industrialized countries stimulated trade and may well have encouraged the specialization in both intermediate products and services. An international orientation was, no doubt, furthered by the great value Dutch businessmen attached to speaking several languages. It might have made the Dutch into an interesting partner for the British. The longstanding and successful combination of Dutch and British interests in Shell and Unilever is really a remarkable feature. More research is needed to explain these successful combinations satisfactorily. Whether or not the Dutch possessed technological advantages is unclear. Dutch companies often used borrowed technology; inventions were imitated or licences bought. The entrepreneurs, however, did not restrict themselves to imitation; they adapted and improved products or processes. The import of technology became a substantial source of technological change. Inward and outward flows of knowledge under licence were in equilibrium in 1970. By the end of the 1980s, direct investment of 9.7 billion guilders going abroad, twice as high as the inward flow, can be confronted with imports of knowledge valued at 3.2 billion guilders, twice as high as the 1.9 billion exported.[99] As multinationals often have major research laboratories near their headquarters, a great amount of R. & D. happened within the Netherlands. However, on the whole, Dutch manufacturing did not seem to have a distinct comparative advantage in R. & D. intensive products.[100] The cause was that the industries in which the Netherlands had a comparative advantage were R. & D. extensive. Compared with similar industries elsewhere, Dutch industries have been technologically advanced, at least since the early 1970s.[101]

The same advantages which furthered fdi also stimulated trade. Revealed comparative advantages in trade were concentrated in the same sectors as the Dutch multinationals.[102] Both inward and outward fdi went to the same sectors: food processing, oil and chemicals, electrical engineering and some metal industries. Exceptions were agriculture and the metal industries in general, which performed well with exports without substantial foreign investment. In a recent book inspired by the theories of Porter, agriculture and food manufacturing were singled out particularly: measured by their share in world exports, the ten most competitive Dutch products apart from natural gas all belonged to that industry.[103] On the world competitive scoreboard the Netherlands occupied the tenth place in 1990. The Netherlands scored best in efficiency, financial dynamic, international orientation and socio-political stability. The dynamic of the economy and of human resources were unfavourable factors.[104]

Instead of looking for 'pull-factors', advantages the Dutch might have over other countries, we can also look at 'push-factors', disadvantages which motivated the Dutch to go abroad. The small size of the home market drove ambitious entrepreneurs out of the country; a high level of savings provided them with capital. For more than a century, the Dutch have been prepared to face world competition and, if necessary, visit the lion in its den.

Notes

1. The authors are grateful to Rainer Fremdling, Geoffrey Jones and Joost Jonker for comments on an earlier draft.
2. **Foreign private investment** 1900 and 1914: see for Dutch investment outside the colonies: CBS, 'Berekeningen over het nationale inkomen van Nederland voor de periode 1900–1920', *De Nederlandsche Conjunctuur. Speciale Onderzoekingen no. 4*, 's-Gravenhage, 1941, p. 13. See also de Jonge, J.A., *De industrialisatie in Nederland tussen 1850 en 1914*, Nijmegen, 1976, p. 306. Dutch investment in the colonies: used is the estimate for 1910 of Baudet, H., 'Nederland en de rang van Denemarken', *Bijdragen en Mededelingen betreffende de Geschiedenis der Nederlanden*, 1975, 90, p. 440. See also Baudet, H. and Fasseur C., 'Koloniale bedrijvigheid', in J.H. van Stuijvenberg (ed.), *De economische geschiedenis van Nederland*, Groningen, 1977, p. 334. Both higher and lower estimates exist. A recent one is Wilterdink, N., *Vermogensverhoudingen in Nederland. Ontwikkelingen sinds de negentiende eeuw*, Amsterdam, 1984, p. 456, note 8 giving a lower estimate for investment in the colonies. It is unclear whether he took into account investment in bonds of colonial central and local government. Idem 1938: CBS., 'Uitkomsten van enige berekeningen betreffende het nationale vermogen in Nederland in 1938', *Statistische en Econometrische Onderzoekingen Nieuwe Reeks*, 1947, 2, pp. 66–74. Foreign private investment exclusive of assets etc. of banks. The figure is almost the same as C. Lewis's estimate of long-term investment as cited in Baudet, 'Nederland', p. 439. She gives also a geographical breakdown. Idem 1947: CBS, 'Het nationale vermogen van Nederland en zijn verdeling eind 1947', *Statistische en Econometrische Onderzoekingen Nieuwe Reeks*, 1949, 4, pp. 3–13. Idem 1985: van Nieuwkerk, M., 'De internationalisering van de Nederlandse economie', *Economisch-Statistische Berichten (ESB)* 12 November 1986, p. 1089. **Foreign direct investment in the Dutch East Indies** 1900 and 1914: estimated by extrapolation between data for 1910 and 1920 given by Baudet, 'Nederland', p. 440 and Baudet and Fasseur, 'Koloniale bedrijvigheid', p. 334. Direct investment is taken as 75 per cent of total Dutch private investment. See for estimates on this share around 1920 and 1938 Van Lynden, C.D.A., *Directe investeringen in het buitenland*, 's-Gravenhage, 1945, p. 122; Derksen, J.B.D. and Tinbergen, J., 'Berekeningen over de economische betekenis van Nederlandsch-Indië voor Nederland', *Maandschrift van het Centraal Bureau voor de Statistiek*, 1945, 40, p. 215. Idem 1938: CBS, 'Uitkomsten', p. 74. A higher estimate can be found in de Bosch Kemper, M.J., *De tegenwoordige staat van Nederland*, Utrecht, 1950, p. 103. Idem 1947: CBS: 'Het nationale vermogen', p. 13. **Foreign direct investment in the USA 1900, 1914, 1938:** Bosch, K.D., *De Nederlandse beleggingen in de Verenigde Staten*, Amsterdam/Brussel, 1948, pp. 481, 499. Despite some hesitation, Bosch classifies foreign activities of mortgage banks as fdi. See idem p. 408 and Wilkins, M., *The History of Foreign Investment in the United States to 1914*, Cambridge/Mass, London, 1989, p. 512. These bonds were included in the figure for 1900 and probably not in those for 1914 and 1939. We have subtracted these bonds ($m 10) off the estimate for 1900. Bosch, *Nederlandsche beleggingen*, pp. 469–71, 479. Idem 1973: Van Nieuwkerk, M. and Sparling R.P., *De internationale investeringspositie van Nederland*, Deventer 1985, p. 116. Idem 1985: 'Standen van de directe investeringen van Nederland in het buitenland en van het buitenland in Nederland in 1984–1989', *De Nederlandsche Bank, Kwartaalbericht* 1991/1, pp. 58–9. **Total foreign direct investment** 1900 and 1914: guestimates by the authors, taking into account fdi in the Dutch Indies and the USA. The premium reserves of the life insurance companies due to obligations outside the Netherlands but including the colonies were estimated at 17 million dollars in 1900 and 40 in 1914. Idem 1938: CBS, 'Uitkomsten', p. 74. Idem 1947: CBS: 'Het nationale vermogen', p. 13. Idem 1960: Dunning, J.H., *Explaining International Production*, London, 1988, Table 3.1. Idem 1973: Van Nieuwkerk and Sparling, *Investeringspositie*, p. 116. Idem 1985: 'Standen', *De Nederlandsche Bank, Kwartaalbericht* 1991/1, pp. 58–9. **The world's total of foreign direct investment** 1914, 1938, 1960, 1973, 1983: Dunning, *Explaining*, Table 3.1

3.   Dunning's figures suggest that Germany had overtaken the Netherlands in 1983. See: Dunning, *Explaining*, idem note 2, Table 3.1. The Dutch Central Bank calculated an accumulated stock of US$ 42 billion in 1983, Dunning's estimate is 36.5. The bank's figures suggest a third position of the Netherlands. According to experts of the bank, the Netherlands ranked third in 1985: Van Nieuwkerk and Sparling, *Investeringspositie*, idem note 2, p. 10 and Van Nieuwkerk, *De internationalisering*, idem note 2, p. 1091.
4.   Van Rietbergen, T., Bosman, J. and de Smidt, M., *Internationalisering van de dienstensector. Nederlandse ondernemingen in mondiaal perspectief*, Muiderberg, 1990, p. 77.
5.   Bosch, *Nederlandse beleggingen*, idem note 2, p. 488.
6.   Van Nieuwkerk and Sparling, *Investeringspositie*, idem note 2, p. 10.
7.   Lawrence, P., *Management in the Netherlands*, Oxford, 1991, p. 2.
8.   Van der Zwaag, J., *Verloren tropische jaren. De opkomst en ondergang van de Nederlandse handel en cultuurmaatschappijen in het voormalige Nederlands-Indië*, (Meppel), 1991; see also *Van Oss' Effectenboek*, 1904–1914; Korthals Altes, W.L., *De betalingsbalans van Nederlandsch-Indië 1822–1939*, Rotterdam, 1986, pp. 191–7; Goedkoop, J.A.M., 'Handelsvereeniging "Amsterdam" 1945–1958, "herstel en oriëntatie"', *Jaarboek voor de Geschiedenis van Bedrijf en Techniek*, 1990, 7, pp. 219–40.
9.   Wilkins, M., 'European Multinationals in the United States: 1875–1914', in A. Teichova, M. Lévy-Leboyer, and H. Nussbaum, (eds), *Multinational Enterprise in Historical Perspective*, Cambridge, 1986, pp. 55–63.
10. Kamerling, R.N.J., *De N.V. Oliefabrieken Insulinde in Nederlands Indië: Bedrijfsvoering in het Onbekende*, Franeker, 1982.
11. The following is based upon Gerretson, F.C., *History of the Royal Dutch*, 4 vols, Leiden, 1955. In 1973 two volumes with notes left by Gerretson were added to a reprint: Gerretson, C. *Geschiedenis der 'Koninklijke'*, 5 vols, Baarn, 1973. Gabriëls, H., *Koninklijke Olie: de eerste honderd jaar 1890–1990*, Den Haag, 1990. See also Lindblad, J.Th., 'The Petroleum Industry in Indonesia before the Second World War', *Bulletin of Indonesian Economic Studies* 1989, 25, pp. 53–77.
12. Kooij, P., *Groningen 1870–1914. Sociale verandering en economische ontwikkeling in een regionaal centrum*, Assen, Maastricht, 1987, pp. 339–45; Wilson, C., *The History of Unilever*, London, 1954, vol. II, pp. 24–84; Glavimans, A., *Een halve eeuw Berkel*, Rotterdam, 1948; *Van Oss Effectenboek*, 1912. For a detailed survey of the Dutch manufacturing multinationals before 1914, see Schröter, H., *Multinationale Unternehmen aus kleine Staaten bis 1914*, forthcoming.
13. Eisfeld, C., *Das niederländische Bankwesen*, Den Haag, 1916, pp. 109–11. The following paragraph is mainly based upon this book and: Verrijn Stuart, G.M., *Bankpolitiek. Geld Crediet en Bankwezen. Vol II*, 's-Gravenhage, 1949, pp. 210–87.
14. Wilkins, *History of Foreign Investment*, pp. 34–6, 56–8, 70, 120, 205, 484, 510–11. Investment companies or administrative bureaux already existed in the 18th century, holding diversified portfolios of life-annuities.
15. The Nederlandsche Crediet- en Depositobank of 1863 merged with the Banque de Paris in 1872, a merger across national borders. French interests in the former bank, however, were of importance from the beginning and the French market had become of prime importance before the merger. The Banque de Paris et des Pays-Bas had offices in France, the Netherlands and Belgium. French business, however, dominated and the bank became one of the leading French, not Dutch, *banques d'affaires*.
16. *Mrs. Van Nierop & Baak's Naamlooze Vennootschappen* 1912, 31, p. 708. In the late 1930s, the bank had 15 offices in the Indies, nine elsewhere in Asia and one in Surinam: Verrijn Stuart, idem note 13, p. 229. The society had an agency in New York for a short period around 1880: Wilkins, *History of Foreign Investment*, idem note 2, pp. 855–6, note 93.
17. The Twentsche Bankvereeniging B.W. Blijdenstein & Co. of 1861, closely associated with the Dutch textiles industry, was represented in London by B.W. Blijdenstein & Co., a private bank established in 1858. The Twentsche owned 88 per cent of the shares. This connection with London remained intact during the inter-war years, though by then management considered the office in London of slight value: Wijtvliet, C.A.M., *De overgang van Commanditaire naar Naamloze Vennootschap bij de Twentsche Bankvereeniging. In de ban van B.W. Blijdenstein 1861–1917*, Amsterdam, 1988, p. 50. Till the 1920s, the Twentsche Bank also participated in three German banks which operated in the textile industry at the other side of the border. The

Amsterdamsche Bank, itself established with mainly German and Austrian capital in 1871, participated extensively in international lending. Its first foreign office opened with an unrecognizable name, the Amsterdam Diamond Office, in 1937. The bank had traditionally close ties with the diamond industry of Amsterdam: Brouwer, S. *De Amsterdamsche Bank 1871–1946*, Amsterdam, 1946, pp. 300-1. The Rotterdamsche Bank of 1863 was designed as a colonial bank, but concentrated soon upon business in the Netherlands. Later, during the First World War and its aftermath, this bank tried hardest to internationalize, by establishing subsidiaries alone or in co-operation with other, foreign banks. Success was, however, limited.

18. Like the Dutch banks, the Indian banks worked with agents abroad. The Nederlandsch Indische Handelsbank too was represented in New York in 1881. Wilkins, *History of Foreign Investment*, idem note 2, pp. 855–6, note 93. The bank, however, was almost insolvent in 1884 and might have curtailed its foreign business. In 1911, the bank, officially registered in the Netherlands, had two Dutch offices, nine in the Indies and two elsewhere in Asia: Eisfeld, *Das niederländische Bankwesen*, idem note 13, p. 202.

19. Jones, G., 'Competitive advantages in British multinational banking since 1890', in G. Jones, (ed.), *Banks as Multinationals*, London, 1990, pp. 33–4.

20. Eisfeld, *Das niederländische Bankwesen*, idem note 13, pp. 228–36. On the land companies and mortgage banks operating in the USA: Bosch, *Nederlandse beleggingen*, idem note 2, pp. 178–90, 437–50. The Dutch interest rate was higher than the British rate and became higher than the French rate in the late 1890s. One can claim that the Dutch level was relatively high around the turn of the century: De Roos, F. and Wieringa, W.J., *Een halve eeuw rente in Nederland*, Schiedam, 1953, pp. 36, 62.

21. Bosch, *Nederlandse beleggingen*, idem note 2, pp. 439–41. See also Wilkins, *History of Foreign Investment*, idem note 2, p. 512.

22. Bosch, *Nederlandse beleggingen*, idem note 2, p. 442.

23. Wilkins, *History of Foreign Investment*, idem note 2, p. 512.

24. Derksen, J.B.D., 'De samenstelling van het nationale vermogen', *De Nederlandsche Conjunctuur* 1939, X, pp. 123–5. Measurement of the portfolio in dollars undervalues the decline.

25. The following is mainly based upon: Gales, B.P.A., *Werken aan zekerheid. Een terugblik over de schouders van AEGON op twee eeuwen verzekeringsgeschiedenis*, 's-Gravenhage 1986, pp. 135–49.

26. Commissie voor de Monopoliseering van het Levensverzekeringbedrijf, *Rapport in zake de bedrijfsresultaten van het levensverzekeringbedrijf in Nederland*, 's-Gravenhage, 1918, p. 13, appendix XIII and XIV; Gales, B.P.A. and van Gerwen, J.L.J.M., *Sporen van leven en schade. Een geschiedenis en bronnenoverzicht van het Nederlandse verzekeringswezen*, Amsterdam, 1988, p. 70.

27. In life insurance, high growth rates can cause 'strain' costs as commissions might initially be larger than premium income.

28. Calculated from: Wiebes, W., *Jaarcijfers van Levensverzekering-Maatschappijen en Begrafenisfondsen 1906–1910*, Amsterdam, 1911.

29. Gales and Gerwen, idem note 26, pp. 29, 97.

30. For these paragraphs was used: Wilson, *History of Unilever*, idem note 12, vol. II, pp. 195–358.

31. In 1929 both parties had agreed to pay the same dividend to the shareholders of the respective companies. Protectionist measures on the Continent had an adverse effect on the profitability of Unilever NV, which made it necessary to regroup the interests belonging to both parts of the company in 1937, otherwise fiscal problems might arise. All interests outside the British empire were formally brought under Unilever NV.

32. Fieldhouse, D.K., *Unilever Overseas. The Anatomy of a Multinational 1895–1965*, London, 1978, p. 40. The margarine experts could be found mainly in Rotterdam and the soap experts in London. This situation still existed in 1977: Reader, W.J., *Fifty years of Unilever*, London, 1980, p. 106.

33. Dendermonde, M., *Nieuwe tijden, nieuwe schakels: de eerste vijftig jaren van de A.K.U*, Arnhem, 1961; Klaverstijn, B., *Samentwijnen. Via fusie naar integratie*, Arnhem, 1986, pp. 11–27; Verstegen, W., *Innovatie in de Nederlandse katoenindustrie. Een historisch profiel van twee diffusieprocessen*, Den Haag, 1990, pp. 9–19.

34. The SHV was initially a consortium of eight Dutch wholesalers, founded in 1896 to act as the

selling agency of the German Rheinisch-Westfälische Kohlen-Syndikat in the Netherlands. The SHV acquired interests of its own in Germany during the First World War.

35. Co-operation between the two companies in the American market may well have influenced this merger: Bosch, *Nederlandse beleggingen*, idem note 2, pp. 432–5.

36. There is some discussion about who actually managed the AKU in the 1930s. In his book about Courtaulds, Coleman published an interesting letter, which indicated that the older and larger VGF had not succeeded in getting control over the Dutch business: Coleman, D.C., *Courtaulds. An Economic and Social History*, Vol. II, *Rayon*, Oxford, 1969, p. 376. See also, Chandler, A.D., *Scale and Scope. The Dynamics of Industrial Capitalism*, Cambridge (Mass), 1990, p. 523.

37. General Electric gave up its participation in Philips in 1952. Philips bought the shares from GE and sold these again: *Van Oss 'effectenboek*, 1960.

38. Heerding, A., *Geschiedenis van de N.V. Philips Gloeilampenfabrieken: een onderneming van vele markten thuis*, Leiden, 1986, pp. 63–145, 175–82, 208–24, 359–417; Bouman, P.J., *Anton Philips, de mens, de ondernemer*, Utrecht/Antwerpen, 1966, pp. 116-24.

39. *Van Oss 'effectenboek*, 1912, 1925, 1932; Glavimans, idem note 12; Tausk, M, *Organon. geschiedenis van een bijzondere Nederlandse onderneming*, Nijmegen, 1978; *De geschiedenis en betekenis van een Deventer bedrijf. Kon. Ind. Mij. Noury & van der Lande NV*, Deventer, n.d.; *Vijftig jaar Hollandsche Aanneming Maatschappij*, 1959.

40. De Vries, Joh., *Hoogovens IJmuiden 1918–1968. Ontstaan en groei van een basisindustrie*, n.p., 1968, pp. 233–7, 347–65.

41. Sluyterman, K.E., 'From Licensor to Multinational Enterprise, the Small Dutch Firm Océ-van der Grinten in the International World, 1920–1966', *Business History*, April 1992, pp. 28–49.

42. Patent laws in many countries obliged the patentholder to work his patents or give a third-party licence to do so. Van der Grinten took this threat to heart, even though it is unsure whether it really would have been forced to give licence. See also, Haber, L.F., *The Chemical Industry. 1900–1930. International Growth and Technological Change*, Oxford, 1971, pp. 146–7.

43. Mira Wilkins kindly provided the following information. A census of foreign assets in the United States (in 1941) identified more than 60 000 'patents and cross-licensing and other patent agreements'; about 12 per cent (= 7 200) involved Dutch nationals. This interesting information suggests that the Océ company was far from alone in its US arrangements.

44. The influence of politics on business between German companies and the countries in eastern Europe is shown in Teichova, A. and Cottrell, P.L. (eds), *International Business and Central Europe. 1918–1939*, Leicester, 1983, part II.

45. Organon was a subsidiary of Zwijnenburg's Vleesfabrieken, a company led by Jewish managers.

46. Dendermonde, idem note 33, pp. 93–137; Klaverstijn, idem note 33, pp. 20–26; Bouman, idem note 38, pp. 151–88, 191–209; Gabriëls, idem note 11, pp. 107–9; Wilson, idem note 12, vol. II, part II, ch. 3; Tausk, idem note 39, pp. 157–63; Sluyterman, idem note 41.

47. Van der Zwaag, idem note 8, pp. 287–95; Franko, L.G., *The European Multinationals. A Renewed Challenge to American and British Big Business*, London/New York, 1976, p. 112; Baudet, H. and Fennema, M. (eds), *Het Nederlands belang bij Indië*, Utrecht/Antwerpen, 1983, pp. 36–7, 136–75; Wilterdink, *Vermogensverhoudingen*, idem note 2, p. 102.

48. Van Nieuwkerk, M. and Sparling, R.P., *De betalingsbalans van Nederland: Methoden, begrippen en gegevens (1946-1985)*, Deventer, 1987, pp. 104–11. The data from 1980 onwards have been taken from the most recent annual report of De Nederlandsche Bank.

49. A substantial part of investment leaving the Netherlands is transit traffic. In 1985, foreign savings contributed to more than half of outward investment. Van Nieuwkerk, *De internationalisering*, idem note 3, p . 1089.

50. De Nederlandsche Bank, *Verslag over het boekjaar 1958*, Amsterdam, 1959, pp. 49–50; De Nederlandsche Bank, *Verslag over het boekjaar 1959*, Amsterdam, 1960, p. 53; Gabriëls, idem note 11, p. 154.

51. De Jong, H.W. and De Mare, J.T., *Multinational Enterprises and the Structure of the Dutch Economy. University of Amsterdam. Department of Economics. Research Memorandum no. 8415*, Amsterdam, 1984, pp. 24–6; Belderbos, R.A., *De internationalisering van de Nederlandse economie: een studie naar omvang en determinanten van directe buitenlandse investeringen, SEO Research Memorandum 8801*, Amsterdam, 1988, pp. 6, 15–19; Jacobs, D., Boekholt, P. and Zegveld, W., *De economische kracht van Nederland. Een toepassing van Porters benadering van de concurrentiekracht van landen*, 's-Gravenhage, 1990, p. 84.

52. Van Nieuwkerk and Sparling, *Investeringspositie*, idem note 2, pp. 116–26; 'Standen van de directe investeringen van Nederland in het buitenland en van het buitenland in Nederland in 1984–1989', *De Nederlandsche Bank Kwartaalbericht* 1991/1, pp. 55–67.
53. Van Nieuwkerk, M., 'De Europeanisering van de Nederlandse economie', *De Nederlandsche Bank. Kwartaalbericht* 1991/2, p. 24.
54. Van Zanden, J.L. and Griffiths, R.T., *Economische geschiedenis van Nederland in de 20e eeuw*, Utrecht, 1989, p. 271; De Jong and De Mare, idem note 51, pp. 18–22, 30–4. See also De Jong, H.W., 'De internationalisatie van het Nederlandse bedrÿf sleven', in *Ondernemen in Nederland: mislukkingen en mogelijkheden*, Deventer, 1985, pp. 137–9; Van Nieuwkerk and Sparling, *Investeringspositie*, idem note 2, p. 76.
55. Besides the Netherlands, Switzerland and Belgium had a ratio above one, but the latter at a much lower level. Van den Bulcke, D., 'Multinationale ondernemingen en de Europese Gemeenschap: impact en respons', *Maandschrift Economie* 1983, 47, p. 309.
56. De Mare, J.T., 'De multinationalisatie van de Nederlandse economie', *ESB*, 28 August 1985, pp. 840–7.
57. The German-Dutch merger between Hoesch and Hoogovens in Estel in 1972 is not considered because the co-operation ended in 1982 before a real integration of both concerns had taken place. See for the participations of Hoogovens in the German iron and steel industry from 1945 till the early 1970s: De Vries, idem note 40, pp. 588–92.
58. Gabriëls, idem note 11, p. 153.
59. Wilson, idem note 12, vol. II, pp. 156-60; Fieldhouse, idem note 32, pp. 568–9.
60. Teulings, A., *Philips. Geschiedenis en praktijk van een wereldconcern*, Amsterdam, 1977, pp. 181–96.
61. Klaverstijn, idem note 33, pp. 22–37; Crone, F. and Overbeek, H., *Nederlands kapitaal over de grenzen. Verplaatsing van produktie en gevolgen voor de nationale economie*, Amsterdam, 1981, p. 171.
62. Sluyterman, idem note 41.
63. Lawrence, idem note 7, pp. 3-4, 111–12.
64. Williamson, O.E., 'The Modern Corporation: Origins, Evolution, Attributes', *Journal of Economic Literature*, 1981, XIX, pp. 1537-40. See also Dunning, J.A., Cantwell, J.A. and Corley, T.A.B., 'The Theory of International Production: Some Historical Antecedents', in P. Hertner, and G. Jones, (eds), *Multinationals. Theory and History*, Aldershot, 1986, pp. 19–40.
65. Teulings, idem note 60, pp. 280-2; Prahalad, C.K. and Doz, Y., *The Multinational Mission. Balancing Local Demands and Global Vision*, New York, 1987, pp. 55-8; Metze, M., *Kortsluiting; hoe Philips zijn talenten verspilde*, Nijmegen, 1991, pp. 55–72.
66. The case has often been analysed, among others by: Van den Bucke, D., *et al.*, *Investment and Divestment Policies of Multinational Corporations in Europe*, Brussels, Westmead, 1979, pp. 67–72.
67. Franko, idem note 47, pp. 141. Despite rising wages and labour shortages, few firms transferred their production in the 1960s. An occasional subsidiary was set up in Ireland, because the government of this country gave a lot of financial encouragement to foreign investors. Ireland had the extra attraction that it offered access to the EFTA market. However, it was not a massive movement. Instead, Mediterranean workers were brought to the Netherlands.
68. Franko, idem note 47, pp. 108–9, concluded from figures dating from 1971 that enterprises based in the smaller European countries had undertaken the least manufacturing in the LDCs.
69. Crone and Overbeek, idem note 61, chapters 5, 6, 7; Van Zanden and Griffiths, idem note 54, pp. 271–2.
70. De Jong and De Mare, idem note 51, pp. 14, 25, 27–9.
71. O'Brien, P. and Tullis, M., 'Strategic Alliances: The Shifting Boundaries between Collaboration and Competing', *Multinational Business*, 1989, No. 4, pp. 10-17. Long before it became an acknowledged policy, Océ-van der Grinten already made use of 'strategic alliances'.
72. *Annual Reports Océ-van der Grinten*, 1960–1990; internal strategic plans Océ-van der Grinten, 1970, 1975 and 1981; *Océ Brief*, 1989–1991.
73. This section is based mainly on the *Annual Reports*, 1989–1990 of AKZO, Philips, Royal Dutch/Shell and Unilever.
74. 'Unilever in Pratauer deal', *Financial Times*, 25 September 1991 p. 31.
75. Some of the insurance companies will start business in Eastern Europe soon.

76. Van der Zee, P.R., *Van winkelnering tot wereldbedrijf. Douwe Egberts van 1753 to 1987*, Utrecht, 1987, pp. 269.
77. The history of subcontracting by Philips in the Netherlands and the relations between internal and external suppliers is the subject of Van Royen, E.J.G., *Philips en zijn toeleveranciers: uitbesteden en toeleveren in de regio Brabant. 1945–1991*, Eindhoven 1991. The book, however, confines itself to external suppliers established close to Philips's head-office and production units in Eindhoven.
78. De Jong and De Mare, idem note 51, p. 19. See also Van Rietbergen a.o., idem note 4, p. 124.
79. Rietbergen, idem note 4, p. 119.
80. Grubel, H.G., 'Multinational Banking', in P. Enderwick (ed.), *Multinational Service Firms*, London, 1989, pp. 64–5. Evidence, however, is mixed. The share of assets owned abroad by Dutch banks in the world's total was halved between 1971 and the late 1980s. The share of the Swiss banks decreased more. Van Rietbergen, idem note 4, p. 116.
81. Dankers, J.J. and Verheul, J., *Zekerheid in verandering. Nationale-Nederlanden 1963–1988*, Maarssenbroek, 1988, p. 20; Eppink, D.J. and van Rhijn, B.A. 'The Internationalization of Dutch Insurance Companies', *Long Range Planning*, 1988, 21, p. 55.
82. Van Oijen, A.L. *The Netherlands in the World. Business, Economy, Markets*, Groningen, 1990, p. 75.
83. Van Laar, P.Th. and Vleesenbeek, H.H., *Van Oude naar Nieuwe Hoofdpoort. De geschiedenis van het Assurantieconcern Stad Rotterdam Anno 1720 N.V., 1720-1990*, Rotterdam, 1990, pp. 206–7.
84. Price Waterhouse, *The 'Cost of Non-Europe' in Financial Services. Research on the 'Cost of Non-Europe'. Basic Findings Volume 9*, Luxembourg, 1988, p. 59.
85. In Table 4.4, AEGON's 'Other European' includes countries outside Europe: Surinam and the Antilles.
86. Van Rietbergen, idem note 4, p. 142.
87. Peters, J.F.M. and Segaar, P.F., 'Aspecten van de internationalisatie van de Nederlandse verzekeringsconcerns', *Maandblad voor Accountancy and Bedrijfshuishoudkunde*, 1988, 62, p. 595.
88. Besides the annual reports of the companies: Van Nieuwkerk and Sparling, *Investeringspositie*, idem note 2, pp. 58–9; Peters, idem note 87, pp. 592–3; Eppink and Rhijn, idem note 81, pp. 54-60; Van Rietbergen, idem note 4, pp. 135–8.
89. *Gedenkboek ter gelegenheid van het honderdvijftig jarig bestaan van de Hollandsche Societeit van Levensverzekeringen NV*, Amsterdam, 1957, p. 109; Dankers and Verheul, idem note 81, pp. 15–17, 20–1, 194–5; Gales, idem note 25, p. 326.
90. Verzekeringskamer, *Verslag over 1989*, p. 9; Aaronovitch, S. and Samson, P., *The Insurance Industry in the Countries of the EEC. Structure, Conduct and Performance*, Luxembourg, 1985, pp. 13, 17; Price Waterhouse, idem note 84, pp. 20–21, 164.
91. The share of more profitable life insurance in total business is larger in the Netherlands than elsewhere. The European markets, however, have been converging in this respect.
92. Price Waterhouse, idem note 84, pp. 111–16, 127–8. Commissions, however, earned by intermediaries were substantially higher than in other European countries of which data were available.
93. Price Waterhouse, idem note 84, pp. 139–64.
94. Price Waterhouse, idem note 84, pp. 180-1, 246; Geehan, R., 'Economies of Scale in Insurance: Implications for Regulation', in Wasow, B. and Hill, R.D. (eds), *The Insurance Industry in Economic Development*, New York, 1986, pp. 137–59.
95. Wasow, B., 'Insurance and the Balance of Payments', in Wasow and Hill, idem note 94, pp. 87–103 .
96. Pelkmans, J. and Vanheukelen, M., *The Internal Markets of North America. Fragmentation and Integration in the US and Canada. Research on the Cost of Non-Europe'. Basic Findings. Vol. 16*, Luxembourg, 1988, pp. 65–9.
97. Jones, G. (ed.), *British Multinationals: Origins. Management and Performance*, Aldershot, 1986, pp. 9–12.
98. Van Zanden and Griffiths, idem note 54, pp. 42–3.
99. Within trade of technological knowledge, Dutch performance in 'technical services' contrasts markedly with R. & D. Van Nieuwkerk, idem note 53, pp. 24-7; 'De betalingsbalans van Nederland in het jaar 1988', *De Nederlandsche Bank. Kwartaalbericht*, 1988/4, p. 52; De Bruijn-

Schintz, H.J.M. and Jannink, J.M.J., 'Het technologisch kennisverkeer met het buitenland', *De Nederlandsche Bank. Kwartaalbericht* 1989/2, pp. 43–55.

100. Koekkoek, K.A. and Mennes, L.B.M., 'Revealed Comparative Advantage in Manufacturing Industry: the Case of the Netherlands', *De Economist*, 1984, vol. 132, pp. 30–48. Measured in exports of hi-tech products and relative to the deteriorating overall EC performance in the world, Dutch competitiveness increased in industrial hi-tech products since the 1970s: Pelkmans, J., *De interne EG-markt voor industriële produkten. WRR Voorstudies en achtergronden V47*, 's-Gravenhage, 1985, pp. 114–5, 147.

101. Van Hulst, N. and Soete, L.L.G., 'Export en technologische ontwikkeling in de industrie', Koninklijke Vereniging voor Staathuishoudkunde, *Export. Praeadviezen 1989*, Leiden, Antwerpen, 1989, pp. 63–85.

102. Financial services are an exception in this respect.

103. Jacobs, Boekholt and Zegveld, idem note 51, pp. 25–43. See also Jacobs, D., 'De concurrentievoordelen van landen', *ESB*, 30 May 1990, pp. 501–3.

104. IMD and The World Economic Forum, Lausanne/Genève, 1990, as cited in Uitterhoeve, W. (ed.), *De staat van Nederland: Nederland en zijn bewoners*, Nijmegen, 1990, p. 134.

5 Securing the markets. Swedish multinationals in a historical perspective

Ulf Olsson

In the early 1990s, Sweden accounts for 4 per cent of the world's total foreign direct investment (fdi) while contributing less than 2 per cent of world trade and a mere fraction of a per cent of the total world GDP. Sweden's share in foreign direct investment is mainly represented by a rather small and amazingly stable group of Swedish multinational firms (mnes), that is, companies with one or more manufacturing subsidiaries outside Sweden.[1] Three-quarters of Sweden's total manufacturing abroad is carried out by Swedish companies that were already multinationals three decades ago. These companies by tradition have a strong position in Swedish economic life; they employ more than half of the domestic industrial workforce and they account for more than half of the country's export. As long as mnes have existed in Sweden they have held an equally important position in Swedish exports. The picture of these enterprises is thus more or less a mirror image of the Swedish export industry, regardless of the causal nature of the relationship between exporting and producing abroad.

In order to understand the present structure of Swedish mnes, it is thus necessary both to explain how the Swedish export industries have evolved and why some of these industries have become international firms by establishing producing subsidiaries outside Sweden. A historical approach is natural, given the pronounced continuity of Swedish mnes. Several theories have been developed to explain their internationalization on a more generalized level.[2] There is hardly any reason to recapitulate these theoretical approaches here. In this chapter, however, a general perspective is chosen to discuss internationalization mainly in the context of the firm or industry rather than from a macro-economic perspective. This approach comes close to those theories that focus on the possibilities for firms to exploit their specific advantages by moving activities outside the home country. Many of those advantages, in their turn, are connected with country-specific factors that explain why Sweden has become a relatively significant source of fdi. Working on the firm level allows us to take into account a number of factors that are obscured by working on an aggregate level. Studies from this perspective are specially attractive, due to the dominant role of the rather small number of firms involved. Furthermore, a number of company histories exist, covering an earlier period of time, from which there exist few studies done by economists.

The first part of this chapter therefore consists of a historical background, including a number of examples of early Swedish mnes. The second part covers the period after 1960, from which we have better statistics and more comprehensive studies of the internationalization process to build on. Throughout the text, the L. M. Ericsson Telephone Co. or later just Ericsson, is used as an example, as it is one of the older and larger of the Swedish mnes.[3]

The industrialization phase

The Swedish industrialization process took place between 1870 and the First World War, with two great leaps during the 1870s and the 1890s. Sweden had for centuries traded with leading European economic centres. From being an exporter of staple or semi-manufactured products, the country succeeded surprisingly quickly in developing a more advanced export industry. There is no room here to go deeper into explaining how this was achieved, but one main result of the industrialization process was the establishment of a rather versatile engineering export industry in addition to the more traditional, staple oriented ones.

Two main groups of Swedish export industries could therefore be identified at the beginning of the 20th century. One was based on raw materials, and mainly geared to supplying the more industrialized parts of Europe. Apart from agricultural products such as oats and butter, it was dominated by forest products which were mainly sold to Great Britain, and iron ore which was bought by Germany. Capitalists from the industrial centres of Europe had been actively investing in Sweden to get direct access to these raw materials, but they were soon to be restricted by new legislation prohibiting foreigners from owning Swedish land. The Swedish staple industries thus remained mainly in domestic hands. These firms developed their production, selling pulp, high quality steel, etc., but they became mnes only to a very restricted extent. In a few cases Swedish forest industries tried to enlarge their own timber supplies by establishing subsidiaries in Finland and Russia. To these exceptions belonged also the firms that integrated backwards outside Sweden to secure the supply of aspen splint for match fabrication (Swedish Match), cork (Wicander) and an attempt to produce chromium for steel production (Sandvik) (see Table 5.1). Within the staple sector, the tradition of passive foreign trade was, however, strong and the establishment even of selling units on the export markets unusual. The process of forward integration by staple industries in order to establish production closer to the final markets abroad belongs to a much later stage in Swedish economic history.

The other main group of export industries consisted of the modern engineering firms. There existed in Sweden a tradition of metal manufacturing, originally based on the production of iron from local sources of high-quality iron ore. There also existed other country-specific advantages such as good technical schools and

Table 5.1 Some Swedish mnes in 1922

Company	Manufacturing subsidiaries in:				Product
	Nordic countries	Rest of Europe	USA	Rest of world	
AGA	3	6	1	4	Beacons, railway signals
ASEA	1	2			Electrical machinery
Baltic		1	1		Dairy equipment
C.E. Johansson		1	1		Precision gauges
Electrolux		1		2	Domestic electrical equipment
ESAB		2			Electric welding
Junger (NIFE)	1	1			Alkaline accumulators (batteries)
L. M. Ericsson		6		2	Telephone equipment and operation
Pump-Separator			2		Dairy equipment
Separator/Alfa Laval		2	2		Cream separators, dairy equipment
SKF		3	1		Ball/roller bearings
Sv. Konservfabr	1		1		Preserves and methods
Swedish Match	(see text)				Matches
Wicander	2		4	1	Cork, linoleum

Source
Lundström, R., 'Swedish Multinational Growth before 1930', in P. Hertner and G. Jones (eds), *Multinationals: Theory and History*, Aldershot, 1986, pp. 138–9.

an educated and literate workforce. The Swedish society by the mid-19th century has been called 'the impoverished sophisticate'. These circumstances partly explain why the Swedes were so quickly able to absorb new technology, make successful innovations and apply them in modern industrial production. Bringing the engineering industry into the picture, Sweden's role in international trade was no longer clearly on the periphery. In addition to exporting to leading industrial countries, these companies found important markets in economically less developed parts of the world. Russia was in fact the largest foreign market for the Swedish engineering industry at the turn of the century. Sweden had, in this respect, already become a part of the European industrial centre.

In some cases these innovative engineering firms developed in a way that has been regarded normal for firms with larger domestic markets: they mechanized and specialized in a technically advanced product, secured the home base, turned to more and more distant foreign markets in order to reach better economies of scale, established their own commercial outlets abroad and finally started to produce outside Sweden as well. This evolutionary model has partly been developed from the recent experience of Swedish mnes, and no doubt has a certain explanatory power.[4]

However, among the firms that finally became multinational, that is started production abroad, it was more normal to develop substantial foreign markets before having a Swedish market that could make the new production profitable. They often had to wait for the domestic market to be large or modern enough to form the basis for a more specialized product. Sometimes foreign products were already well established in Sweden and hard to beat from the beginning. This was the case for Svenska Kullagerfabriken (SKF), which started in 1907 and had to build up markets for their ball and roller bearings in Britain, France and the US before they could beat the established German brands in Sweden.

When it came to products such as separators and telephone equipment, the home market was also too small to allow the building up of efficient production. From the very start, therefore, a company such as Separator exported most of its cream separators. The limited size and relative backwardness of the Swedish market thus seems to have been a blessing in disguise for Swedish firms. The difference in size of the home markets significantly influences the development of small country mnes as compared to, for example, their American counterparts. The eventual victory of several of the Swedish mnes on their domestic battleground was rather a result of the ongoing development of their products in stimulating international competition.

The rapid international establishment of these Swedish engineering firms took place during the decades around 1900, a period of international industrial protectionism. Sweden belonged to the countries with the highest protective tariffs, which were in the neighbourhood of 15 per cent of the product value. Nonetheless, Swedish firms in many cases had more problems in holding their own at home than abroad. Tariff barriers did not prevent the Swedish firms from expanding their export and should probably only be given a marginal role in this period of dynamic industrial change. Seen from the perspective of the firm, daring entrepreneurs and skilful organizers were able to expand their activities, regardless of national boundaries. It should not be forgotten, on the other hand, that the export industry was actively supported by strong and internationally oriented investment banks as well as by the government, which not only imported capital for infrastructural investment but also aggressively promoted Swedish shipping and exports.

There was generally a clear and direct connection between Swedish exports and production abroad. Foreign production was often started in countries where a market for the product had already been developed by the mother companies. For the exporting firm to achieve a quick, market-oriented expansion it was in many cases most efficient to produce locally. This was normally done by building a new factory, that is a greenfield investment, but also by buying an already existing one, or by forming some sort of joint venture with a local partner. Sometimes, an acquired firm was not a direct competitor, but simply represented production facilities. Sometimes, a producer of similar goods was bought up. In the latter case, the Swedish firm obviously had an advantage over the local producer in some respect: be it a more attractive product, improved production methods or better financial resources. Such a move could also be a way of reducing international competition, especially when the Swedish mne in question entered fields where highly-specialized products were sold on an oligopolistic world market.

Normally, the establishment of a foreign production unit was regarded as necessary not only to increase production capacity but to get access to a specific market as well. Sometimes this was an outright requirement, especially when the customer was a public authority, buying, for example, equipment for hydro-electric plants (ASEA), lighthouses (AGA) or telephone systems (Ericsson).[5] In other cases, the barriers to trade were protective tariffs or other less visible obstacles that had to be overcome. These engineering firms succeeded in developing international markets in spite of existing trade barriers, but such barriers nevertheless encouraged some of the firms to turn multinational at an early stage.

The development of L.M. Ericsson Telephone Co. forms an excellent illustration of the history of the early Swedish mnes. At the beginning of this century, the 25-year-old firm employed about 1000 workers in Stockholm, producing some 50 000 telephone sets a year. Forced to compete with other Swedish producers, which in addition owned the domestic networks, Ericsson found its main markets abroad. Of the production in Sweden, 95 per cent was thus exported, half of which went to Great Britain. Public authorities abroad were normally involved in giving concessions for telephone operating companies and therefore were influential in decisions to import equipment. As a result political pressure was brought to bear on Ericsson, which soon established producing subsidiaries abroad. The two most important ones grew up in St Petersburg and in Beeston, England. These were efficient units with substantial and profitable production of telephone exchanges and sets, designed mainly for the local market. Before the First World War, Ericsson factories also existed in Paris, Vienna, Budapest and Buffalo, USA. These were less important from the production point of view, but opened the national markets and marked the presence of Ericsson in the area. The American company never got a real foothold, basically because of the strong position of the Bell group, and was sold in 1923.

Just before the First World War, almost half of the Ericsson group's total sales were outside Sweden. The firm had markets all over the world, but the largest was the Russian market, which included Poland.

Wars and depressions

The First World War reinforced 'nationalistic' influences on the structure of the Swedish mnes. To be established with a producing unit inside the important markets was more vital than ever, both for political reasons and because of the physical barriers to trade that were a result of the hostilities. Since Sweden stayed neutral during the war, the Swedish mnes normally fared better than those that had belligerent countries as their home countries. In some cases the Swedes could, no doubt, profit from the situation; SKF was for example able to establish itself on *entente* markets such as the US, while German producers of ball-bearings were being stopped.

· The Russian revolution of 1917 probably had a more profound and direct effect on the Swedish mnes than had the First World War. Not only did important export markets in practice disappear, several subsidiaries within the Soviet Union were also nationalized without compensation to the owners. This happened, for example, to ASEA, Separator/Alfa Laval, SAT, a telephone operating company, and Ericsson, which lost its large factory in St Petersburg.

Sweden experienced a net economic growth during the 1920s as well as during the 1930s, although the country was hit first by a severe but brief post-war depression in 1921–23 and then by the deep international depression of the 1930s. The comparatively positive development between the wars was partly due to the fact that Sweden was an industrial latecomer. Older industrial areas in Europe, dominated by industries like steel, coal, textiles and shipbuilding, were severely struck by the depressions and vested interests in these areas acted as brakes on industrial transformation. In Sweden, with a younger industrial base and cheap hydroelectric power, the renewal was easier. As a result, Sweden moved up the ladder of modern industrial nations both in terms of standard of living and in terms of a technological knowledge base.

During the fundamentally liberal and export-oriented 1920s, several new Swedish mnes established themselves. From having imported much capital before the war, Sweden had become a net exporter of capital, much of it in the form of fdi. At the end of the decade there were at least 50 companies running producing subsidiaries abroad.[6] Most notable was the nebulous Kreuger match empire, which for a time included no less than 144 producing units, many of them owned via strawmen, in 33 different countries. Even after Ivar Kreuger's suicide in 1932 and the reconstruction of the collapsed Swedish Match, the group consisted of 70 manufacturing companies in 31 countries. At the end of the 1930s it accounted for about 60 per cent of world export of matches.[7]

In many ways the Kreuger group was an exception to the normal Swedish mnes of the time. The dramatic conquering of distant markets through large acquisitions and the volume of the business remind us of more recent periods. The cornerstone of the Kreuger empire was a knowledge of how to manufacture and sell matches, but the spectacular growth of the group was accomplished by offering state loans against national match monopolies and a ruthless, oligopolistic power play. The ability to raise capital was thus a key to success in this business, a situation not unlike that of the rather few multinational telephone companies that competed for the rights to build and operate costly telephone networks in order to control local markets.

One effect of the upheaval of the inter-war period was the creation of industrial spheres centered around the leading commercial banks. They had become owners of industrial shares, used as collateral for loans that could not be paid back. Stockholm's Enskilda Bank, owned by the Wallenberg family, gradually became the nucleus of the largest industrial group.

The 1930s were in Sweden, as in most countries, influenced by the reduction of international trade, increasing tariff barriers and formidable trade wars. The export quota, that is the value of exports in relation to GNP, went down to lower levels during this decade than during the two preceding ones – not until the 1960s was it to come back to the level of the 1920s. This development was accompanied by a smaller number of new Swedish mnes being established abroad than during the previous decades, which demonstrates that export growth was the *sine qua non* of fdis. For those few firms, however, that established production units outside Sweden – and for those which already had them – trade barriers and political factors in the host countries became still more important as motives for manufacturing abroad.

The Second World War had its most important influence on Swedish mnes through the destruction and loss of property in Eastern Europe. To name some examples, Esab, SKF, Sandvik, Alfa Laval, AGA and Swedish Match all lost assets in Poland, Czechoslovakia, Hungary and in what later became the parts of Germany with communist rule. It has been pointed out that the effects of the world wars must be kept in mind when discussing the history of the mnes in different countries; certainly the confiscation of foreign assets during the wars has been an important factor for the German industry as well as for the British. Swiss and Swedish mnes, based in neutral countries, have normally been spared from such experiences. Development during and after the Second World War, however, illustrates that undertaking international business also involved risks for Swedish mnes. SKF, for example, running strategically important production subsidiaries in both Germany and the US could not escape the conflict. SKF's American subsidiary was supervised by the US government during the war because of its connections with the enemy. The SKF parent company was put under heavy pressure by the American government towards the end of the war, including an open threat to bomb the main factory in Sweden if it did not stop doing business with Germany completely. Equally remarkable was the fact that the parent company as late as 1950 was forced to make a special deal, according to which it could not freely exercise its rights as owner of its American branch, but had to accept American intervention. Not until 1980 did this agreement finally end.[8]

The tendency from the 1930s for fewer manufacturing mnes to be established abroad grew still stronger during the 1940s. Not until the next decade did the figures reach those of the liberal period before the crisis of the 1930s.[9]

To a substantial degree, the Swedish engineering industry was mobilized for the national rearmament process from the middle of the 1930s. Not only was the volume of production and profits kept up during the war, in spite of the reduced foreign trade, but in some cases the production of defence material also gave an important technological impetus. SAAB, later SAAB-Scania, was, for example, born with the government as a midwife and given a much privileged start as a producer of aircraft. Some of the most research-intensive sectors of the post-war engineering industry profited from getting large state orders. Thus in many cases the period of rearmament was an important stepping-stone for Swedish industry in the years to come. In the post-war confrontation between the eastern and western blocs, Sweden stayed non-aligned. It therefore had to continue investing heavily in a domestic, technologically advanced armaments production, which involved many leading engineering firms.[10]

Ericsson had developed a collaboration with a private Swedish telephone oper-ating company, SAT, with which it merged in 1918, when the Swedish telephone network became united and publicly owned. After that, Ericsson was dominating the Swedish market. Following the generally expansive 1920s, the depression reduced sales, mainly on the export markets. Hence, during the 1930s, a larger proportion of the domestic production was sold at home, culminating with almost two-thirds during the late 1930s. In the long history of Ericsson, this was the only period apart from the war years, when the company was not a pronounced export firm.

During the inter-war years, Ericsson also involved itself in running telephone networks in Mexico, Argentina, Italy and Poland. This was a way of securing a wider market, but the capital costs involved in building up new networks later became too heavy a burden and the company decided to withdraw from these activities after the Second World War.

Ericsson managed, however, to hold its own on the world market during the depression, covering roughly 15 per cent of the world's total production of telephone equipment. The international market was more or less divided during this period through cartel agreements. Of the group's total production, one-third was produced in factories outside Sweden by the end of the 1930s. This figure was lower than before the First World War. In fact, the 1930s and 1940s saw a decline in the proportion of foreign employees in the group; not until the mid-1960s did the foreign workers once more form the majority. Still, the Ericsson group owned 11 manufacturing companies abroad just before the Second World War. Most of the newcomers in this group were small and established or purchased in order to obtain orders for equipment in the country concerned.

The Second World War meant a rapid increase in Ericsson invoicing on the domestic market, of which around 20 per cent was equipment for the Swedish armed forces. Export quantities remained stable, which means that they formed a smaller proportion of the total invoicing. Profits were good, and a financially strong Ericsson faced the post-war period.

Foreign direct investments 1960–90

Swedish industry received a flying start, serving a world market hungry for goods as the immediate disruptions of the Second World War were overcome. The export industry could harvest the fruits of an unparalleled long period of post-war international economic growth. For a small, open economy like the Swedish one, the liberalization of world trade had profound, positive effects. The export quota increased and reached 35 per cent during the 1970s, although a large proportion of the rapidly growing GDP was allocated to the public sector and domestic housing programmes. The foreign trade, however, by this time, was a smaller part of the international economic activities, since the mnes played an ever-increasing role in the economy.

One of the characteristics of Swedish internationalization was the dramatic acceleration in fdi. This increase took place in two distinct waves. The first occurred before 1977, when the yearly net outflow of such capital increased eight times in fixed prices. After a couple of years of stagnation during the recession of the late 1970s, direct investment abroad exploded during the 1980s, with a yearly growth in the value of fdi of almost 30 per cent between 1979 and 1988.[11] This development reflected a global trend, explained not only by the general economic upswing, but also by the general liberalization of the rules for capital movement. The total OECD outflow of fdi was twice as high in the 1980s as in the 1970s.[12] As Table 5.2 shows, Sweden seems, however, to have experienced an extremely quick relative growth in this respect, at least in comparison with the larger industrial nations.

Swedish direct investments have traditionally been carried out mainly by industrial firms, even if lately other sectors have increased in importance. In the middle of the 1980s, three-quarters of the total stock of investment abroad was still industrial, while the remaining part was owned by companies within the financial and service sectors. The number of employees outside Sweden in the mnes increased almost three times during the three decades, approaching half a million or a quarter of all employees in Swedish-owned trade and industry. Close to 300 000 of these employees worked in manufacturing affiliates, compared to just over 100 000 three decades earlier (see Table 5.3).[13]

An extra outflow of capital was added after 1987, when foreign exchange control was liberalized, and Swedes were allowed to invest in financial assets and real estate abroad.[14] Much of the annual growth since then is thus explained by large real-estate investments. During a single year such as 1989, however, Swedish

Table 5.2   Swedish outward and inward fdi, 1961–90 (US $ billion)

Year	Net export	Net import
1961–65	342	87
1966–70	703	622
1971–75	1556	368
1976–80	2864	507
1981–85	5115	848
1986–90	21332	5107

Note
Reinvestment of local earnings by Swedish mnes abroad is not included in this table but has increased considerably lately. According to calculations by Sveriges Riksbank for 1986–1988, the yearly Swedish direct investments abroad are roughly 30 per cent higher if this reinvestment is included.

Source
Sveriges Riksbanks Årsbok. Svensk industri och industripolitik (1990).

mnes acquired more companies abroad than the mnes of any other country. The yearly outflow of direct investments in manufacturing industry stabilized at around US$ 3 billion per year during the second half of the 1980s. This chapter concentrates on these industrial investments. First, let us consider the distribution between different industrial sectors.

As at the beginning of the century, the engineering industry has been totally dominant among the Swedish mnes during the last three decades (see Table 5.3). In 1960, companies within the 'machinery' and 'transportation equipment' sector employed 67 per cent of the total workforce abroad, a figure that had declined somewhat to 63 per cent in 1986. Within the engineering sector, the car industry has been the fastest growing, reducing the relative role of 'non-electric machinery'.[15]

The slight relative shift away from engineering industry among the mnes was mainly due to the production abroad of finished products from the forest industry. There were still very few examples of firms establishing themselves abroad to get access to raw materials, the most important of them being forest industries investing in Canada and the US.

Clothing and textiles were the only industries where firms moved production out of Sweden to find cheaper labour. In an attempt to survive competition from non-European producers, not least in the Swedish market, some Swedish firms started production in Finland and Portugal.

More often than during earlier periods, the rapid growth of fdi after 1960 took the form of purchasing already existing firms. This tendency increased over time; between 1979 and 1986 three-quarters of all foreign subsidiaries were bought

Table 5.3   Swedish manufacturing subsidiaries abroad in 1960, 1974 and 1986 (employees and total assets)

Industry	Employees (%)			Assets (%)			Total number in 1986
	1960	1974	1986	1960	1974	1986	
Food		1	2		1	2	19
Textile and clothing		3	1		1	0	11
Pulp and paper	0	3	3	1	6	3	16
Paper products and printing		3	8		4	11	50
Chemicals	21	10	11	14	8	10	123
Metals and metal goods	7	11	9	11	13	7	105
Machinery	47	34	34	50	32	36	171
Electrical machinery	19	24	22	18	22	19	69
Transportation	1	5	7	1	7	9	28
Other industry	5	6	4	5	6	3	54
All industries	100	100	100	100	100	100	646
Total number of employees	105 511	211 111	259 821				
Total assets in US$ billion				742	6 131	20 147	

Source
Swedenborg, B. *et al., Den svenska industrins utlandsinvesteringar* 1960–1986, Stockholm, 1988, pp. 182–3.

rather than started as greenfield projects, including those developed out of sales or service companies.[16] The implication of this fact is that the Swedish mnes no longer just wanted to produce a 'Swedish' product closer to an existing market, but aimed at getting hold of something else as well: a new technology, a net of subcontractors, a sales organization, a supplementary product or simply an additional slice of a basically saturated market. The last case is obvious with Electrolux, which in the early 1990s has the highest number of employees abroad of all Swedish mnes, and which has become a major world producer of electrical household appliances mainly by acquiring competitors like Zanussi in Italy (1984), White Consolidated in the US (1986) or Thorn EMI in Great Britain (1987).

Let us now turn to the question of in which geographical areas Swedish direct investment has taken place, as shown in Table 5.4. It is first worth noticing that the industrialized parts of the world dominate the picture. This fact reflects the rather advanced demand structure on the Swedish market, early formed by factors such as long hauling distances and a harsh climate, later by a general demand for a healthy environment, safe traffic or public welfare. Here, Sweden might have had some of its country-specific advantages.

As a further point of departure, let us assume that the foreign demand for Swedish goods can be satisfied either by exporting from Sweden or by producing locally. When comparing the main markets, we find that the proportions between the two ways of furnishing the market differ. These differences and changes in the proportions indicate the motives behind establishing production subsidiaries.

Table 5.4   Regional distribution of employment in Swedish manufacturing subsidiaries abroad, 1960, 1974 and 1986

	1960	1974	1986
Industrialized countries			
Original EEC countries	46	44	36
Denmark, Ireland, UK	14	11	11
EFTA (inc. Portugal)	7	9	8
Remaining Western Europe	1	3	3
North America	12	8	21
Other industrialized countries	3	5	4
Developing countries			
Latin America	7	13	12
Asia, Africa	10	7	5
All countries	100	100	100
Total number	105 511	221 111	259 821

Source
Swedenborg *et al.*, *Den svenska industrins utlandsinvesteringar 1960–1986*, Stockholm, 1988, p. 71.

In such a comparison, Latin America first stands out as the region with the highest proportion of local production in relation to total sales. The reason for this is, no doubt, the fact that the governments in this region, which soon after the war became regarded as very promising by Swedish exporting firms, demanded local production to open themselves for import. Many Swedish mnes such as SAAB, Volvo, Ericsson, Alfa Laval, etc., established themselves here, mainly in Brazil, Mexico and Argentina. In 1974 there were already 60 Swedish production subsidiaries established, covering 63 per cent of total Swedish sales on this market. Political considerations in this case thus caused a substitution of local production for exports from Sweden.[17]

A similar pattern is visible as well when we look at the figures for the original EEC countries, that is France, West Germany, Italy, Belgium, The Netherlands and Luxembourg. During the late 1950s and the 1960s, Swedish industry regarded it as necessary to invest within the tariff walls of the emerging Common Market, while Sweden as a member of the free trade area could supply the EFTA countries more easily directly through exports. Of the total sales to the original EEC in 1970, 42 per cent was produced locally, while the figure for EFTA was only 15 per cent.

The economic integration of this protected part of Western Europe was thus an important factor in the internationalization of production. This conclusion is further supported by the development during the following period. The negotiations between EFTA and the EEC resulted in a free trade agreement in 1972, after which the effects of the economic division of Western Europe was less threatening for Swedish exports. Consequently, the flow of direct investment towards the EEC dried up.

The main direction of fdi thus partly shifted away from Europe during the 1970s. Instead, the main flow headed westward for about a decade, reaching a peak in 1986, when one-third of the yearly investments went to the US, which soon became the country with the highest number of Swedish-owned subsidiaries.

This expansion was much more forceful than the increase in the total demand for Swedish goods from the US market; while the value of production by these US subsidiaries increased eight times between 1978 and 1986, Swedish export to the US increased only four times. The reasons behind the development lay mainly within the host country. The American market was regarded as interesting because of its size, its technical sophistication and its growth potential. The American economic vitality was starkly contrasted during these years against the relative stagnation of the European; 'Eurosclerosis' was the catchword of the day. Swedish firms were primarily attracted by the market potential and even inexperienced companies moved very quickly; the US was chosen as a first country in which to start production as often as Finland and Denmark, thus disregarding physical and 'psychic' distance.[18]

Sweden was not the only country to invest in the US. In fact, although Swedish firms invested amazingly large sums, the Swedish relative part of the stock of foreign investment in the US declined during the first half of the 1980s.[19] Direct investment was attracted from many areas; during this period a share of almost 40 per cent of the world's total direct investment capital went to the US, which had replaced Europe as the main recipient.[20] The feeling was that 'the train was leaving' and no world business leader with ambitions wanted to miss it.

Looking closer at the group of about 70 Swedish production subsidiaries in the US established before 1987, we find that an unexpectedly large number of rather small and inexperienced firms had joined the scramble for the US market.[21] However, we can also notice that the large, already widely established mnes were in place. For these firms, acquisitions were preferred as opposed to greenfield investment. The barriers to entry were probably higher in the US market than in European countries and it was often regarded a prerequisite to take a decisive, although expensive, initial step. It was necessary not only to create production facilities, but also to get hold of a distribution network and a reasonable slice of the market. Volvo bought White Motor Corporation in 1981 in order to attain a volume large enough to make the production and selling of trucks profitable. The company was reasonably successful in this third attempt to enter the US market.[22] The acquisition of White Consolidated by Electrolux in 1986, as mentioned above, is another important case in point.

After the publication of the White Paper on the internal market by the EEC in 1985, Europe was once more in focus. The shift in the global attention from the US to Europe, where now the most rapid growth and dynamic industrial development was expected, illustrates how international direct investments had become a highly sensitive market for capital accumulation.

Just as 30 years earlier, Sweden was threatened with exclusion from its main market, the difference being that this market now accounted for half of the country's export instead of a third, since Great Britain and Denmark also belonged to the EEC now. The same political uncertainty was once more at hand. Should Sweden join the Common Market; could, as an alternative, a favourable free trade agreement be negotiated, and, in that case, when?

The industrial crisis of the 1970s did severely hit parts of the Swedish economy, which lost much of its international competitiveness. The traditional industries, producing products such as pulp and paper, minerals, metal and steel, ships, etc., experienced heavy setbacks and went through painful restructuring processes. The technologically more advanced and more internationalized engineering firms showed a better ability to adjust to the new situation. After the crisis, therefore, the emphasis of the Swedish export industry was further shifted towards specialized and rather advanced products. Sweden's relative weakness on the international market was for a time overcome through a stepwise devaluation of the Swedish crown by no less than 40 per cent between 1977 and 1982. During the prolonged international boom of the 1980s, Swedish industry was expansive and profitable. Firms chose to invest a substantial part of their surplus abroad. The question was, where?

According to a large survey, Swedish firms in general expected the integrated EEC area to become the most dynamic and fastest growing region in the world.[23] For industries with their main markets in Sweden, producing textiles, food, energy, etc., these expectations did not fundamentally change their investment plans. For the exporting process industries such as pulp and paper, the uncertainty about Sweden's future relations to the Common Market made them more inclined to invest within that area, preferably in the late stage of the production process. Good examples are the purchases of the German company Feldmuehle by Stora and the British company Reedpack by SCA in 1990. The largest Swedish forest industry groups thereby secured parts of the final consumers' markets. It was not possible, for obvious reasons, to move the basic processes out of Sweden; large-scale production units had to stay close to raw materials.

Most sensitive to Sweden's future relations to the EEC were the engineering firms, both because they had the highest hopes of profiting from the integration of this market and because they had most to fear from being cut off from international flows of goods and capital. The old, skill-intensive engineering firms thus went on investing in Europe, but younger, highly specialized and R. & D.-intensive firms also became multinational.

Figures reveal that the EEC internal market project made the Swedish investors react quickly. Sweden doubled its flow of investments to the EEC in current dollars every year from 1985 to 1988.[24] The EEC share of Swedish fdi increased from 41 per cent in the period 1982 to 1985 to 51 per cent during 1986 to 1988. For firms already established within the Common Market, it was interesting to get access to larger shares of a growing market. For smaller and younger firms, it was a matter of getting a foothold inside the walls of the Common Market. The appearance of a number of rather small Swedish firms outside their home country was a new experience. In many cases these firms were subcontractors to the bigger mnes and simply followed them abroad. Partly thanks to systematic education through schools and industrial organizations, Swedish entrepreneurs learned to master the difficulties of investing abroad. Old economic and cultural ties with Europe made this process possible on a relatively large scale.

From time to time, the exodus of industrial capital in different directions caused alarm within Sweden. Was fdi leading to a deindustrialization of the country? Several investigations were made, showing that the Swedish mnes have, as a group, been more dynamic than other firms within Sweden. Between 1970 and 1986, for example, employment in those industrial firms that only invested at home declined by almost 24 per cent, while domestic employment in the mnes declined by only 5 per cent. The total number of employees in the Swedish mnes increased by 10 per cent during the same period, indicating their general dynamism.[25]

However, as illustrated in Table 5.2, fdi increasingly became a one-way traffic for Sweden. Until the late 1960s, a rough balance used to exist between export and import of industrial investment, but since then Sweden has been a net exporter of such capital. Lately the export of capital has grown dramatically, causing some alarm amongst Swedish public opinion. During the 1980s, Swedish mnes invested around US $ 30 billion abroad, while foreign companies invested only around US $ 5 billion in Sweden. After taking into account that these imbalances might be of a temporary character, caused by the recent changes in the foreign exchange regulations, they have been nonetheless regarded as the writing on the wall. To a certain extent this development can be explained by discontentment with the climate for industrial investments in Sweden, pushing domestic capital out of Sweden, but not attracting foreign capital. In addition to uncertainty about future relations to the Common Market came uncertainty about energy policy, high interest rates, high costs for labour, etc. The positive effects of the devaluations around 1980 were gradually reduced and Sweden once more became a country with low growth figures and high inflation compared to most OECD countries. For international industrial capital, Sweden by the end of the decade hardly looked attractive. Partly as a result of changes in economic policy, including an application for membership in the Common Market, partly due to the recession, the picture changed dramatically during 1991. The net sum of Swedish fdi was reduced from about US $ 15 billion to about 1.5 billion.

The Ericsson group

Three tendencies characterized the development of the Ericsson group after the Second World War. The first was rapid growth. The number of employees increased from less than 20 000 in the beginning of the 1950s to more than 80 000 two decades later. During the same period, sales from the parent company increased by more than 9 per cent yearly, allowing for changes in the value of the money. The expansion in sales for the whole Ericsson group was still faster. After a period of slower growth and reduction of the number of employees, the sales figures for the group increased very dramatically again during the late 1980s, reaching almost US $ 10 billion in 1990. Ericsson was by then number four among the world's largest producers of telecommunications equipment, covering around 7 per cent of the total market and having 70 000 employees, most of them outside Sweden. [26]

Of fundamental significance in this growth process was the breakthrough of two generations of new technology; the electromechanical crossbar system around 1960 and the electronic AXE system for digital public switches two decades later. Using these technological advantages, Ericsson was able to hold its own on the expanding world markets.

This expansion went together with successful concentration on the field of public telephone switches and, lately, mobile radio communications. The second main feature of Ericsson's post-war development was thus specialization, which meant that the company abandoned the policy of diversification that had characterized the preceding period. The last step in the concentration process took place in the 1980s, when Ericsson was more or less forced to leave the business area of office data and information systems as a result of costly concentration on the explosively expanding market for public telecommunications (see Table 5.5).

The third tendency in the post-war development of the Ericsson group was the 'reinternationalization' of Ericsson. After more or less enforced concentration on the domestic market during the 1930s and 1940s, Ericsson found more and more

Table 5.5   The Ericsson group. Distribution of external sales by business area, 1989

Public telecommunications	44
Radio communications	21
Business communications	12
Cables and network	13
Defence systems	8
Components	2
Total	100

Source
Ericsson Annual Report, 1989.

of its markets abroad. The Swedish parent company increased the export share of its sales from one-third to two-thirds between 1946 and 1970. The non-Swedish market became still more important for the entire Ericsson group.

As part of specialization policy, Ericsson gradually withdrew from the telephone operating business, wanting to avoid competing with its own customers. Already in the 1950s, the number of telephone operating companies in the group was reduced to three, and in 1990 there remained only one, situated in Argentina.

Non-Swedish manufacturing companies, on the other hand, increased in number and importance. After a dynamic decade of growth, Ericsson in 1970 had 21 production units outside Sweden, including a number of separate cable-works (see Table 5.6). After that, the number stabilized around 20. The majority of the non-Swedish Ericsson employees thus worked in manufacturing affiliates. Compared to the well-established pre-war European situation, the factories in Eastern Europe were lost and the British was sold, while the French and Italian factories increased in importance. More than half of the foreign factories were now situated outside Europe, most of them set up during the 1960s.

As between the wars, the main reason for manufacturing abroad was demand from buyers. Brazil, Australia and Mexico were the most important examples of countries where a large market, in combination with the demands from the authorities for local production, forced Ericsson to invest in factories for telephone exchange equipment and sets. Competition on the market made it impossible to resist such political pressure, although Ericsson, at least during the 1960s, could produce the equipment more cheaply in Sweden. Ericsson was reluctant to use the alternative to exploit its technological lead by letting other companies produce the equipment under licence. It was afraid of losing control of quality, and of the identity of the company being watered down. Without a basis in the form of a subsidiary, it was regarded harder to stay on the market in the long run.

Table 5.6   Foreign manufacturing companies within the Ericsson group, 1970

Country	Number of employees
Denmark	313
	1816
Norway	1733
	323
Finland	744
Holland	788
France	5039
Spain	834
Italy	3144
Brazil	3398
	463
Argentina	290
Mexico	369
	684
Columbia	170
	67
Venezuela	243
Australia	2530
	266
	195

Note
Several separate factories existed in some countries.

Source
Attman, A. *et al.*, *L. M. Ericsson 100 Years*, vol. II, Stockholm, p. 273.

The Swedish market still played a role as a first testing ground for new technology, but had become rather unimportant in volume; the home market accounted for less than 10 per cent of the total external sales of the group towards the end of the 1980s. Western Europe still dominated as a market for Ericsson, with more than half of the volume, but South America became more important during the 1960s and other continents increased their share. Only in North America was it difficult for a long time to break into the market.

The attraction of the American telecommunications market was partly due to its size – about one-third of the world market – but also because new services for customers and other technological novelties were first developed there. Ericsson wanted not only to conquer another market, it wanted to take part in the dynamic development of the telecommunications of the future.

Ericsson had tried to get a foothold in the US market on two earlier occasions. As was mentioned earlier, the first attempt took place at the beginning of the century when Ericsson opened a sales office in order to offer Swedish telephone equipment to 'independent' companies, that is the companies outside the dominating Bell Group. This office was expanded into a factory in Buffalo, New York, where production started in 1907. It proved hard to sell telephone equipment in the US even with heavy support from the parent company, and the American venture was finally wound up in 1920 after heavy losses.[27]

A second attempt was made after the Second World War. Experiences during the war had shown the value of having a qualified production unit in the western hemisphere, which could supply the markets in Latin America in case of new political problems or a blockade. Once more, Ericsson was also hoping for the 'independent' market in the US. In 1951 Ericsson bought a majority of the shares in North Electric Co. in Ohio, a company with about 1000 employees, producing equipment for American telephone companies, mainly General Telephone Corporation and United Utilities, but also for the US Government. It soon proved to be an unexpectedly costly and time-consuming process to develop an American version of the Ericsson crossbar system and produce it at the local factory. After more than a decade and two changes of management the company was still running at a constant loss. Only after an agreement with United Utilities in the middle of the 1960s, which included large orders but also an option for the takeover by the American company of North Electric Co., did a definite improvement take place. United Utilities became the sole owner of North Electric in 1967 and the shares in United that Ericsson received in compensation were sold the year after. The second attempt to establish Ericsson as a supplier on the independent US market thus also ended in a retreat, though of an orderly kind. On the positive side, indirect advantages were no doubt gained from the close contact with American technology and the American telephone market.[28]

When the third serious attempt was made in the US at the beginning of the 1980s, the market situation was brighter in one respect: as a result of an antitrust case in 1983 there now existed seven independent Bell Operating Companies, formally separated from their main supplier, Western Electric Co., which was owned by AT & T, now deprived of its virtual monopoly. As a result, the seven regional Bell Companies, which controlled the bulk of the local traffic, became free to buy from outside suppliers. Confident of the quality of its well-established AXE system Ericsson decided on a massive offensive with the target of conquering 10 per cent of the market by 1990. A bridgehead had been created in 1980 in the form of Anaconda-Ericsson, a joint venture between an American cable producer and Ericsson.[29]

Starting in 1983, Ericsson put large resources into two organizations, one which adapted the AXE switch systems to the US market and another that worked in the field to sell the system. Partly because of simultaneous competition for important orders on the British market, Ericsson almost overstretched its resources. There were also clear 'cultural' complications in melding together, on the one hand, different groups of American technicans with Swedish experts and, on the other, these product specialists and the entirely locally staffed market organization. The whole Ericsson group faced a severe crisis around 1985, not only of a financial nature, and the expensive US strategy was put in question. The Data Systems and Office Equipment divisions were sold off in order to concentrate on telecommunications. Something of a restart of the US venture was then accomplished, including an 'Americanization' of the US subsidiary, a change in management, more formalized goal-setting and stricter financial control. This policy indicated a further deviation from the traditional Ericsson way of cautious step-by-step entrance into new markets under full control from Stockholm. The policy was at the same time an example of the general need for a more market-oriented organization of a subsidiary in the US than in other countries.

Ericsson received its first American order for the AXE system during 1986 and at the end of the next year 200 000 lines had been ordered by a number of different American operating companies. The breakthrough came later than hoped for and the costs were much higher. Nevertheless, the strategy must be regarded as successful.

Although the fruits from the American market were not yet ripe, the group was firmly established by the end of the decade as one of the world's leading telecommunication companies with rapid growth and good profitability. In its positioning for future expansion, Ericsson had, since 1985, increased its production facilities through acquisitions not only in the US but also in Norway, France, Spain and Great Britain. The group sold 40 per cent of its production in the EEC and employed 30 per cent of its personnel there. Beside public telecommunication, mobile radio communication had become a very important business area, in which Ericsson formed an alliance with General Electric in the US, becoming a leading supplier there and elsewhere.

Despite the American venture, Ericsson remained a rather hierarchical group with a strong position with the Stockholm headquarters and a close cultural identity. The recent concentration on a small number of technically advanced products is probably one explanation for the duration of this tradition.[30] Only about 20 per cent of the R. & D. expenses were still used outside Sweden in the 1980s, which is roughly the same figure as in the 1960s.[31] Only in a few cases have more fundamental R. & D. groups been formed outside Sweden. One of these exceptions was the Ericsson laboratory working in Darmstadt, Germany, between 1954 and 1963, motivated by the existing surplus of qualified technicians in the country. North Electric Company during the same period was another important non-Swedish research centre within the group. Tendencies of moving at least some of the more applied development work closer to the market became visible in the late 1980s. A new R. & D. centre was, for example, opened in North Carolina, USA in 1990.

The modern Swedish multinational firm

Swedish industry in the early 1990s is dominated by a rather small number of firms, most of them operating internationally. Around 20 large companies employ one-third of the industrial workforce in Sweden and account for one-half of the total Swedish exports. These companies, at the same time, employ more of their total personnel outside Sweden than inside. One-half of their export consists of internal deliveries within the mnes themselves. Of the investments made by this small, leading group of Swedish mnes, 40 per cent went abroad during the period from 1978 to 1985. The figure has since increased to around 50 per cent. The leading Swedish mnes are growing fast and primarily outside Sweden.[32]

All except four of the companies in Table 5.7 had established production abroad before 1960; eight of them were running foreign manufacturing units in 1986 that had been started around 1920. The leading group of Swedish mnes tends to be long-lived, which reflects the fact that the structure of Swedish industry has stayed unchanged.

If we look at the total group of mnes producing abroad both in 1965 and in 1986, it is clear that they had become more and more dependent on foreign markets; the role of the domestic market was reduced from 47 to 23 per cent, while an increasing proportion of the production took place outside Sweden (see Table 5.8). In addition to this stable group there emerged new mnes, increasing the pace of the internationalization process.

In discussions of the structure of the contemporary Swedish mnes, continuity has rightly been stressed. In a way, this is what could be expected. Historical investments are rather binding in the sense that it is cheaper to add to existing production facilities than to build something completely new; a 'path dependence' is normal. Some radical structural changes have taken place, but they have mainly had to do with strong external political influences, such as wars, the establishment of socialist regimes or drastic changes in the system of trade barriers. The structural stability reflects the stability of the Swedish foreign trade pattern and more or less constant political pressure to produce close to the market. The gradually increasing degree of internationalization to a certain degree thus seems to be a natural result of the growth of the firms themselves. Normally, in the case of Swedish firms, expanding in volume means increased exports and/or local production. In addition to these factors, however, certain recent changes in corporate behaviour have to be mentioned.

One reason for the stronger tendency to develop giant, international firms is the interdependence between the different activities of a firm. Competition and risks in the international business community have gradually increased. A new product takes more time and money to develop, while at the same time it tends to have a shorter life on the market. Consequently, more and more effort must be put into R. & D., while at the same time international markets have to be secured and the financial basis for the firm has to be large and stable. The ambition to grow is thus not so much a matter of reaching economies of scale in production as of covering

Table 5.7   The 20 largest Swedish multinational manufacturing firms, 1986

Name of company	Total employment	Foreign employment	First affiliate	Main products
Electrolux	129 192	100 477	1921	Household appliances, office machines
SKF	44 887	37 037	1910	Roller bearings, steel
Ericsson	68 176	32 444	1911	Telephone stations, exchanges, equipment
ASEA	63 124	25 797	1916	Electric equipment, engines, turbines
Volvo	71 213	18 904	1958	Motor vehicles, machinery
Swedish Match	25 556	17 917	1912	Building materials, packaging, matches
Sandvik	24 033	13 449	1920	Steel, steel manufactures
Atlas Copco	16 498	12 091	1943	Pneumatic drills, compressors
Esselte	18 046	11 993	1962	Office equipment, printing, publishing
Alfa Laval	15 460	9 833	1885	Separators, dairy and farm machinery
Saab-Scania	47 407	9 519	1957	Motor vehicles
AGA	14 584	9 466	1900	Gas and gas energy (heating, freezing, welding)
SCA	18 114	6 344	1960	Paper and allied products
ESAB	6480	4 642	1931	Electrical welding machinery
PLM	7575	4 354	1961	Packaging (glass, metal, paper)
Stora	17 242	3 666	1956	Pulp and paper
Euroc	8 192	3 526	1953	Cement, machinery
Astra	6 768	3 485	1942	Pharmaceuticals
Nobel	16 256	2 824	1967	Military equipment, chemicals
Assi	8 213	2 559	1967	Wood, pulp and paper

Source
Swedenborg , B. *et al., Den svenska industrins utlandsinvesteringar 1960–1986*, Stockholm, 1988, p. 29.

Table 5.8   Swedish multinational manufacturing companies. Distribution of sales and production in Sweden and abroad, 1965, 1974 and 1986

	1965	1974	1986
Sales in Sweden	47	35	23
abroad	53	65	77
	100	100	100
Production in Sweden	72	67	53
abroad	28	33	47
	100	100	100

Note
Deliveries from Sweden to foreign affiliates are included in 'Production in Sweden' but not in 'Production abroad'.

Source
Idem Table 5.7, p. 37.

the technological development with massive R. & D. and of being present on the most important markets. A giant firm can also reduce risks by being its own bank, insurance company, etc.[33]

The decision to invest in production abroad thus still has relatively little to do with optimal allocation of production in the strict economic sense.[34] Most mnes would normally have preferred to concentrate production to make it more rational, but because of political and strategic considerations, they have been forced to build a less efficient production organization. Atlas Copco, to take one obvious example, pursues a not very optimal production of pneumatic compressors in several less developed countries. Wage costs are relatively insignificant for the location of the production of technologically advanced capital good of this kind.

The Swedish mnes have traditionally seldom competed with low prices on standardized products. The quality of the product, the ability to stay in the market for a long time and give service to the buyer, and general credibility have been more important factors. To this might be added the need to take part in development in the most dynamic markets, including local production and R. & D., as demonstrated in the case of Ericsson establishing itself on the US market. The turbulent telecommunications industry is a good example of how the leading multinational firms organize themselves in rather similar formations when manoeuvring in the global forum.

The behaviour of the modern mne can no longer as easily be understood in terms of evolutionary sequences of internationalization, but rather as strategic management decisions in an already internationalized market-place. While the establishment of foreign production earlier, normally was a way of defending an established market, it later – in a more liberal economic environment – became part of a market strategy.

We can thus conclude that the Swedish mnes have grown in size lately and become still less domestically oriented in their sales as well as in their production. The question then arises as to what this tendency has meant for the decision-making and management of the companies.

Swedish mnes are known to have been managed in a way typical for the mnes of continental Europe rather then US companies. A more strict 'parent-child' relationship has been upheld, which means that foreign subsidiaries have reported directly to corporate headquarters and there has been no special international division, regional headquarters or specific division for a certain product or technology. To this 'Swedish model' belong certain other characteristics. The subsidiaries have, for example, formally been autonomous, but in fact well integrated into the group through informal, personalized relations, reinforced by intensive international rotation of personnel. Such an organization contrasts with the American tradition of formal 'bibles of rules' and frequent use of host country nationals as presidents in the subsidiaries.

Many explanations can be found for this 'Swedish model'. One is the fact that most of the Swedish mnes have been based on technological innovations or inventions made a long time ago. Technological identity has been in focus during the international growth. Since the market often consisted of public authorities or industries rather than individual consumers, there had to exist a strong support from the top technical and service levels in Sweden. It was also easier to have a direct insight in each business deal and therefore less important to organize formal and running checks of costs etc. Furthermore, before the 1970s, international expansion was often gradual, following the traditional chain from selling via an agent, establishing an own market organization and, finally, building up production facilities through 'greenfield' investment. In such a sequence, knowledge about policies and norms could be transferred gradually, with the help of managers sent abroad. It has also been pointed out that Swedish capital owners and banks traditionally have been more actively involved in industrial entrepreneurship than in most comparable countries. This fact might have strengthened the very integrated and close network that forms the Swedish business community.[35]

Strong ownership ties existed between several of the Swedish mnes. The Wallenberg group had a dominant position in half of the companies in Table 5.7, including most of the engineering firms except Volvo. This position simply reflects the fact that the group during the 1970s included one-quarter of the total Swedish industry and one-half of the engineering industry. The existence of this integrated group of industries, partly combined in 'clusters' of supporting production and marketing, probably added strength to the Swedish mnes, which, after all, were small by international comparison. At the same time, much decision-making was centralized on a 'meso' level and firmly based in Stockholm.[36]

As was illustrated in the case of Ericsson's activities in the US, there have, however, recently been signs that the strict 'parent-child' relationship within Swedish mnes is being broken up. We find similar patterns also in other companies, which are leapfrogging stages in the traditional internationalization process, growing very quickly through acquisitions and becoming increasingly dependent on accommodating to important foreign markets. R. & D. and other qualified functions within the mne are more often than earlier being performed outside Sweden. We have also seen a general tendency of appointing more non-Swedish presidents in foreign subsidiaries after the mid-1970s.[37]

A certain movement away from a traditionally centralized system of decision-making towards more freedom for foreign units within the Swedish mnes can thus be seen, but only within strict limits. The headquarters are normally still in command when it comes to finding optimal strategic solutions concerning markets, brand names, distribution channels or financial policy. The global, 'geocentric' character of mnes, such as Ericsson or SKF, involved as they are in worldwide competition for highly-specialized products, seems to demand a central command. SKF for a period consisted of several national producers of the whole range of bearings, called the 'the five kingdoms'. These kingdoms were broken up during the 1970s, and the European factories were forced to specialize according to a global strategy, while the group's new research facilities were located in the 'neutral' Netherlands. Sweden did not become more important as a producing country through this operation, but the headquarters in Sweden nevertheless regained a stricter managerial control over the battlefields.[38]

Foreign parts of Swedish mnes, on the other hand, occasionally emerge as centres which are not only allowed to develop local strategies but become instrumental parts in forming the overall strategy of the whole mne. A hierarchical pattern of organization is in such cases changed into a 'heterarchical'.[39] The development and production of a certain product is, for example, centred in an affiliated company with full responsibility. Atlas Copco's centre for air power is, to take one example, situated in Belgium. In other cases centres for the marketing and general management of a product division have been put outside Sweden, normally as a result of an acquisition by the mother company. One such example is Esselte, which has several of its divisions for office equipment, publishing and printing based abroad. Independent research centres have so far more seldom been created outside Sweden, SKF being one of the exceptions. More than three-quarters of the mnes' total research volume is still carried out in Sweden.[40]

In spite of some signs of an emerging 'heterachical' structure of Swedish mnes there are so far few examples of Swedish mnes leaving Sweden and becoming domiciled outside the country. Some family-owned companies, responding to the unfavourable taxation rules, have done so. The most well-known cases are IKEA, a worldwide supplier of furniture, and Tetra-Pak, a successful producer of packaging machinery. The latter in 1991 even purchased another old and large Swedish mne, Alfa Laval, and moved its headquarters to its new home country, Switzerland, as well.

Shares in the most well-known Swedish mnes are quoted on leading foreign stock exchanges, but ownership of the companies has normally stayed firmly in Sweden. This is partly explained for several companies by an old practice of issuing differentiated shares, of which only a certain number with restricted voting power are accessible to non-Swedes. Every attempt by a foreign interest to buy a Swedish company is, furthermore, scrutinized by the Swedish government before obtaining the necessary approval. Such laws and practices are hardly compatible with Swedish integration in an economically liberalized Europe and there are changes under way. The Swedish mnes will not stay as protected from foreign buyers in the future.

The process of global integration into giant firms thus poses potential threats to the national identity of the Swedish mnes. Swedish industry is highly concentrated, but its mnes are seldom large by international standards. Volvo is one of Sweden's largest companies, but a dwarf compared to American, Japanese or German car producers. In the present regrouping of the international car industry where Volvo is developing links with Renault, and the second Swedish car producer, Saab-Scania, is co-operating with General Motors, the centre of the new groups might easily end up outside Sweden. The country is, after all, both small and in a peripheral geographical position. ASEA, an important Swedish mne since 1916, is another case in point. After the merger with the Swiss company Brown Boveri, 50 per cent of the international business of Asea Brown Boveri is owned by the Swedish company, but the company is formally based in Switzerland.

Conclusion

Certain country-specific advantages help us to understand why Sweden developed an advanced manufacturing industry toward the end of the 19th century. Local natural resources, no doubt, played an important role. Ferrous metals for centuries had been the base for the dominant export product, the bar iron, and the technical and metallurgical know-how spilled over into the engineering industry. A high level of literacy and an advanced system of technical education were additional important advantages at this early stage.

Sweden had a very restricted home market, but an easy access to the large European markets. Swedish entrepreneurs, innovators and bankers have been part of a European network for a long time. From very early on, the specialized engineering firms turned outwards, exported and learnt to feel at home on foreign markets. Most of the early fdi is explained by the need for these early exporters to establish themselves firmly abroad.

The companies rooted in the forest sector much later found it necessary to invest abroad. Basic processes were kept in Sweden for obvious reasons, but by integrating vertically and forward the Swedish companies secured important segments of the final markets in Europe. Country-specific advantages were instrumental also in the case of pulp and paper: rich and accessible forests, cheap hydroelectric power and the geographical proximity to important markets. As in the case of the engineering firms, the collaboration with commercial banks and the general good capital supply in Sweden after the First World War helped the forest industries to form strong, integrated units and grow internationally.

Once established, the Swedish mnes succeeded in holding their own on the cartel influenced and protected international markets of the 1930s and 1940s. When the international economy expanded after the Second World War, Sweden, as a small, open economy, not only increased its export but also strengthened its position as a prolific international investor. The number of employees outside Sweden in Swedish mnes has increased three times since the early 1960s, reaching one-quarter of the total employees in Swedish trade and industry. Most of the fdi has taken place within the engineering sector, mainly in the fields of machinery and transport. These engineering firms were established exporters of industrial products and chose to produce abroad to secure their markets. The consumer industries and service sectors are, on the other hand, more or less lacking. This Swedish profile goes back to the turn of the century, when many of the companies involved were in fact started. The Swedish mnes are thus concentrated in a rather narrow segment, where they form clusters, often held together through common ownership.

Compared with fdi from the USA, Japan, the UK and Germany, Swedish mnes tend to be research intensive rather than capital intensive and to a high degree based on technology and skill.[41]

The Swedish political tradition of promoting R. & D. at the universities as well as within industries fits well with the fact that the country's mnes are technologically relatively advanced and have their main markets in industrialized areas with high demands for quality and product sophistication.

While the size and character of Swedish fdi in general might be explained by a number of country-specific advantages, the geographical direction of these investments has been mainly determined by the traditional structure of Swedish exports and the real or expected barriers to this export. The large numbers of Swedish mnes existing in Latin America can only be explained by political pressure in combination with a promising market situation. The establishing of the Common Market in Europe around 1960 resulted in an increase of Swedish fdi within the six EEC countries. During the 1980s, capital for fdi has moved more quickly and in larger quantities out of Sweden. The dynamic US market attracted many Swedish mnes during the first half of the decade, while later, when Europe promised more rapid growth, the investments there increased most quickly. Instead of securing already conquered markets by establishing local production, Swedish industry has lately nervously moved in any direction where the prospects for growth and technological dynamism have looked brightest. While the ageing group of Swedish mnes has kept on growing, Sweden's general competitiveness seems to have decreased. The inward flow of fdi has more or less dried up and few new industrial companies of importance are being established.

By growing in size, the Swedish mnes are becoming – in a quantitative sense – less Swedish. There are still few signs that their national identity is being watered down or that their headquarters are moving out of Sweden. It has, nevertheless, become increasingly easy for them to cut loose from their source country, a situation that should be disquieting for a country which is more than ever economically dependent on its mnes.

Notes

1. Other definitions are discussed in Hertner, P. and Jones, G., 'Multinationals: Theory and History', in P. Hertner and G. Jones, (eds), *Multinationals: Theory and History*, Aldershot, 1986; Blomström, M., 'Competitiveness of firms and countries', in *Globalization of Firms and the Competitiveness of Nations. Crafoord Lectures 2*, Institute of Economic Research, University of Lund, 1990.
2. Caves, R.E., *Multinational Enterprise and Economic Analysis*, Cambridge, 1982. The history of the early Swedish multinationals has been presented in Lundström, R., 'Swedish Multinational Growth before 1930', in Hertner, P. and Jones, G. (eds), *Multinationals: Theory and History*, Aldershot, 1986.
3. Attman, A., Kuuse, J., and Olsson, U., *L. M. Ericsson 100 Years*, vols I and II, Stockholm, 1976.
4. A recent summary of this line of theoretical thought can be found in Nordström, K.A., *The Internationalization Process of the Firm – Searching for New Patterns and Explanations*, Institute of International Business at the Stockholm School of Economics, Stockholm, 1991.
5. For ASEA, see Glete, J., *ASEA under 100 år 1883–1983. En studie i ett storföretags organisatoriska, tekniska och ekonomiska utveckling*, Västerås, 1983.
6. Lundström, idem note 2, p. 147.
7. Ibid.
8. SKF Annual Report, 1980.
9. Swedenborg, B., Johansson-Grahn, G. and Kinnwall, M., *Den svenska industrins utlandsinvesteringar 1960–1986*, Stockholm, 1988, pp. 59–61.
10. Olsson, U., *The Creation of a Modern Arms Industry. Sweden 1939-1974*, Publication of the Institute of Economic History of Gothenburg University, no. 37, Gothenburg, 1977.
11. *Sveriges Riksbanks Årsbok* (Bank of Sweden's Yearbook).
12. EFTA countries' fdi, *EFTA Economic Affairs Department, Occasional Paper No. 34*, 1990.
13. *Svensk industri och industripolitik*, Stockholm: Industridepartementet, 1990, *passim*.
14. The last remaining part of the foreign exchange control was abandoned in 1989, after 50 years.
15. Idem note 9, p. 178; Swedenborg, B., *The Multinational Operations of Swedish Firms. An Analysis of Determinants and Effects*, Stockholm, 1979, p. 268.
16. Idem note 9, pp. 110–15.
17. For country-specific advantages, see Porter, M.E., *The Competitive Advantage of Nations*, London, 1990, pp. 345–55. For political considerations, see Swedenborg, idem note 9, pp. 104–5.
18. Idem note 4, pp 227–8.
19. Ågren, L., *Swedish Direct Investment in the US*, Institute of International Business at the Stockholm School of Economics, Stockholm, 1990, p. 35.
20. Spero, J.D., *The Politics of International Economic Relations*, New York, 1990, p. 251.
21. Idem note 9, p. 77; idem note 9, pp. 41–2.
22. Idem note 19, pp. 149–73.
23. Braunerhielm, P., *Svenska industriföretag inför 1992*, Stockholm, 1990, pp. 117–18.
24. Idem note 12, (1990), p. 11.
25. Idem note 12, p. 13.
26. *Svenska Dagbladet*, 9 September 1990, p. 4.
27. Idem note 3, I, pp. 203–7.
28. Idem note 3, II, pp. 287–91.
29. Idem note 19, pp. 174–85.

30. Idem note 19, pp. 123–45.
31. Jagrén, L., 'Svenska utlandsetablerade företags marknadsandelar' in *De svenska storföretagen – en studie av internationaliseringens konsekvenser för den svenska ekonomin*, Stockholm, 1985, p. 137; idem note 3, II, p. 266.
32. Idem note 13, pp. 56–7.
33. Eliasson, G., *The International Firm: A Vehicle for Overcoming Barriers to Trade and a Global Intelligence Organization Diffusing the Notion of a Nation*, working paper no. 201, Stockholm: IUI, 1990, *passim*.
34. Hörnell, E., Vahlne, J. and Weidersheim-Paul, F., *Export och utlandsetableringar*, Stockholm, 1985, *passim*; Bergholm, F. and Jagrén, L., 'Det utlandsinvesterande företaget – en empirisk studie', in *De svenska storföretagen – en studie av internationaliseringens konsekvenser*, Stockholm: IUI, 1985, pp. 142–3.
35. Hedlund, 'Organizing in-between. The Evolution of the Mother-Daughter Structure of Managing Foreign Subsidiaries in Swedish MNFs', *Journal of International Business Studies*, Autumn, 1984.
36. On the role of 'clustering', see Porter, *Competitive Advantage of Nations*, idem note 17, pp. 148–54; Olsson, U., *Bank, familj och företagande. Stockholms Enskilda Bank 1946-1971*, Stockholm, 1986, *passim*.
37. Hedlund, G., Danielsson, K. and Synnerstad, K., *Who Manages the Global Corporation? Changes in the Nationality of Presidents of Foreign Subsidiaries of Swedish MNCs during the 1980's*, Institute of International Business at the Stockholm School of Economics (mimeo), 1990.
38. SKF Annual Report, 1972 and 1973.
39. Idem note 35.
40. Foreign centres for production, marketing and management appear more frequent than foreign centres for research. Forsgren, M., Holm, U. and Johanson, J., 'Internationalisering av andra graden', in *Internationalisering, företagen och det lokala samhället*, Stockholm, 1991.
41. Clegg, J. *Multinational Enterprise and World Competition. A Comparative Study of the USA, Japan, the UK, Sweden and West Germany*, London, 1991, p. 143 and *passim*.

6 The multinational companies of Norway

Fritz Hodne

The colonial heritage

In general, one may say that the stable trade characteristics of any country reflect the combined impact of history and natural resources. Take history first. The outstanding historical feature is that Norway was in a political union with Denmark from 1450 to 1814, thereafter in a dynastic union with Sweden from 1814 to 1905. Lacking the substance and trappings of sovereignty, the country failed to foster a national military and political aristocracy, and with it, the kind of capital accumulation associated with a native *haute bourgeoisie*. For similar reasons its Jewish immigrants, granted citizenship from the 1850s, were always a marginal group. By contrast they were a fairly strong element in the other Scandinavian countries. Unlike Danish and Swedish merchants, Norwegian entrepreneurs in the 19th century lacked access to the Jewish networks of international banking and finance. A general consequence has been the absence of a self-confident upper middle class, and a disproportionately strong Labour party. As a result, government and government initiative has come to play a disproportionate role in the modernization of the economy during the last 150 years. The distinctive feature of the colonial heritage was perhaps the anomaly that for four hundred years the nation's political centre was always foreign. Instead, its national identity decamped to the regions with their local peasant culture. This historical twist sets Norway apart from both Sweden and Denmark.[1] A related aspect should be considered: unlike its neighbours, Norway's provincial status meant that it possessed no colonies. A moral advantage perhaps, but the absence of colonies meant that Norway missed the usual trade channels that during the 17th and 18th centuries helped foster a merchant class, familiar with marketing goods on world markets.[2]

What about resources? Reinforcing the facts of history, natural resources played their part as well in shaping the nation's culture and economy. Traditionally, the country exported fish, timber, and ores, which were in abundance, in exchange for grain, salt, brandy, cloth, and capital goods. The country was also blessed with abundant waterfalls that provided energy for a variety of industrial processes, the most important of which till the advent of hydro electricity was sawing timber and milling grain. The external trade was borne on keels, made at local yards from local materials; thus the origins of the present international shipping empire. When Britain pioneered free trade from 1850, Norwegian shippers seized on the opportunity. By 1878, Norway was the world's third largest shipping nation, trailing Britain and the United States. Its share of world tonnage climbed from 3.6 per cent in 1851, when it held eighth place, to 6.8 per cent in 1878, the top year, when it held third place.[3] During these years the country's merchant fleet emancipated from the confines of the country's export business and made its way into the international carrying trade. By 1880 its size far exceeded the capacity of its home yards and the needs of its own foreign trade. Since then, despite losses during two world wars, constant technological change and rising capital demands, the nation has preserved its position in international shipping as one of the major players.

Consider next the dominant technologies of the 19th century. In the age of steam, manufacturing skills usually built directly on domestic deposits of coal and iron. Exploitation of these resources bred familiarity with the dominant machine culture. In these respects Norwegian entrepreneurs were handicapped, since the country has no coal and its iron deposits are low-grade, scattered and hard to exploit. Looking at national figures for value creation, employment, investment, and foreign trade, we may say that it was not till around the first decade of the 20th century that Norway became an industrial economy of sorts. It was of a very special kind. The impulse came with the new turbine technology that harnessed waterfalls to produce hydroelectric energy. The country's numerous waterfalls gave the country a potentially absolute advantage. According to international statistics four of the world's ten highest waterfalls are located in Norway.[4] Foreign capital, first British capital, then mostly German, Swedish and French capital, entered just after the turn of the century to utilize these natural resources, this time in the form of foreign direct investment (fdi) rather than portfolio investments. Cheap hydroelectric energy served as a basis for broadly three types of new industries: the electrometal, the electrochemical, and the electrotechnical.

Looking at the main facts of history and resources, then, we expect to see Norwegian multinationals particularly in areas such as fishing, shipping, forestry and energy intensive industries. The facts bear out the expectation. Two multinationals appeared in the period 1890–1914, one British-owned, the second Norwegian. First, the water power and forest reserves were utilized by British capital in the formation of the British multinational firm, The Kellner Partington Paper Pulp Co. Ltd (Borregaard), which began operations in 1889 at Sarpsborg, Norway, at Hallein, Austria, and at Manchester, and acquired forest reserves and additional pulp plant facilities in Sweden in 1907.[5] The other multinational to appear in this period was a domestic firm, O. Mustad & Son A/S, which in the period 1890 to 1914 launched production plants in Sweden, Germany, Great Britain, France, Italy, Spain and Austria-Hungary to produce fish hooks of all sizes and descriptions, a forerunner of international specialization by market segment rather than geographical sovereignty as a compensation for a small home market.[6] What about imitators?

The third wave

With a few exceptions, Norwegian manufacturing industry remained homebound till the advent of the EFTA period which began in 1960. The signing of the EFTA free trade agreement by Austria, Denmark, Norway, Portugal, Sweden, Switzerland and the UK changed the competitive position for the home industry. Till 1960 it had been sheltered by tariffs and shortages, and had served the home market pretty much without foreign competition.

The EFTA agreement, which came into force on 1 July 1960, aimed at a gradual removal of tariff barriers for manufactured goods. The process was to be completed by 1 January 1967. This promised to eliminate the border line between the home market industries and the export industries; henceforth both experienced the effects of competition. Thus began a new era. Faced with competition, many domestic manufacturers gave up, notably those making consumer goods. Those that survived resorted to various forms of adaptations. One way to stay ahead was to slim the product range. Managing Director Morten Hansen of A/S Protan, a post-war firm making a long list of PVC coated materials, plastics and speciality products for the food industry on the basis of seaweed, in 1964 summed up the new situation in the following words: 'The shedding of several products is as we all know a result of the new market conditions; having earlier made a variety of products for a small market, our company is forced to change over to making a few speciality products for a larger market'.[7] Manufacturing companies, always hampered by the small home market, were set back by German occupation during the Second World War. Expertise and reputation had to be rebuilt by degrees in the post-war period. The effects of war and occupation may be gauged by looking at Sweden and Switzerland. Their machinery intact, they expanded abroad shortly after 1945. With a few exceptions, among them A/S Protan above, Norwegian companies turned to foreign markets only when they had mastered the home market. In general this occurred in the 1970s. By and large Norwegian industry missed out on both the first wave of internationalization after the Second World War, 1946 to 1960 – and the second wave – 1960 to 1970 – the former dominated by American multinationals, the second by British and American companies.[8] By and large so did Denmark and Finland. Till that decade there were severe restrictions in force on cross-country currency movements. Equally, the Oslo Stock Exchange, dormant since the 1930s, had no foreign operators, and consequently in the period 1945 to 1970 had a minimal role in underwriting industrial investments in private industry. Whatever the explanation, apart from some tentative steps in setting up sales offices abroad in the 1960s, Norwegian industrial companies began to invest in production facilities abroad only in the following decade.

By contrast, other small countries like Sweden, Switzerland, or the Netherlands, operated a broad range of multinational companies, in some cases as far back as 1870. As may be learnt from the article on Sweden in this book (Chapter 5), Sweden already had by 1922 at least 50 companies running manufacturing plants in foreign countries; the notorious Kreuger group of the 1920s alone controlled 70 manufacturing companies in 33 countries. Similarly, Switzerland's Nestlé turned to multinational production from the 1920s. The multinational giant in consumer electronics, Philips of Holland, dates back to the turn of the century.

Up till 1980 the Norwegian literature on the subject of fdis is limited to a handful of minor articles and reports.[9] From 1978 there are two short articles which report on Norges Bank's licensing of investments in manufacturing facilities abroad, in which Norwegian companies held more than 10 per cent of the equity. A total of 146 such licences had been granted to manufacturing companies as against a total of 2000 in all; however, the manufacturing investments represented a workforce of over 20 000 in 1977, and a total capital investment of 5 billion NOK (around US$ 830 million), all in all a substantial addition to the domestic economy.[10] At the opening of the 1980s 'deindustrialization' loomed on the horizon. The political establishment cheered the outgoing movement. A Labour government report of 1980 spoke of the need to 'strengthen our competitive stance, maintain high investment levels, improve productivity, and stimulate profitability'.[11] A select committee was appointed in 1981 to propose ways by which the government could help business achieve these targets.[12] The title of the report: *The Need for Internationalization of the Norwegian Economy*, points to the political urgency felt at the time when the second oil shock in 1979 had induced stagnation of employment and output in domestic industry. Because the new oil sector in the Norwegian sector of the North Sea had boosted cost levels way above its competitors, Norwegian industry needed to improve its competitive performance in world markets. The mandate spoke of 'the need to improve our export structure, and through export of services, transfer of technology, and purchases of industrial holdings abroad, increase our access to the larger foreign markets that alone could offer a future for Norwegian industry'. Valuable from our point of view was the fact that in preparing their report, the authors interviewed 27 domestic parent companies with a total of 41 daughter companies in the EC area. The time period was 1958 to 1980, and included launchings in which the parent company held a minimum of 25 per cent of the share capital. By sector, nine of the investor firms were in engineering, four in primary metals, and four in the chemical industry. Of their 41 daughter companies, 23 had been launched by the Norwegian mother company while 18 represented purchases of existing foreign firms. Note that apart from the terminal points, 1958 to 1980, nothing further is said about timing of the foreign ventures, nor about the volume of the investments, the size of the foreign work force or about profitability. Information on these points can only be obtained from the individual annual company reports.

The government followed up the 1981 report by a special proposition in 1985, that offered various forms of government assistance to internationalization, the most important of which were guarantees against the risks involved in exports to socialist and Third World countries.[13] Next, according to a Norges Bank report from 1984 there were a total of 2956 foreign companies in which the Norwegian share exceeded 10 per cent by 1 November 1984.[14] In 2187 of these companies the Norwegian owners were represented directly; in the remaining 769 companies the

Table 6.1   Foreign companies in which the Norwegian share exceeded 10 per cent at 1 November 1984

Sector	No. of companies	%
Manufacturing	385	13.0
Shipping	486	16.4
Trade	994	33.6
Banking	27	0.9
Insurance	33	1.1
Other financials	194	6.6
Commercial services	410	13.9
Others	208	7.0
None	219	7.5
Total	2956	100.0

Source
Norges Bank Report 1984

Norwegian interest was channelled through foreign agents. In the previous year, 264 companies had been added (9.8 per cent), which suggests that the outgoing wave had become a scramble, probably aided by generous loans, credits and guarantees from the government and its agencies, among them The Guarantee Institute for Export Credits (GIEK), Norway's Export Council, and the government's industrial fund. The generosity of the terms may even have induced some domestic companies to enter into deals abroad that in terms of prospective profitability were unwarranted. A breakdown by sector of the above 2956 companies is given in Table 6.1.

A perspective on this 1984 report is provided by an OECD survey from 1985, offering information on fdis by the major players, and, incidentally, on Danish, Finnish, Norwegian, and Swedish outgoing aggregate investments for the years 1979 and 1984 (see Table 6.2).

Table 6.2 documents that till the mid-1980s the UK, the United States, Japan, and West Germany had been responsible for the bulk of fdis during the previous 15 years; second, that apart from Sweden the Scandinavian countries in net terms had only marginal business investments abroad both in 1979 and 1984; yet they were obviously increasing these investments at a time when the old dominant players were reducing theirs. In relation to gross domestic capital information Norway and Sweden in 1984 placed a bigger share in fdis than both the UK and USA. Norway was part of the third wave. In the period 1981 to 1985 Norwegian net fdis increased from 1.1 to 7.5 per cent of gross domestic capital formation. The result is based on investments by a handful of big Norwegian industrial companies,

Table 6.2   Direct net investments abroad, by investor country, 1979 and 1984 (US $ Million)

	1979	1984
USA	25 220	4 500
UK	12 484	8 658
Japan	2 898	5 695
West Germany	4 493	3 308
Sweden	606	1 044
Denmark	0	96
Norway	44	542
Finland	125	413

Source
OECD, 'Balances of OECD countries 1965-1984', Paris 1985, cited from M. Carlsen and Ingrid Rasmussen, 'Norske næringslivsinvesteringer i utlandet', *Penger og kreditt* 1988, p. 18.

including Aker, Dyno, Elkem, Freia, Hydro, Jotun, Kongsberg Våpenfabrikk and Norsk Data. (See the survey of the Norwegian mne family below.)

A report from 1988, based on data collected by the Norges Bank research staff shows that the fdis stemmed from the eight biggest companies. It is worth noticing that the companies pioneering the internationalization movement were themselves in the process of formation in the 1980s, through mergers, buy-outs, purchases, and joint ventures. These eight industrial companies had 70 per cent of total foreign sales by Norwegian daughter companies abroad in 1979. Their share increased to 77 per cent by 1983. In that year they owned 85 per cent of their share capital. As for employment, Norwegian-owned companies abroad employed 21 000 workers in 1979 against 29 000 in 1983, an increase of 70 per cent. Of this, the eight biggest above increased their foreign workforce from 11 000 to 19 000 in the period. Shipping companies, running service operations, were omitted. As shipping investments loomed large, the results cited here are somewhat lopsided. Of greater significance perhaps, in 1979 the foreign workforce of these eight companies represented 10 per cent of their total employment as against an average 40 per cent by 1985. While their total sales trebled from 1979 to 1985, their daughter companies increased their sales by more. Foreign sales increased from 60 to 76 per cent of their total turnovers, almost all of the increase attributable to their foreign daughter companies. Due to the weakness of the data, nothing worthwhile can be said about profits.[15]

Norwegian fdis, 1986–1991

Table 6.3 reports on the further trend in outgoing long-term investments, with data for the years 1986 through the first six months of 1991, collected by the central bank staff. Short-term portfolio investments are excluded; they were minor anyway. The gross foreign investment figures in Table 6.3 for the years 1986 to 1991, published here for the first time, indicate a rapidly rising trend in Norwegian outgoing investments, up from about 20 billion in 1986 to 36 billion NOK in 1990, an 80 per cent increase. Judging from the figure for the first half of 1991, the upward trend promises to continue. Provided the second part of 1991 matches the first half, total Norwegian outgoing investments in 1991 should exceed 50 billion NOK (US$ 7.7 billion). The gross figures thus suggest a dramatic upward trend in Norwegian fdis from 1986 to 1991. In net terms, however, the outgoing investment figures in Table 6.3 provide no clear trend; also the net outgoing balances are relatively small in aggregate terms. A better clue to uncovering motives and trends in the figures would be to look at the foreign stock purchases alone, which, in fact, is possible on the basis of the published figures. Again, no clear trend is discernible. Gross stock purchases rose from 5165 million NOK in 1986 to 8997 million in 1990, having peaked at 19 998 million in 1989. Deducting desinvestments, we arrive at a net figure of 4 855 million for 1986, which just about matched the 1990 figure of 4 574 million NOK. Clearly, in so far as Norwegian stock purchases abroad reflect long-term designs, they do not reveal any dramatic upward trend for the period 1986 to 1990, whether one looks at the gross or the net figures. As for the direction of the Norwegian investments, we turn to Table 6.4.

Table 6.3   *Norwegian direct investments abroad, stocks and long-term loans, 1986–91 (million current NOK)*

Year	Gross investments	Desinvestments	Net investments
1986	20 356	8 212	12 144
1987	25 986	17 494	8 474
1988	33 914	28 363	5 551
1989	35 324	25 746	9 578
1990	36 080	29 955	6 125
1991[1]	24 971	21 469	3 502

Note
1. 1 January–30 June 1991.

Source
Norges Bank, Department of Statistics. 'Desinvestment' is the term used by the Norwegian Central Bank to mean selling off assets, both stock bonds and paying back loans.

Table 6.4   Norwegian direct investments abroad, by country and area, 1986–91 (%).

Country	1986	1987	1988	1989	1990	1991[1]
Scandinavia	18.6	8.5	6.4	29.3	37.0	42.1
UK	19.5	18.5	6.3	13.3	20.9	6.7
EC	46.1	40.3	26.8	43.4	59.1	40.2
USA	5.9	6.5	3.5	13.7	7.8	9.2
Industrialized countries	70.0	75.7	86.5	94.0	94.6	96.0
Non-industrialized	30.0	24.3	13.5	6.0	5.4	4.0

Note
1. First half of 1991.

Source
Norges Bank, Department of Statistics.

As shown in Table 6.4, the overwhelming proportion of the Norwegian direct investments during this period 1986 to 1991 have gone into industrialized countries and a rapidly dwindling proportion into non-industrialized nations. Among the former, the EC countries have been the most important investment area, taking between 27 and 59 per cent of total long-term investments abroad in this period. Of these again, the UK has been the preferred country, followed by France and the Netherlands. A growing proportion has found its way into neighbouring Scandinavian countries, with Denmark taking a total of 17 591 and Sweden 22 071 million NOK of a total of 177 million NOK invested long term in the period (Table 6.3). In relative terms Denmark has taken about 10 per cent and Sweden 13 per cent of the total from 1986 to 1991. It may come as a surprise that the United States have received such a modest share, below ten per cent except for 1988. This points to a fairly common observation in the annual company reports in question that the US market has proved to be difficult to penetrate for foreign companies. We turn to the question of size, and compare the outgoing capital flow with gross investments in fixed capital (see Table 6.5).

An obvious comment on the volume of the fdis relative to gross capital formation would be that the outgoing capital flow from 1986 to 1990 just about doubled, up from 14 per cent in 1986 to 28.9 per cent in 1990. Gross fdis in 1990 thus run close to one-third of total investments in the domestic economy. Norwegian industry certainly has taken to heart the government urge from 1981 to go international. As noted above in Table 6.3, the net figures fail to suggest any dramatic capital flight from Norway during 1986 to 1990.

Finally, on the basis of a questionnaire in 1989, Norges Bank in September 1991 published figures for the first time, showing the total Norwegian holdings abroad.

Table 6.5   Norwegian gross direct investments abroad in relation to gross fixed capital formation, 1986–90 (million NOK in %)

Year	Foreign investments	Gross investments	Foreign (%)
1986	20 365	145 539	14.0
1987	25 986	157 364	16.5
1988	33 914	169 359	20.0
1989	35 324	170 530	20.7
1990	36 080	125 059	28.9

Sources
Foreign investments: Norges Bank, Department of Statistics. Gross investments: *National Accounts.*

Holdings here imply a minimum share of 10 per cent of the equity capital of the companies in question. The holdings totalled 28 billion NOK in 1988, increasing to 35.9 billion at the end of 1989.[16] Norwegian investors received 1.0 billion in 1988 and 1.3 billion NOK in the form of dividends and net interest, which is no surprise. Of the total in 1989, the UK topped the list with 22.9 per cent of the investments, followed by Sweden (14.7), Denmark (14.2), the Netherlands (11.4) and the United States (11.4 per cent). By sector, the biggest was banking with 14.6 billion NOK, followed by manufacturing 10.3, and trade 7.1 billion NOK. The companies in question represented a total of 79 921 man years.

The Norwegian foreign holdings may be compared with the foreign holdings in Norway. In 1987 and 1988 Norges Bank conducted a survey of foreign direct holdings in Norwegian companies. At end of 1988 they amounted to a total of NOK 41 billion, which yielded a reinvested return of NOK 4.8 billion. Of the total, the United States held 27.1 per cent, Sweden 24.1, France 20.5, followed by the Netherlands, Switzerland, Great Britain and Germany. The EC countries represented 40.5 per cent of the total. By sector the fdis were concentrated in three areas: trade, hotel and catering (34.1 per cent), oil (22.2 per cent) and bank, insurance, commercial property and other financial services (21.7 per cent). The fdi provided employment for a total of 118 500 employees, or 5.4 per cent of the nation's work force of 2 183 000 in 1988.[17]

Identifying the players 1965–90

By way of introducing the actual players, we review current theories that seek to explain why companies move abroad. Recent contributions to the theory of fdis come under three headings: market imperfections, defensive investments, and the product cycle theory. During the 1980s they have been refined in various directions, without as yet providing an international consensus encompassing all the phenomena observed.[18] The first theory explains fdis as a response to imperfect product and factor markets, which the company despite the risk and handicaps seeks to exploit to its advantage. Among internal factors prompting a decision to go abroad one could point to competent leadership, raw materials, new products, the desire to find a use for old machinery, the opportunity to capture economies of scale and secure competitive advantage, or easy access to capital. Among external factors one could mention the influence of customers, the expansion of competitors, tariff barriers abroad, the need to follow suit in order to be present in all markets, notably in oligopolistic markets with high entry costs, or the formation of the European Common Market, a chance to obtain regional subsidies in that area, or exploit tax benefits in the Bahamas. In either case the costs of operating through the ordinary export channels are deemed higher than setting up a daughter company abroad. By so doing the company creates an internal market for the sale of its goods or services, and stands a better chance to appropriate any potential gains from its patents, its research or other competitive assets. The second theory assumes defensive motives. Companies go abroad in order not to maximize short-term profits on any individual product, but to maintain a given market power balance for the entire company in the longer term. Several respondents gave this motive in a questionnaire conducted in 1978 by Norges Bank.[19] However, the above considerations pertain to expansion both on the home market and foreign markets; indeed, going abroad is reduced to a special case of the general internalization theory, according to which firms in a given situation obtain lower transaction costs by extending their internal operations rather than using external markets. The third theory invoked to explain fdis and international trade is called the product cycle theory. This theory assumes a systematic relation between foreign trade and location of production; both are seen as successive stages in the life cycle of a product. New products tend to appear in the most advanced economy. After an initial phase the product moves from an experimental to a standardized form, and finally to a mature stage. *Pari passu* price competiveness becomes decisive, which dictates that by degrees production will shift from high-to medium-to low-cost locations in low-income countries, from whence the good will be exported back to the original home market or other high-cost countries.

If we view the Norwegian multinationals against the theoretical background sketched above, we observe that they have followed mostly the route suggested by the market imperfection model. Four stages recur, each tracing increasing commitments of resources abroad: (1) direct exports, (2) foreign agents, (3) sales subsidiaries, (4) foreign production company.[20] By 1970 the companies above were nearly all dominant and well established on the domestic market. They had developed their own company culture, they controlled assets such as patented technology, products, and boasted their own management style. Operating mostly in oligopolistic markets, they obtained economies of scale by launching or acquiring a daughter company abroad rather than relying on external exports. Most of the Norwegian fdis during the 1970s pertain to horizontal investments, whereby the mother companies were able to penetrate new markets, achieve bigger market shares and overall market power. In other words, defensive considerations were present. Horizontal investments are aimed at companies producing goods of the same degree of value adding as that of the mother company. The other entry method involves vertical integration, whereby the mother company secures a market for finished products abroad, based on its own semi-finished manufactures at home.

Two strategies are observed. As far as Europe and the United States are concerned, the fdis usually involved purchases of existing firms. In the Middle East and the Far East, notably in the Singapore area, they usually involved investments in new companies. Beginning in 1969, Viking-Askim, Moss, faced with high wage costs at home, in a joint 65-35 venture with the Danish Øst Asiatiske Kompagni, in 1973 moved its footwear plant and machinery to Malaysia, where rubber was a local raw material and there was a relatively stable political environment. The product cycle model found illustration here, in that a standardized product technology was relocated from a high cost to a low cost wage market. Norsk Hydro in 1969 established chemical fertilizer production in Qatar. This was followed up in the 1970s when Jotun and Dyno launched new companies in Singapore. And Norcem, now part of Aker, organized cement production in the Middle East.[21] The other strategy is exemplified by purchases of existing plants in Europe and the US. In the 1980s Dyno bought up civil explosives plants in Sweden and the US, ending up as one of the largest manufacturers of explosives for civil purposes in the world. Hydro bought up fertilizer plants in Western Europe and is now the world's dominant player in the field of fertilizers. With a basis in North Sea oil resources Hydro and state-owned Statoil in the 1980s bought up gas station chains in Sweden and Denmark, while Elkem following the same strategy became one of the largest ferro alloy manufacturers in the world. Norcem bought into Swedish fireplace and tile companies, and shares in the Swedish cement industry. Aker merged with Norcem in 1987; the deal turned the new company Aker into one of Europe's leading cement concerns. To cap its ambitions Aker together with Sweden's AB EUROC in 1988 bought the Castle Cement Ltd, Britain's second largest cement producer.[22]

A variety of risks are involved, including currency, financial and political risks. The early Norwegian ventures in the 1960s involved Third World countries, usually with government guarantees. It was part of the foreign aid optimism of the decade, that has run so strongly in social democratic Scandinavia. In several cases the political risks in the host countries were undervalued. The following examples were typical. On the assumption that the Nigerian government would grant a concession, Kværner in 1964 leased a British engine factory in Lagos, Nigeria, for three years. After three years Kværner had achieved a turn around. Rather than grant a concession, the Nigerian government expropriated the factory, and Kværner had to relinquish its Nigerian engagement, with considerable loss to GIEK, the Government Guarantee Institute for Export Credits. Other Norwegian companies also burnt their fingers in Nigeria, following a wave of nationalization there in the 1970s, during which 121 foreign companies were nationalized by 1976. Similarly, when Peru nationalized its fish industry in 1973, the Norwegian-owned Pesquera Tambo de Mora S.A., was expropriated as a result. Ghana's changing political regimes during the 1960s and 1970s also involved Aker in loss-producing enterprises, until in 1975 Ghana's government, wishing to control its own fishery resources, abrogated its agreement with Aker to operate its deep-sea trawlers, built with Norwegian aid money. It is also clear that Borregaard, operating a pulp plant in Brazil, was forced out by local political pressure motivated by nationalist jealousies.[23]

The examples point to the tendency apparent after 1973, to make foreign trade again a bilateral affair, with its attendant claims that imports balance export, for each country and even for each industry. The return to discriminatory practices despite GATT was pretty universal by 1991. Whatever the moral of the matter, bilateralism favours trade with neighbouring countries, with OECD countries or EC members, which by 1990 present minimal risks, political or financial. The facts bear out the contention: of Norway's total fdis at end of 1989, 76 per cent were invested in Europe, another 11 per cent in the United States.[24] Similarly, of the Danish foreign investments in 1983 more than four-fifths, 86 per cent, were invested in OECD countries, against 14 per cent in Third World nations, despite liberal guarantees and export credits from the Danish government.[25]

Having now followed the overall aspects of the subject in some detail and offered concrete examples, we turn to the question of identifying the players. The basis for making a list of Norwegian mne companies as of May 1991 are the published annual reports of the biggest Norwegian manufacturing companies. The following criteria are observed: membership in the mne family requires a minimum of three foreign production plants and sales of a minimum of two billion NOK. On the basis of this definition, a search through the annual reports of the biggest manufacturing companies yields a list of 11 Norwegian multinationals as of May 1991. Two companies, Norske Skogindustrier A/S and Freia-Marabou, are about to enter the group. Norske Skogindustrier A.S, for instance, reported exports of 6.9 and Freia-Marabou of 3.2 billion NOK for 1990, though the latter mostly to neighbouring Scandinavian countries. However, they disqualify for mne-membership since they operate production facilities in less than three foreign countries. Several smaller companies, among them Mustad A.S, NEK Kabel A/S, Stentofon AS, Frank Mohn AS, Jac. Jacobsen Industrier A.S, and Jordan A.S, though operating production plants in several foreign countries, are disqualified, as their sales fall short of the two billion mark. Borregaard, the former flagship in this context, is out of the race entirely, having been merged with other companies twice during the last four years, during which even the name has disappeared. The leading companies are presented in Table 6.6, and briefs on each are provided in Appendix 1 at end of this chapter.

In the 1988 edition of *The Times 1000* one finds two of the companies listed in Table 6.6 among the 50 leading companies in Europe. They are Statoil and Norsk Hydro, ranked number 46 and 48 respectively. In that group one finds three Swedish companies: Volvo (24), Electrolux (34), and ASEA AB (47), two Swiss companies: Nestlé SA (9), Ciba Geigy AG (36); one Belgian: Petrofina (33), but

Table 6.6   Norwegian multinationals, May 1991 (sales in million NOK (1990))

Company	Sales	Abroad	%	Employment	Abroad	%
Aker	13 413	5 486	41	12 500	3 852	31
AL	2 405	1 851	77	2 340	1 800	77
Dyno	7 095	5 742	81	7 273	5.071	70
EB	10 071	4 535	45	13 000	4 000	31
Elkem	8 008	7 528	94	7 454	2 000	27
Hafslund Nycomed	4 340	3 042	70	3 035	1 400	46
Kværner	13 088	7 543	58	17 000	9 000	53
Nora	9 048	1 810	20	7 727	1 925	25
Norsk Hydro	60 972	53 486	88	33 042	16 297	49
Statoil	81 475	53 000	65	13 222	4 400	33
Tiedemanns	4 121[1]	2 817	68	2 323	1 510	65

Note
1. After tobacco taxes.

Sources
Annual company reports, *Eksport-Aktuelt* No. 12, 1991, p. 3.

no Danish or Finnish companies. Updated information on ownership networks among European multinationals is easily available.[26]

Some generalizations

The present survey of the Norwegian mnes throws light on three salient trends in European manufacturing industries in the 1980s. One is the liberalization of markets, both regarding tariffs, company legislation and standards. Another is the increasing size of operating units, necessary to achieve cost-effective production in deregulated markets. A third is internationalization. Naturally, with a small, open, specialized market economy, Norway was influenced by these politically inspired changes. Thus, Norway exported NOK 187 billion of goods in 1988; of this 65 per cent went to the EC area, 20 per cent to the Nordic countries, including Denmark, and 16 per cent to EFTA countries.[27] Notably its export-competing industries underwent a transformation, characterized by mergers, consolidation, concentration and internationalization. In consequence, manufacturing has been shedding workers from about 1970, though the lay-offs have been offset to some extent by the rise of the oil and gas industry, and more importantly by public sector jobs. The production value of manufacturing as a share of national income dropped from 25 per cent in 1951 to 14 per cent in 1985, a bottom year, a decline that is conveniently downplayed if one instead of the manufacturing figures, uses the Clark-Fourastié term for all the secondary activities, including manufacturing, mining, oil and gas, energy and construction.[28] Also the entire political climate changed in the 1980s, both regarding ideology, economic policy goals and instruments, as the full employment-high inflation regime was replaced by monetarism.

The rise of 11 Norwegian multinational industrials in the twenty year period, 1970 to 1990 should be seen against this broader background. Expectedly, market considerations have been the single most important motive for the decisions by the Norwegian industrial companies to enter the multinational band wagon. Earlier, specialized in accordance with state geographical lines, Norwegian manufacturing companies in the 1980s began to line up along product lines to position themselves in niches in international, deregulated markets for goods and services. There is thus an obvious linkage between the international deregulation in the 1980s and the bunching of Norwegian mnes in the decades 1970 to 1990, six in the 1970s, another five in the 1980s. The 11 multinationals represent the biggest and oldest firms among Norwegian manufacturing companies. Their combined sales for 1990 were 52 per cent of total sales from manufacturing, and they employed 32 per cent of all workers in manufacturing. Running their own finance divisions, several of them have emancipated from the former dependence on domestic banks.

By ownership, nine are privately owned, Statoil is wholly government-owned, Norsk Hydro is government controlled, but only in the formal sense that 51 per cent of its stock is in government hands. Foreign ownership is restricted in part by the concession laws cited above, but also by the practice of issuing A-shares with full voting rights for Norwegian citizens and B-shares with restricted voting rights to foreigners.

By fields of operation, the Norwegian mnes produce mainly semi-finished goods. Apart from Norgessalpeter, hardly any of their products command instant recognition in the international markets. However, several of their products enjoy high-income elasticities, among them fresh salmon, pharmaceuticals and oil. Two of the firms are engaged in oil: Statoil, Hydro; two, AL and Hafslund Nycomed, are in pharmaceuticals; two are mainly in foods and beverages: Nora and Tiedemanns; two, Elkem and Hydro, are in basic metals, and engineering is prominent in at least four: Aker, Hydro, Kværner and Statoil. The original natural assets of hydropower and oil are visible in the activities of Hydro, Elkem, Hafslund and Statoil, and so were forest reserves in the case of Borregaard, now a has-been.

The Norwegian industrial mnes provide a somewhat incomplete picture of fdis in the 1980s. This is because Norwegian shipping is ignored, and shipping investments constituted 31.6 per cent of net fdis in the period 1986 to 1988. Thus, the impression gained from the industrials alone is somewhat lopsided.[29]

As for timing, several factors help explain why all the above 11 companies made it into the mne family in the 20-year period, 1970 to 1990. For one thing, they rose to dominance in the home market just prior to that period. Seeking new markets, their boards quite easily took to the idea of international operations. The slogan of internationalization was increasingly popular; imitating competitors was probably the sufficient motive in several instances. More seriously, both Hydro and Elkem faced energy shortages at home from around 1970. Their call for more energy went unanswered. The government was besieged by conservationist groups, who called for a ban on further despoliation of nature. Their protests were overruled during two spectacular confrontations between demonstrators and the police in 1970 and 1981, but the demonstrators converted the general public to their view. As a result by 1991 the energy-intensive industry, threatened by too little energy at uncompetitive prices, has announced its intention to desert the home country and move abroad. Also in 1970 the value added tax system was introduced, together with changes in company taxation and both increased the attractiveness of foreign operations. By 1977, rising production costs pushed Norwegian cost levels 12 per cent higher than neighbouring countries, resulting in loss of market shares at home and abroad. Kværner's purchase of the Scottish shipyard Govan in 1988 was an attempt to escape from the excessive cost levels in Norway.[30] Moreover, the currency regulations were gradually lifted in the 1980s which opened the domestic market and the Oslo Stock Exchange to foreign capital and foreign players. The currency deregulation, complete from 1 July 1990, was welcomed by the government as a means to stop the creeping deindustrialization, following the first oil shock in 1973. Deindustrialization so far has meant a 50 per cent reduction in engineering employment in less than 20 years. Similar figures are reported from Sweden and Denmark and from all the advanced industrial countries, though interpretations differ.[31] Undoubtedly, another retarding factor was the rapid rise of the Norwegian oil sector. It offered bonanza orders for the big engineering companies like Kværner, Aker, EB, and Hydro. In the 1970s they had no incentive to go abroad. However, when they did go, one should not overlook the consistently higher net earnings per share on operations abroad during 1986 to 1988, compared to domestic earnings.

Finally, it should be recalled that domestic capital owners tended to find shipping in comparison with manufacturing a better investment choice; in general this was certainly the case up to 1920, but shipping continued to enjoy tax breaks throughout the post-war period as well, which helped give shipping a continued edge over competing investment alternatives.[32] The government decision in 1987 to establish a Norwegian international ship register attests to the force of this point. When the tax concessions eroded during the 1980s, due to the depressed freight levels in the international carrying trade, a growing number of domestic shipping companies started registering their ships in convenience flag countries that offered better tax conditions, in Panama, Liberia, the Bahamas and others, in order to escape the high operation costs imposed by the Norwegian trade unions. In an attempt to stop the haemorrhage a Norwegian Labour government set up a Norwegian International Ship Register (NIS), offering international registry conditions. Amidst trade union protests the register went into operation in 1987. By 1990 it had signed up 90 per cent of the merchant fleet.[33] These comments on shipping merely remind us that unlike Sweden, Norway, never a manufacturing country anyway, has simply chosen a trade strategy rather than a manufacturing strategy in its race to achieve economic growth in the modern era. To the extent that this is the case, the question of laggardness on the part of domestic industry in going abroad becomes trivial, in as much as in shipping Norway has been a player in international business since before the turn of the century.[34]

In the longer term perspective, the list of multinationals in Table 6.6 documents the rule that in the beginning all companies were national. Basing their genealogy on the age of the oldest member, we find that the 11 Norwegian mnes in 1991 represent a total of 1425 operating years, or an average of 119 years each. Clearly, with an average apprentice period of 119 years, the Norwegian mnes bear out the proposition that whatever the myth says, the rational policy for achieving success in international business is to work long-term.

Appendix 1

The Norwegian Multinational Companies in 1991

Aker
As a multinational industrial group Aker was launched as late as 1987. A result of a merger between Aker (est. 1841), an engineering and shipbuilding company, and Norcem, a cement and construction group, Aker at the time ranked as the biggest privately-owned industrial corporation in Norway. Aker is active in cement and building materials, engineering, offshore projects and constructions, landbased construction and commercial property development. With the Swedish company Industri AB EUROC, it holds majority interests in cement-related businesses in the US, Jamaica, Togo, Liberia, Ghana, and Tanzania, it owns plants in Norway and Sweden for prefabricated expanded clay blocks, and operates four tiles works in Sweden. Aker is active in oil exploration, oil drilling, and oil rig construction internationally. It owns sizeable commercial and industrial properties at home. Beside its home and foreign production facilities, the concern operates numerous sales offices and sales agencies in at least a dozen countries.[35] In April 1988, Aker in a joint deal with the Swedish company Industri AB EUROC bought the British cement group Castle Cement Ltd, each taking 50 per cent of the stock. The British cement company had a market share in Britain of 25 per cent. Aker already held an equity share of 24.8 per cent in the Spanish cement giant Cia. Valenciana de Cementos Portland, the biggest cement group in Spain with six operating cement mills in Spain, and 75 concrete plants along the Mediterranean coast. The entry into the mne family may be set at 1986 when Aker and Norcem merged.

AL
Based in Oslo, AL acts as parent company for a multinational group of companies engaged mainly in the development, manufacture and distribution of drugs and diagnostic methods for human patients, animals and fish. Its products also include foods and animal feeds, vaccines, animal health products and food additives. AL

ranks as the world's biggest manufacturer of fish vaccines. A daughter company, AL Laboratories Inc., was launched in the United States in 1975. The American daughter company is listed on the New York Stock Exchange (NYSE).[36] Through production and marketing of its own products, and through purchases of other American drug companies, the American company, AL Laboratories, headquartered in New Jersey, acted as locomotive in the overall rapid growth of the AL group in the 15 years, 1975 to 1990. The entry into the multinational family may be set in the mid-1980s. In a joint 50-50 venture with Dyno, AL in 1986 launched Dynal A/S, a research company holding world patent rights to develop the 'Ugelstad beads' (magnetizable, monodisperse polymer particles) which are expected to have considerable future market potentials in biomedicine, including cancer and Aids diagnosis. AL operates its own production plants in Norway, Denmark, the United States, and Indonesia; and through its American daughter company, AL controls daughter companies active in drugs, foods, and diagnostics in USA, Europe, Japan and Australia.

Dyno
Dyno Industrier A/S, dates back to 1865 when Alfred Nobel, the Swedish inventor of dynamite and father of the Nobel prize, registered a Norwegian daughter company at Lysaker outside Oslo, under the name Nitroglycerin Compagniet, to produce dynamite, his patented explosive. In 1917 the company changed its name to Norsk Sprængstofindustri A/S. By 1935 it included a group of seven affiliated companies, all domestic, engaged in explosives.[37] After the Second World War Dyno diversified from explosives into liquid glues, adhesives, resins, plastic films, paints, and finished plastics products. By 1970 it had acquired a dominant position on the home market. In 1969 Dyno set up a factory in Singapore, Dyno Industries Singapore Pte Ltd, in which Dyno held 65 per cent of the share capital, to produce formaldehyde and synthetic resins. In 1971 Dyno acquired majority interests in Cooper, Pegler & Co. Ltd, an English machine company, based in Sussex. At the same time Dyno entered contracts to build formaldehyde and glues factories in Denmark and Finland, on-line in 1972. From 1971, then, Dyno entered the multinational corporate family, as yet in a very small way. The company claims their big breakthrough to multinational status took place in 1984 when Dyno bought the US company Ireco Inc., Utah, a producer of civil explosives. By 1990, Dyno Industrier A/S operated 120 plants, of which 100 were based abroad in more than 30 countries.

EB
Elektrisk Bureau (EB), established in 1882, at first sold imported telephones and telephone equipment locally. By 1885 it manufactured its own telephones. EB expanded its product portfolio; by 1914 it included telephones, telephone exchanges and electric household goods; in addition EB maintained a retail activity for its own and its imported electrical goods. In the 1920s EB went into partnership with L.M. Ericsson. The company also diversified into cables. The years 1930 to 1935

proved difficult. However, despite several writedowns of Ericsson's stake in EB, the symbiosis between Ericsson and EB continued. After 1945 EB began a systematic program of diversification, while maintaining a high level of investments and R. & D. A major source of demand was Televerket, the state monopoly in telecommunication. EB continued its domestic expansion in telephones, cables, and diversified into maritime telecommunication, process control and signal systems. Foreign sales increased from 12.9 to 20.4 per cent of turnover between 1970 and 1980. The road to mne-status proceeded via exports, selling agencies and service offices abroad, the first two of which were established in 1972 in London and Hamburg, to full-scale production plants abroad. The first two foreign production plants were acquired in 1977. The third foreign daughter company was EB Communications (Singapore) Pte. Ltd, registered in Singapore in 1979.[38]

Elkem
Incorporated in 1905, A/S Det Norske Aktieselskap for Elektrokemisk Industri, began as a water power company and a manufacturer of chemical fertilizers. From the start, Elkem was involved in industrial development, research and engineering in the metallurgical field. An early patent was the Søderberg Electrode System. Patented in 1919, it was developed by Elkem, initially for the smelting of ferro alloys, pig iron, etc., and gradually adapted to the electrolytic aluminium furnace. The Søderberg's electrode has been adopted all over the world, and by 1970 produced 60 per cent of the world's total output of aluminium and steel. After 1945 Elkem diversified into production of metals and materials, above all aluminium, but also into ferro silicium, electrode paste, calcium carbide, manganese alloys, silicium metal, etc. All operations were in the domestic market, but about 80 per cent of the products were exported to Canada, Brazil and the United States. Through a merger with Christiania Spigerverk in 1972, a veteran steel company from 1853, Elkem swelled employment, sales and sales offices abroad. The first step to multinational production was taken in 1968. To meet the German and British expansion in crude aluminium, Elkem in 1968, in collaboration with Alcoa, bought majority positions in both the British and the Dutch aluminium industry. The decision aimed at securing stable outlets for Elkem's production of crude aluminium from its plant at Mosjøen and from 1970 from its Lista plant, owned jointly by Elkem and Alcoa.[39] The acquisitions in 1968 also gave Elkem a position in the EC market for finished aluminium products. Next, the 1965 report mentions the purchase of shares in an English company, Kings Lynn Steel Co. Ltd. In 1973, at a time when Elkem had acquired 50 per cent of that company's share capital, Kings Lynn built a steel plant in Manchester, while changing its name to Manchester Steel Ltd.[40] By our criteria these three acquisitions established Elkem as a multinational.

Hafslund Nycomed
Hafslund Nycomed A/S (HN) was launched in June 1988, when A/S Hafslund purchased a controlling position in A/S Nycomed. Hafslund traced its origin back

to a hydroelectric company established in 1898; Nycomed (est. 1874) was a pharmaceutical company. At the time of the merger A/S Hafslund was involved in engineering and ferro alloys, mostly for the export markets; Nycomed had developed patented products in the field of contrast fluids. Nycomed's product, sold under the trade name Omnipaque, was used for medical imaging diagnostics. The method eliminated the risks of invasive surgery. After the merger in 1988, HN acquired daughter companies in Austria, France, Denmark, and the US; it arranged licensing production agreements with other pharmaceutical companies in Finland, Japan and elsewhere for Omnipaque, and set up subsidiaries to market its products in Europe, USA, Japan and the Far East. HN turned into a multinational in 1990, owning production facilities in France, Denmark, and Austria, a laboratory plant at Sunnyvale, California, in addition to operating its plant in Norway. HN is also building a production plant in Ireland, expected to come on-line in 1992. One sign of internationalization is that in June 1989 the company raised US$ 761 million on the international capital market, in 1990 a new capital issue brought in US $ 111 million. Another sign is that in 1990, 33 per cent of the stock is foreign owned. The top ten owners include Morgan Guaranty Trust Co., Royal Bank of Scotland, Skandinaviska Enskilda and Chase Manhattan Bank. A third is that 70 per cent of gross sales are now outside Norway (74 per cent in 1989). By the end of 1990 Hafslund Nycomed was listed on the stock exchanges of Oslo, London, Frankfurt and Vienna, and was listed on the Copenhagen Stock Exchange in 1991.

Kværner
Kværner Industrier A/S, dating back to 1853, is Norway's leading engineering company. Its products at first included agricultural tools and simple mechanical constructions. To these were added around 1900 water turbines, electric generators and other high-voltage equipment as well as machinery for pulp and paper factories. In the 1970s Kværner was involved in several mergers and buy-out operations, which brought it into shipbuilding, marine engines, refrigeration equipment and liquified natural gas (LNG) carriers. A result of its own R. & D., Kværner from the 1970s held world patent rights for the LNG carriers. The start up of oil and gas production in the North Sea in the 1970s opened up a rapidly-expanding market for offshore operations. Kværner bought into two oil companies and took up positions in shipping. By 1983 oil-related activities accounted for 51 per cent of total operating revenue.[41] Diversification and acquisitions were accompanied by changes in organizational structure, whereby Kværner Industrier A/S became a holding company for a growing family of independent engineering firms. A Spanish daughter company, Thune-Eureka Espanola SA, located in Villagarcia de Arosa, came on-line in 1974. It represented Kvæmer's first production plant abroad. Kværner held 75 per cent. In 1976 daughter companies followed in Japan, Switzerland, the US and Sweden, at the same time as licence agreements with foreign companies multiplied. In the late 1970s the 100 per cent owned German daughter company, Kværner Brug (Deutschland) GmbH, Bremen, started production of Kværner products. So did the 100 per cent owned English daughter company,

Kværner (UK) Ltd, located in Newcastle. Thus by 1978 Kværner may be said to have stepped up the ladder to fully-fledged multinational status. Exports as a percentage of sales averaged 43 per cent during the period 1974 to 1978 and 56 per cent during the period 1981 to 1985.[42] Expansion abroad continued unabated in the 1980s, when Kværner bought Kamyr AB, a Swedish wood processing plant, and the Scottish company, The Govan Shipyard Ltd. By 1986 Kværner had additional daughter companies in South Korea, Brunei, Australia, India, Nepal and Malaysia. A sign of increasing internationalization is that foreigners own a total of 26.4 per cent of the Kværner stock. Among the top ten owners as of 8 March 1991, one finds S.G. Warburg & Co. (3.7 per cent), Chase Manhattan Bank (3.3 per cent), Morgan Guaranty Trust Co. (2.74 per cent) and Royal Bank of Scotland (1.85 per cent). Kværner is listed on The Oslo Stock Exchange, and from 1990 also on The International Stock Exchange of London and Stockholms Fondsbørs.[43]

Nora

Nora Industrier A/S is a Norwegian holding company that joined the multinationals in 1989. Organized along divisional lines, with three main divisions for beverages, foods, and confectionary, Nora also includes Helly Hansen, an international sportswear company with 75 per cent of its sales abroad, a commercial property division, the country's biggest flour milling division and a string of industrial bakeries in the biggest urban areas around Oslo and Bergen. After a series of purchases, mergers, closures and consolidations, Nora by the end of the 1980s ranked as Norway's largest food and beverage corporation, a parent company for among others the Martens Bakery, Bergen, dating back to 1753. An example of the concentration that took place was that the number of chocolate manufacturers was reduced from 12 to four between 1980 and 1990.[44] Indeed, having outgrown the national market by 1985, Nora entered a phase of internationalization. The strategy involved buying up domestic and foreign companies in familiar fields, with growth potential in a bigger, liberalized European market, including products, brand names, franchises, distribution channels, or access to new markets for other Nora products. As part of the campaign, Nora in 1985 bought Helly Hansen, an international sportswear company, with roots in Norway, and operating factories in Norway, USA, Ireland and Portugal. This was followed by the acquisition of the Coca Cola franchise for Norway, and purchases of food factories in Denmark and England in 1989. These secured membership in the multinational family.

Norsk Hydro

Norsk Hydro was founded in 1905 under the name Norsk Hydro Elektrisk Kvælstof Aktieselskab A/S. Its first product was Norgessalpeter, a nitrogen fertilizer, produced by high amounts of electric energy. Hydro owned its own waterfalls and hydro stations. Hydro from the start combined absolute natural advantages, commercial products with scientific research, export orientation and capital-intensive methods. During the Second World War Hydro entered into non-ferrous alloys. Magnesium a 'light metal', became a permanent addition. On liberation in 1945 the Norwegian government came into possession of the former German stock as war reparations. The government in 1990 still holds 51 per cent of the stock. Hydro entered aluminium in the 1970s, and moved into oil exploration and production in the same decade in the North Sea oil field, which led to ammonia, plastics and petro chemicals. Hydro by 1974 had acquired controlling positions in industrial companies in Wales, Sweden, Austria, and France, which bestowed membership in the mne family. Hydro in the 1980s phased out old, antiquated, or loss-producing fertilizer plants in France, Germany, Great Britain, Norway and Sweden, while investing heavily in new plants in Tobago, Trinidad, France and the Netherlands, besides building a magnesium plant in Canada. Seeing new opportunities, Hydro in the 1980s established pioneering companies in Norwegian aquaculture, a new sunrise industry, to serve a rapidly growing fresh fish market in the United States, Japan and Western Europe. As part of its drive for internationalization, Hydro obtained listing on 12 major stock exchanges in Europe and USA, including The New York Stock Exchange (1986), Tokyo (1989), London, Paris, Frankfurt, Basel, Amsterdam and Stockholms Fondsbörs, in addition to Oslo.[45] Hydro was able to raise long term loans in all the major currencies to underwrite its investments. To cut transaction costs, Hydro operates its own finance division. Of the total sales of 61 billion NOK for 1990, the division for agriculture contributed 43 per cent, light metals 30, oil and gas 20 and petrochemicals 7 per cent.[46] About 64 per cent of the share capital is held by Norwegians. About 61 per cent of its total sales are in the EC area. With 112 daughter companies, and 202 offices in 36 countries in all four continents, Hydro was a fully fledged multinational by 1990.

Statoil
Norway's state-owned oil company, Den norske stats oljeselskap as, was launched in 1972 to handle the Norwegian government's interests in the North Sea oil fields, discovered by the American oil company Phillips Petroleum in 1969, after three years' drilling. After serving its apprentice years under the big international oil companies, Mobil, Phillips Petroleum, Shell and Elf Aquitaine, Statoil in 1987 assumed responsibility for Statfjord, the vast undersea field bordering on the British Murchison field. In 1990 Statoil is involved in all aspects of the oil business, including exploration, drilling, production, transportation, refining and marketing. Statoil is engaged mainly in the North Sea fields, but takes part through daughter companies in exploration and production also in the Dutch, Danish, UK and German sectors. Statoil is active in China, and has exploration acreage in Malaysia, the Netherlands and in four other countries. The Ekkofisk oil is transported through a pipeline to Teesside, England, the Statfjord oil further north, by carriers to customers in Europe and the USA. The gas is sent by pipeline to St Fergus in Scotland and to Emden in Germany. Part of the gas is shipped by way of the Kårstø terminal, located north of Stavanger. Statoil has two refineries, at Mongstad north of Bergen and at Kalundborg, Denmark. Statoil is moreover responsible for the construction and operation of Zeepipe, a new pipeline system which will transport Norwegian gas to buyers in continental Europe from a terminal at

Zeebrugge, the Netherlands. In Scandinavia, Statoil operates a network of 450 gas stations in Sweden, and in Denmark a network of 400, and plans further expansion. Headquartered at Forus outside Stavanger, Statoil has daughter companies in Norway, UK, Denmark, Sweden, Finland, France, Germany, Belgium, the Netherlands and the US, both for exploration, production, refining, marketing and distribution of oil, gas, and petrochemical products. With sales of 88 billion NOK for 1990, assets of 74 207 million NOK, Statoil is a money machine that now accounts for about 12 per cent of the entire GNP of Norway.[47]

Tiedemanns

Tiedemanns (est. 1778) is a private industrial manufacturing group, organized along modern divisional lines, with divisions for tobacco, beverage cartons (Elopak), recreation, aquaculture, industrial automation and pharmaceuticals, in addition to portfolio investments in ships and commercial properties. Tobacco products and Elopak cardboard cartons are the biggest earners.[48] Tiedemanns owns the world patent rights for the Elopak fresh food cartons, and operates production companies for coated cardboard cartons in rapidly growing markets in 15 countries on four continents. Licence-takers include companies in 11 countries. The diversification policy reflected above, stems in part from increasing restrictions on production, distribution and advertising for tobacco products both at home and abroad. Advertising for tobacco was banned in Norway in 1975, and in 1988 tobacco smoking was restricted in restaurants and other public places. In consequence, Tiedemanns since 1980, in addition to Elopak, has diversified into promising growth industries, including ski and recreation gear, aquaculture and pharmaceutical products. By 1990, Tiedemanns operates fish farms in Norway, Ireland and Portugal, and in 1989 established a pharmaceutical production plant in Malaysia, expected to come on-line in 1991. These give the Tiedemanns group mne membership. It is not listed on any stock exchange.

Notes

1. Christensen, Ø., 'Die norwegischen Bedenken gegen die EG', *Nordeuropa Forum*, no. 1, June 1991, pp. 20–3.
2. Valeur, J., *Internasjonalisering. En global modell og noen empiriske observasjoner i norsk næringsliv*, Bedriftsøkomomisk Institutt, Oslo 1987, p. 129.
3. Hodne, F., *Norges økonomiske historie 1815–1970*, Oslo, 1985 p. 141.
4. *The Economist Pocket World in Figures*, London 1991, p. 13.
5. Bergh, T. and Lange, E., *Foredlet virke. Historien om Borregaard 1889–1989*, Oslo, 1989, pp. 13–15.
6. Wicken, O., *O. Mustad & Søn 150 år*, Oslo, 1982.
7. Johannessen, F.E., *Ingen grenser. Protans historie 1939–1989*, Lillehammer, 1989, p. 54.
8. Robock S.H. and Simmonds K., *International Business and Multinational Enterprises*, Homewood, Illinois, 1989, 4th ed. pp. 26–8.
9. Aronsen, B. and Berg, L., *Norske industrietableringer i EF-landene*, Bedriftsøkonomisk Institutt, Oslo, 1980; Hansen, S.O. and Wamli, B., *Norske investeringer i utenlandsk næringsliv. En undersøkelse basert på regnskapsresultater 1977–78*, Norges Bank, 1980; Samdal, I., *Norsk*

industri i utlandet, Norsk Produktivitetsinstitutt, Oslo, 1976; Smukkested, O., *Erfaringer med norske industrietableringer i Sørøst-Asia*, Industrøkonomisk Institutt, Bergen, 1979.
10. Steina, P., 'Norske investeringer i utlandet', *Penger og Kreditt*, 1978, no. 4, pp. 316–17, and Hansen Svein Olav and Wamli, Bjørn, 'En undersøkelse av norske investeringer i utlandet', ibid., p. 318–25. The dollar/NOK exchange rate has fluctuated considerably over the last fifteen years. It was $1 = NOK 5–6 between 1977–81, $1 = NOK 8–9 during 1984 and 1986, and $1 = NOK 6.50 in 1988–92.
11. St. prp. no. 87 (1984–85), 'Tiltak for internasjonalisering av norsk næringsliv'.
12. NOU 1981: 47, *Behovet for internasjonalisering av norsk næringsliv*, Oslo, 1981, p. 9.
13. Idem note 11.
14. Hansen, S.O., 'Oversikt over norsk deltagelse i utenlandsk næringsliv', *Penger og kreditt*, no. 4, 1984, pp. 298–300.
15. Carlsen, M. and Rasmussen Ingrid, 'Norske næringslivsinvesteringer i utlandet', *Penger og kreditt*, 1988, p. 20. Norsk Data, at the time one of the biggest manufacturing companies, specializing in medium size data machines, was later outcompeted by the big Japanese and American electronics giants. By 1991 Norsk Data was out of the mnc league.
16. Hansen, S.O. and Wamli, B., 'Norske direkte investeringer i utlandet', *Penger og kreditt*, no. 3, 1991, pp. 167–72.
17. Hoel, M., 'Utenlandske direkte investeringer i Norge', *Penger og Kreditt*, 1990, no. 2, pp. 103–8. Workforce: *Statistical Yearbook 1990*, Table 160.
18. This section follows Robock and Simmonds, idem note 8, pp. 41–50.
19. Steina, P. idem note 10, p. 322.
20. For a survey of these strategies, see Root, Franklin R., *Entry Strategies for International Markets*, Lexington, Mass., Toronto, 1987.
21. Smukkestad, O., *Erfaringer med produksjonsetableringer i Sør Øst Asia. En studie av 11 norskeide bedrifter i Singapore, Malaysia og Thailand*, Arbeidsnotat no. 30, Industrøkonomisk Institutt, Bergen, 1979.
22. Examples are provided in Bakka, Bjarne: *Even Smaller Industrial Firms go International: Environmental Challenges, Stages of Internationalization, Marketing Strategies, Company Examples*, Oslo, 1990; Svendsen, Bjørn (ed.), *Internasjonaliserings-strategier for norske industribedrifter*, Industrøkonomisk Institutt, Bergen, 1982.
23. Samdal, I. *Norsk industri utlandet*, Norsk Produktivitets Institutt, Oslo, 1976, pp. 11–13.
24. Hansen, S.O. and Wamli, B., 'Norske direkte investeringer i utlandet', *Penger og kreditt*, 1991, p. 169.
25. Larsen, J.N., 'Direkte investeringer og projekteksport. Danmark og u-landene i den nye internationale arbeidsdeling', in Peter Sjøholt (ed.), *Internasjonalisering av norsk næringsliv. Forutsetninger og muligheter*, Report no. 103 from Industrøkonomisk Institutt (IØI), Bergen, 1988, p. 75.
26. Stafford D.C. and Purkis, R.H.A. (eds), *Macmillan Directory of Multinationals*, 2 vols., new ed. 1989, Macmillan Publishers Ltd, London, Marocchini, P., *et al.* (eds), *Who owns Whom 1990. Continental Europe*, 2 vols, Dun & Bradstreet Ltd, London, 1991.
27. *Statistical Yearbook 1990*, p. 226.
28. NOS, *National Accounts*.
29. Karlsen, J.K., *Business Strategy and National Policy Concerning Integration: Nordic Direct Foreign Investments in the European Community*, Notat, Næringsøkonomisk Institutt, Bergen, 1990, p. 34.
30. Sørlie, K.R., *Velkommen 1992. EF-utfordringer for norsk næringsliv*, Næringslivets Forlag, Oslo/ Gjøvik, 1989, p. 73.
31. Kaelble, H. 'Was Prometheus most unbound in Europe? The Labour Force in Europe during the late XIXth and XXth Centuries', *The Journal of European Economic History*, 1989, **18**, 65–102; Hodne, F., 'Trends in industry in three Scandinavian countries 1950–1990', *Wissenschaftliche Zeitschrift der Humboldt-Universität zu Berlin, Reihe Geistes-und Sozialwissenshaften*, 1991, 40, no. 7, pp. 63–74; Ambrosius, G., 'De-Industrialisierung in westeuropäischen Ländern nach dem zweiten Weltkrieg', *Wissenschaftliche Zeitschrift der Humboldt Universität zu Berlin. Reihe Geistes-und Sozialwissenschaftern*, 1991, 40, no. 7, pp. 65–73.
32. Central Bureau of Statistics, *Historisk statistikk 1978*, Oslo, 1978, Table 274: 'Average share dividends'.
33. Stenmarck, K. 'Norsk internasjonalt skipsregister- bakgrunn og utvikling', *Penger og kreditt*, 1986, pp. 11–17.

34. It is interesting in this context to note that in a recent work on trends in foreign trade, R.E. Rowthorn places Sweden among manufacturing countries, Norway among service economies. See R.E. Rowthorn and J. Wells, *De-industrialization and Foreign Trade*, Cambridge: Cambridge University Press, 1987.
35. *Aker Norcem Konsernpresentasjon 1987.*
36. *Årsrapport A.L 1990*, pp. 5–6.
37. *Norsk Sprængstofindustri Aktieselskap. Beretning og Aarsregnskap for Driftsaaret 1917*, p. 2.
38. *Årsberetning og regnskap 1976 A/S Elektrisk Bureau*, p. 17; *1980* p. 1; *1972* p. 5; *1979* p. 4.
39. *Elektrokemisk A/S. Årsberetning og regnskap 1968*, p. 4–5.
40. *Elkem-Spigerverket a/s. Årsberetning og regnskap 1973*, p. 26.
41. *Kværner Industrier A/S. Årsberetning og regnskap 1976*, p. 6; *1982* p. 9; *1983* p. 8.
42. Ibid., p. 49; *1978* p. 2; *1985* p. 2.
43. Ibid., p. 44; *1990* pp. 10, 42.
44. *Årsrapport 1990 Nora Industrier A/S*, p. 24.
45. *Norsk Hydo Årsberetning 1990*, p. 39.
46. Idem., pp. 8, 19.
47. *Årsberetning og regnskap Statoil* 1988, 1989, 1990; *Økonomisk Rapport*, 1991, no. 11, pp. 20–1, 26.
48. *Årsrapport Tiedemanns 1990*, p. 8.

PART 2
SECTORS AND FIRMS

7   The German electrotechnical industry in the Italian market before the Second World War

Peter Hertner

The German electrotechnical industry in the world market before 1914

Chapter 2 outlined the development of German multinational enterprise (mne) over the long term. This chapter, and the following one, examine specific sectors of German business, and specific time periods. The focus here is the German electrotechnical industry, whose development played such an important part in the industrial growth of Germany in the late 19th century. The major corporate players, Siemens and AEG, were among the most dynamic German manufacturing enterprises of this period. They were also among the most important of the early German mnes. This chapter examines their business strategies in the Italian market, both before the First World War, and in the changed political and economic environment of the inter-war years.

In every year between 1901 and 1913 more than 50 per cent of all electrical generators, motors and transformers imported into Italy came from Germany.[1] In the peak year of 1912 almost 73 per cent came from Germany. By 1908, 70 per cent of all generators installed in the major Italian power plants were of foreign origin, and again most of them had been imported from Germany.[2] The years between 1896 and the outbreak of the First World War established electricity – in Schumpeter's words – as 'the dominating factor' of economic growth, particularly in the two most dynamic economies, the US and Wilhelmine Germany.[3] Production of electric energy in 1912 reached 24.7 billion kWh in the USA and 12.8 billion in Germany. In contrast, Britain produced a mere 2.4 billion kWh, followed rather closely by the latecomer Italy with an annual production of 1.8 billion kWh.[4]

The leading position of the US and Germany was reflected by their share in total world production of electrotechnical goods. In 1913, according to one estimate, the German share was 35 per cent, compared to the US's 29 per cent, and 16 per cent for the UK.[5] Another estimate gives 31 per cent to the German industry, 35 per cent to the American, and only 11 per cent to the British.[6] However, German industry, with its comparatively limited home market, dominated world exports of electrotechnical material before the First World War, with a share of 46 per cent, followed by the British and American industries with shares of 22 and 16 per cent respectively.[7]

A contemporary source indicates that the German electrotechnical industry exported 22 per cent of its yearly production, while its British competitor reached a value of 30 per cent. The Americans, on the other hand, with their huge home market, only reached a level of about 7 per cent.[8]

German strategies in the Italian market before the First World War

From the German point of view, the Italian market was certainly not negligible, yet it was not the most important one. As for electrical machinery, Italy in 1900 occupied, with a share of 14.2 per cent, the second position after Tsarist Russia (23.8 per cent). Four years later, Britain with a 19.5 per cent share became the most important among the receiving countries, followed by Russia (10.9 per cent) and Italy (10.5 per cent).[9] As far as the export of electrotechnical goods from Germany is concerned, Russia and Britain still occupied the leading positions in 1913 with shares of 10.8 and 10.4 per cent respectively, whereas Italy with a mere 6.0 per cent was no longer such an important market; by then it had been over-taken by Austria-Hungary, Argentina and Belgium whose markets for these German goods had been expanding at a faster rate.[10]

In the language of the eclectic paradigm of international production, the success of the German firms in the Italian market can be explained by their comparative ownership advantages vis-à-vis their host country competitors, and by the comparative location endowments of the German and Italian economies.[11] Considering the specific development taken by the industry of electrotechnical material and bearing in mind the way electricity production grew there can be no doubt that, from the beginning of the 1890s, the so-called high-voltage sector was dominant in Italy and Germany like everywhere else in the world.[12] All kinds of urban agglomerations saw the installation of public and private lighting, urban transport was electrified, whereas railway electrification followed much more slowly only after the turn of the century. Again, the change to electrically-driven machinery in industry was only gradually realized and achieved its definite breakthrough in the US as well as in Europe only during the second decade of the 20th century. All this meant that thermoelectric and, afterwards wherever possible, hydroelectric power plants had to be built. Since by the early 1890s the technical problem of transporting electric energy over considerable distances had been solved, these power plants could then be erected on the economically most feasible sites, for example on rivers or adjacent to coal mines, or next to harbours where coal could be shipped at the lowest possible cost.

The industry which constructed the technical material for these purposes was not all of very recent origin. In Germany, for instance, we find a traditional electrotechnical manufacturer in the firm of Siemens & Halske which had already been established in 1847 and which had been thriving for decades, thanks to the construction and maintenance of telegraph machinery and lines. In the 1880s it also moved cautiously into the high-voltage sector where, incidentally, its founder, Werner Siemens, had already played an important role as one of the inventors of the dynamo in 1867.[13] At least until the middle of the 1890s, however, those firms who were newcomers in the electrotechnical field, and particularly in the high-voltage sector, showed a more dynamic performance than Siemens & Halske. Its most dangerous rival proved to be the Allgemeine Elektricitäts-Gesellschaft (AEG), founded in 1883 in Berlin by the industrialist Emil Rathenau and some prominent Berlin and Frankfurt bankers in order to exploit the principal Edison patents in the field of electric lighting. Technically at first dependent on the Edison and Siemens companies, AEG (which until 1887 bore the name of Deutsche Edison-Gesellschaft für angewandte Elektrizität) gradually gained an important position in the German market starting from the electrification of lighting and transport in Berlin itself.[14] Smaller but still quite important companies like Schuckert of Nuremberg, Lahmeyer, Helios, and Bergmann developed rapidly during the 1890s. The dynamic growth of the entire branch came, however, to a provisional end in the crisis of 1901 which caused the disappearance of most of the medium-sized firms leaving AEG and Siemens, the latter having merged its high-voltage business with Schuckert, with a virtual duopoly. This situation then left space for quite a large number – about 350 – of relatively small so-called 'specialized' firms[15] which were very different in size and financial potential from the two big 'full-line manufacturers'.

Siemens as a supplier of electrotechnical material had been present in Italy on a regular basis since the 1870s. It had sold telegraph equipment there sporadically since the 1850s,[16] but its sales figures for the years between 1887 and 1893, when electrification in Italy started slowly to gain momentum, were not very impressive, even allowing for the fact that these were difficult years for the Italian economy as a whole.[17] Its main rival in Europe, AEG, showed much more dynamism when it decided, in 1894/95, to electrify lighting and urban transport in Genoa and its immediate hinterland by taking over the already existing companies and modernizing and extending their networks.[18] This bold move into comprehensive electrification of an entire sub-region already bore all the signs of what contemporary German observers were to call the *Unternehmergeschäft*. Practically, it meant that the large electrotechnical producers – at the beginning the medium-sized ones too – created their own market by founding local and regional electric power, tramway and lighting companies or by taking over and 'electrifying' already existing firms in those countries (for example, Spain, Italy, Russia, the Latin American states) and for those customers (particularly local and regional public authorities) which suffered from a chronic lack of capital or which were too reluctant to adopt this new technology. The newly-founded or transformed companies were then obliged by statute or by more flexible means to buy all or most of their electrotechnical material from their big industrial founders.[19]

Besides creating manufacturing subsidiaries abroad – which both Siemens and AEG did to a limited extent, particularly in high-tariff countries like Russia, Austria-Hungary, Spain and France[20] – the *Unternehmergeschäft* must certainly be considered a parallel step in internalization aimed at reducing the risks of selling in a foreign market which at the same time could thus be considerably enlarged. This new type of strategy was, however, not without its problems. By creating a conspicuous number of energy producing and distributing companies inside Germany but, above all abroad, an increasing amount of equity capital and bonds accumulated in the portfolios of the electrotechnical producers, thus rapidly reducing their respective liquidity status.

A solution to this was eventually found by creating financial holding companies with the help and the financial participation of the great banks both in Germany and abroad. These financial holding companies took over the shares and bonds of the newly-created public utility companies, held them in their portfolios during the period of construction and initial development and sold most of their holdings to the general public as soon as they had 'matured' and yielded a profit, after which they generally only retained and controlled minority holdings. In order to ensure their own liquidity during the 'construction periods' of their various public utility daughter companies the financial holdings issued their own shares; if possible, they even preferred to place bonds on the market in order to guarantee the intake of long-term capital at stable interest rates which was especially important for investment in hydroelectric facilities.[21]

Each of the big German electrotechnical producers was in control of such financial holding companies: AEG had, among others, the Bank für elektrische Unternehmungen which it had founded in 1895 in Zürich together with a number of important German and Swiss and, to a minor extent, French and Italian banks. Incidentally then, the activity of this so-called Elektrobank started with the takeover of the public utility companies which AEG had founded shortly before in several Spanish cities and in Genoa. Siemens followed at short distance with its Basel-based Schweizerische Gesellschaft für elektrische Industrie and its Elektrische Licht-und Kraftanlagen AG of Berlin, both of them established in the same year – 1895. Schuckert and some of the medium-sized electrotechnical producers possessed their own financial holding companies which, in the aftermath of the 1901 crisis, very often ended up by falling under the control of the two 'bigs', Siemens and AEG.

Part of these financial holdings, especially those earmarked for operations outside of Germany, took their legal seat in Switzerland, as we have already seen, or in Belgium – for instance the AEG-controlled the Société Financière de Transports et d'Entreprises Industrielles, commonly called SOFINA. The main reason for this was due to the very liberal company law and stock exchange regulations of these two countries and to some tax advantages they could offer. In part, it may also have owed something to the participation of some of the most important Swiss and Belgian banks in these holdings and to the fact that, where business with France was involved, this could, since 1871, be done much more easily from a neutral country than from Germany itself.[22]

In Italy, apart from Genoa and its hinterland, there was considerable German investment in electricity production and distribution and in electrified urban transport; the regions particularly concerned were Piedmont, Eastern Lombardy, as well as parts of Tuscany, Umbria and Sicily.[23] Almost all of this had been created originally by the electrotechnical producers and in almost all of these cases control was exercised via one of the holding companies described above. There was even the case of the Società per lo sviluppo delle imprese elettriche in Italia which had been brought into being as a regional sub-holding, exclusively for Italy, by AEG, the Elektrobank and its allies from various countries.[24]

According to our calculations, at the end of the year 1900, German capital controlled 40.3 per cent of the total capital of all Italian electric utilities excluding, however, electrified public transport.[25] More than a decade later, at the end of 1913, the percentage of companies controlled by German capital and active in the same field, again according to our estimates, only reached 16.5.[26] This was far removed from contemporary assessments which indicated the German quota as reaching 'about half of the capital invested in the Italian electrical industry'.[27] One should, however, add that the reduced share of 16.5 per cent must be related to a total volume of nominal capital of Italian electric companies which had increased by no less than four times between 1900 and 1913. Besides German there was other, particularly Swiss and Belgian, investment in the Italian electric industry: one might suppose that by 1913 between 25 and 30 per cent of the capital of companies active in this sector was controlled by foreign ownership. The real influence of foreign capital went, however, beyond this percentage figure since almost all of the leading companies at the regional level, with the noteworthy exception of the Italian Edison company which dominated Milan and central Lombardy, had a majority or at least an important minority of foreign-based shareholders.

Looking at these facts and figures one is almost forced to conclude that the predominance of German producers in the Italian market for electrotechnical goods was not only based on a possibly superior quality of management, on advanced technology applied in mass production of certain standardized electrotechnical products like, for instance, light bulbs or small electric motors, but also on thorough marketing efforts and on an extended after-sales service.[28] Evidently, all these 'ownership advantages' did not prove to be sufficient in the case of high-voltage products which – with the exception of steam turbines and turbo-alternators – were essentially 'mature' goods after the middle of the 1890s and which, at least from a short-term perspective, did not seem to head for further important technological breakthroughs. Nor can German predominance in this specific market be totally explained by either the proprietary nature of the industry's technology, which blocked potential competitors with the help of patent legislation and technology co-operation between the industry's leading firms, or by the network quality of electrical equipment, which required system compatibility and thus favoured the position of first-movers.[29]

It was, in fact, the provision of finance, in exchange for contractual commitments to take supplies of electrotechnical material exclusively from the 'founding father', which was the additional condition which enabled the suppliers to offer complete 'package deals' to their various customers. In most cases this 'extra' proved to be decisive for the creation of the market by the suppliers themselves. The fact that the imports of large generators (over 1000 kg of weight) were dominated initially by Swiss suppliers in the mid-1890s (65 per cent of these imports in 1894) before they became the domain of German producers (68 per cent in 1908) seems to point in that direction.[30] The Swiss suppliers consisted mainly of the Maschinenfabrik Oerlikon and the even more important Brown, Boveri & Cie, the latter owning its own financial holding company, the Motor AG für elektrische Unternehmungen, founded in 1895, which in turn controlled an Italian sub-holding, the Dinamo Società per Imprese Elettriche, created in 1907.[31] Until 1914 these Swiss firms, though important and innovative especially in the fields of turbine technology and railway electrification, could only compete with the big German suppliers and their financial holding companies up to a certain extent, and this should explain the figures for Italian generator imports given above.

Among the comparative location endowments of the host country which could eventually favour sales of foreign electrotechnical products one has to specify as a major point in the Italian case the virtual absence of effective tariff protection. As a matter of fact, contemporary observers agreed that the Italian general tariff of 1887, mitigated further by several bilateral treaties ratified during the following two decades, was not particularly effective for the type of goods we are discussing here. Being a weight tariff, its protective consequences were further diminished by technical progress which, for instance, made direct current motors of the same capacity lose half their weight between 1895 and 1910.[32]

Under these conditions, foreign suppliers were not stimulated to increase internalization by moving into direct investment in manufacturing. Besides the Swiss Brown Boveri which took over the Milanese Tecnomasio Italiano in 1903,[33] there was only the German AEG, which in 1904 founded the AEG Thomson-Houston in Milan as a joint venture with the Société Thomson-Houston de la Méditerranée.[34] The establishment of AEG Thomson-Houston was part of the 1903 worldwide agreement between AEG and General Electric which left, among many other results, the Italian market equally divided among the two giant corporations.[35] These two direct investments were certainly much less a result of tariff questions than of the growth of Italian economic nationalism during the last decade before the outbreak of the First World War. State orders went increasingly to national firms, and it was this kind of non-tariff trade discrimination which induced the AEG Thomson-Houston to build a factory in Milan and start production in 1909; three years later it employed about 450 people,[36] whereas the Tecnomasio Italiano Brown Boveri already employed about 1020 in 1908.[37] Siemens which never came to establishing manufacturing unit in Italy before the First World War accused AEG later on, in an internal memorandum, of having gained an advantage *vis-à-vis* all other electrotechnical German firms selling in the Italian market. By building a factory in Milan AEG had become a 'national' Italian supplier while in fact, if we are to believe Siemens, three-quarters of the goods sold under the name of AEG Thomson-Houston Società italiana di elettricità came directly from Berlin.[38]

Siemens obviously considered that it could do without this further internalizing step, also because of its traditionally strong position in the low-voltage sector. In 1907 it obtained access to the patents of the American Strowger who had invented a successful system of automatic telephone exchange.[39] In Italy Siemens had sold telephone equipment on various occasions, for example in 1902 to a non-automatic exchange which was installed in Milan.[40] In 1907 most of the Italian telephone sector was nationalized[41] but this did not really solve its relative backwardness if compared to other European countries. A result of at least a tentative drive for modernization was the installation, by Siemens, of two automatic exchanges, one in Rome and the other in Genoa, which had, however, only been partially completed when Italy entered the war in 1915.[42]

New strategies for the inter-war period

Despite the strong competition exercised by other multinationals, and above all by Western Electric, the manufacturing branch of the US giant American Telephone and Telegraph Company,[43] Siemens had gained such a strong position in this field that the Italian administration did not hesitate to contact it again just a few months after the end of the war, in the spring of 1919,[44] asking the ex-enemy firm to return. In order to get a new hold in the Italian market Siemens had to accept a joint venture with an Italian producer, Società Industrie Telefoniche Italiane 'Doglio', Milan, which then had to produce part of the telephone equipment in Italy while part of it was made in the Siemens factories in Berlin.[45]

In 1923 the Siemens manager in charge tried to persuade his company to buy shares in the capital of the Doglio factory at Milan: this would transform Siemens into a truly 'national' company; part of the telephone production would take place in Italy, but the most qualified work would have to be done in the German Siemens factories.[46] Nothing came out of all this, but the Italian state administration for the telephone sector had already persuaded Siemens in 1921 to invest in the Società Italiana Reti Telefoniche Interurbane (SIRTI) which was to build the long-distance telephone cable network, a sector which had remained with the state after the telephone privatization in 1907. SIRTI had been founded in 1919 by the two major Italian cable producers, Pirelli and Tedeschi, as well as by the Italian branch of Western Electric.[47] The admission to this select 'club', two years after its foundation and only three years after a war in which Italian producers had hoped to eliminate their German competitors once and for all, seems to indicate that Siemens possessed a strong advantage in the field of telephone technology which had by no means been wiped out during the war years.

The Italian telephone business proved to be quite a success, especially when the regional networks had been re-privatized in 1924/25.[48] According to a list set up in 1930, Siemens had installed, and consequently sold its material to, 71 per cent of all telephone connections in Northern Italy, followed by the Swedish Ericsson group with 17 and by Western Electric with 10 per cent.[49] Western Electric had a stronger position in central Italy[50] whereas Ericsson was practically the exclusive supplier to the southern Italian concession area; this zone which also comprised Sicily, but not Sardinia, had been assigned to the Società Esercizi Telefonici (SET), founded in 1924 by Ericsson itself 'with the help of Swedish and British banks ... and some Italian interests'.[51]

By the middle of the 1920s each of these three big multinationals could count on a manufacturing plant established in Italy itself. Siemens could not hope to get its pre-1914 Italian affiliate returned which had been sequestered during the war. In 1921 it founded, therefore, a new Italian company, Siemens Società Anonima, with headquarters in Milan, which in 1926 had a workforce of 282; there, a year earlier, it had started to assemble low-voltage material, probably mostly telephones.[52] According to a report written in 1923, Western Electric operated 'a small shop (250 employees) at Milan' with 'an annual business of $ 250 000 to $ 300 000, ... it has been generally unprofitable'. Nevertheless – and this could only be afforded by a big multinational parent company – we are really holding on in the belief that the Italian telephone system will soon undergo radical change', and this was to be privatization which arrived a year later![53] Already in 1919, Ericsson had taken an interest in a small telephone manufacturer in Rome, the Fabbrica Apparecchi Telefonici e Materiale Elettrico (FATME), which then became its exclusive Italian producing unit.[54]

Thus, Siemens behaved – at least for its stake in the Italian telephone business – like the other two multinationals: in order to be considered a 'national' producer, a manufacturing unit, however small, had to be established. This ran, however, against proclaimed principles of company strategy, for Siemens saw itself during the 1920s, at least in official statements, as 'an export-oriented firm with a manufacturing basis in Germany'.[55] As Carl Friedrich von Siemens, head of the concern between the wars, put it in a speech in 1928, Siemens had

> no interest in investing our money abroad in manufacturing plants .... Nor is it our task to secure profits from capital involvements abroad .... If we have nevertheless done so in this case or that, that was solely in order not to be entirely excluded from the market.[56]

The importance of the Italian telephone market in the 1920s for German industry is quite well reflected in German export figures. Whereas, in 1913, telephone and telegraph equipment worth 1.93 million marks was exported to Russia, followed closely by Italy with 1.74 million, in 1925 Austria had taken the lead with 2.19 million marks, but Italy could boast 2.0 million which was equivalent to 8.2 per cent of total German exports in this field. One year later, when the sector had been privatized in Italy, the Italian share went up to 8.28 million marks – 23.4 per cent of German exports of telephone equipment – which made Italy the largest single receiving country. The same was still true in 1927 (4.97 million marks, 19.0 per cent) and only in 1928 was there a marked downturn with 3.46 million marks (10.0 per cent) which put it behind Britain and the Netherlands as receiving countries of German telephone exports.[57]

Table 7.1   *Share of German exports of telephone and telegraph equipment,*
1925–31

	Total exports	Exports to Italy
1925	14.1	14.6
1928	14.4	24.9
1931	20.8	37.8

Source
See note 58

If we look at the share which exports of telephone and telegraph equipment occupied in total exports of the German electrotechnical industry and if, with regard to Italy alone, we compare the share of telephone and telegraph exports to that of total exports of electrotechnical goods, we end up with the percentages as shown in Table 7.1.[58]

The structural change in German exports from high-voltage to low-voltage products – and within these sectors from simple to highly specialized and higher value-added goods[59] – in the case of exports to Italy, appeared enlarged. Indeed, high-voltage products fared considerably less well in the Italian market of the 1920s. One must not forget that there had been a forced import substitution process during the First World War which was to be supported afterwards by the new protectionist tariff of 1921.[60] This process was reflected by the ratio of imports of electrical machinery into Italy to exports of Italian made machines of the same kind: expressed in percentages it reached 13 in 1913, 75 in 1920 and then fell back again to 43 in 1925 and 37 in 1929.[61] Giving to the figures of 1907 a value of 100, the imports of electrical machines into Italy developed as shown in Table 7.2.[62]

Already in 1922, according to the US commercial attaché at Rome, as to the supply of electrical equipment,

> Germany has succeeded in regaining its dominant position in the Italian market and still represents by all odds the most important source of supply. This situation is due to the fact that the highly developed electrical industry in Germany has been established for many years in the Italian market and also to the depreciation of the mark with reference to the lira, which has materially aided imports of German goods.[63]

This statement is supported by a look to the figures which demonstrate, for instance, that again in 1922, 54 per cent of Italian imports of electric generators and motors were of German origin.[64]

The restoration of pre-1914 conditions was, however, out of the question since the German come-back met, as we have seen, with a sharply diminished overall demand for imports of this class of goods and with completely changed market

Table 7.2   *Italian imports of electrical machines, 1907–29 (1907=100)*

1907	100
1912	84
1920	23
1922	38
1925	53
1929	58

Source
See note 62.

conditions. As a matter of fact, German investment in Italian electricity production and distribution had been lost or, when possible, sold off during the war as enemy property. Furthermore, effective control over the Swiss and Belgian financial holding companies was lost immediately after the war as a consequence of German currency problems and inflation.[65] In a situation where they suffered from an acute lack of foreign exchange, and where the big German banks could not give them any help because of their own liquidity problems, the large German electrotechnical concerns could not intervene in order to restore their influence on their foreign holding companies. Consequently, the whole mechanism of the 'Unternehmergeschäft', as described above, could no longer be used and thus an important – if not the decisive – advantage for the foreign business of German high-voltage goods producers had been cancelled.

New direct investment abroad would have been another possible strategy for the large German electrotechnical producers, but their individual cash flow situations had become rather tight, if not critical, as a consequence of German monetary stabilization in 1923/24. A partial solution to this problem could be found by bringing in American capital. Siemens had several times recourse to this after 1925, for the concern as a whole and also specifically for the telephone business, though never in the form of equity capital.[66] AEG, which suffered from serious liquidity problems, had to cede about 25 per cent of its equity capital to General Electric, its traditional international partner, in 1929.[67] Another possible capital saving way out could have been the setting up of joint ventures abroad, possibly with domestic firms of a particular country.[68] In the high-voltage business with Italy several approaches to this were made. In 1920/21 there were plans for Siemens-Italy and FIAT to amalgamate,[69] and in 1930 joint ventures between Siemens and Ansaldo as well as between Siemens and Westinghouse – in this second case specifically for the Italian market – were discussed,[70] but none of these came to the stage of concrete negotiations.

The sales of the Siemens Milan subsidiary between 1923 and 1930, which do not include the much more dynamic telephone business and are thus influenced

Table 7.3   Sales of Siemens's Milan subsidiary, 1923–30 (000 lire)

Year	Sales
1923/24	43 554
1924/25	54 737
1925/26	67 027
1926/27	35 859
1927/28	34 841
1928/29	38 208
1929/30	38 456

Source
See note 71.

above all by the problems of the high-voltage sector, show this development (see Table 7.3).[71]

The sharp economic crisis following the stabilization of the lira in 1926/27 and the ensuing economic stagnation become more than evident from these figures,[72] and it is not surprising that for Siemens joint ventures with Italian partners were again considered to be a viable solution.

These already quite difficult years were then followed by the world economic crisis of 1929/33 which produced a complete breakdown of demand, especially for heavy electrical machinery, not only in the world market as a whole but, of course, also in Italy. The International Notification and Compensation Agreement of 1931 to which the leading US, British and German electrotechnical concerns as well as the Swiss Brown Boveri group acceded was an attempt to cartelize part of a rapidly shrinking market.[73] In the same year, the most important Italian firms – Ansaldo, Marelli, San Giorgio, Tecnomasio Italiano Brown Boveri and Compagnia Generale di Elettricità, the last two of them subsidiaries of foreign multinationals – subscribed to an agreement which assigned fixed quotas for sales of generators and transformers beyond a certain minimum size for each of them and which tried to regulate the essential sales conditions.[74]

Foreign trade, and especially imports of electrotechnical machinery into Italy, was heavily hit by these developments. Italian imports fell from 61.7 million quintals in 1926 to 13.5 million in 1935, with imports of electrotechnical machinery declining from 5.4 million quintals in 1926 to 4.3 million in 1935.[75] Thanks to the telephone business, however, total German electrotechnical exports to Italy did not show an analogous development. Between 1925 and 1929 they rose from 27 million marks to 37 million marks, before falling to 26 million marks in 1931.[76] Imports declined further with the autarchy campaign of the Fascist government, which slowly gained momentum after 1932.[77] This resulted in a strong tendency towards bilateralization and import quotas.[78]

As for the high-voltage business, Siemens found it increasingly difficult to compete with AEG in the Italian market, the latter having, as we have seen, decisively reinforced its ties with General Electric. In Italy, General Electric had controlled the Compagnia Generale di Elettricità since 1921,[79] and one could have imagined that AEG, in view of its traditional ties with General Electric – renewed in 1923[80] and then again, as we have seen, in 1929 – would have quite naturally closely collaborated with the Italian firm by the exchange of patents or the co-ordination of sales. As it happened, an attempt at such an agreement failed in 1924 after negotiations which had been going on for almost a year.[81] A solution of that kind had to wait for another eight years and became effective only from 1 January 1933. It provided for the exchange of patents and production methods and made the Compagnia Generale sales representative of AEG for Italy.[82]

The other important competitor of Siemens in the Italian high-voltage business was Tecnomasio Italiano Brown Boveri (TIBB), an affiliate, as already mentioned, of the well-known Swiss multinational.[83] As it was, TIBB and Compagnia Generale · were the two most important Italian suppliers for heavy electrical machinery. Both of them were the result of fdi, so the pre-1914 situation had apparently not undergone important changes.

Siemens did not, as we have seen, move into direct investment in the Italian high-voltage sector – with the exception of some highly specialized niches of this market, as will be explained below – and it did not create any joint ventures in this field. On the other hand, switching over to low-voltage products, and this meant especially concentrating efforts on the telephone business, could turn out to be a valid alternative strategy. The numbers are there to prove this case. While about 75 per cent of Siemens's sales in Italy during the period 1921 to 1923 consisted of high-voltage material – and this situation was, one must add, certainly favoured by German hyper-inflation and the ensuing rapid depreciation of the mark – this share had decreased to a little less than 40 per cent by 1936/37. This quota stabilized for the remaining years until Italy's entrance into the First World War, and the share of Siemens-Schuckert, the part of the Siemens concern which produced exclusively high-voltage material, did not decrease any longer. This was also due to the fact that the German share of Italian imports of electrotechnical material had become absolutely dominant in 1936 (67 per cent) and 1937 (64 per cent) as a result of the League of Nations boycott in the wake of Italy's invasion of Ethiopia, of Italian rearmament favouring investment goods imports and of bilateral trade agreements between Fascist Italy and Nazi Germany.[84]

Despite its declared reluctance *vis-à-vis* direct investment and joint ventures, Siemens, as a major concern with extremely diversified output, could try to overcome mounting difficulties in trade during most of the interwar period by switching over to increasing internalization. Even in the increasingly difficult high-voltage business this could be done by falling back on technologically ambitious special products. In the Italian case this was realized, for instance, in 1928 through acquisition of a majority holding in the Società Italiana dei Forni Elettrici e dell'Elettrocarbonium which produced graphite and carbon electrodes for electrochemical and electrometallurgical plants.[85] In the field of medical electricity, Siemens-Reiniger-Werke took over in 1925 the Società Italiana Apparecchi Medicali ed Affini (SIAMA), founded two years previously, and merged in 1929 with the Milan firm of Luigi Gorla & Co.; the Gorla-Siama company thus formed distributed, and later itself also manufactured, X-ray installations and diathermy apparatus.[86]

Individual sub-sectors in the high-voltage area could also be covered by takeovers done abroad. When Siemens & Halske bought the Isaria-Zählerwerke-AG in Munich from Brown Boveri in 1927, it thereby also took over the Italian subsidiary Società anonima Officine Isaria Contatori Elettrici in Milan.[87] In the years before this, it had become increasingly difficult for Siemens to sell electrical meters in Italy because of the growing propaganda in favour of national products; municipally-owned electricity companies in particular had to give their orders exclusively to Italian producers.[88] It was not until the takeover of Isaria that it became possible to shift the manufacture of meters to their Milan factory and be accepted as a national producer for sales to municipal and governmental customers.[89]

In the light-bulb sector, already an extremely cartelized one internationally before 1914, and still more so in the inter-war period, after 1920 Osram-Werke, Berlin, had been represented in Milan through a sales subsidiary. Siemens was involved in Osram, along with AEG and the Auer-Gesellschaft, and partly took over the selling of Osram lamps in Italy. In 1930 the Italian Osram subsidiary merged with the then largest Italian light bulb manufacturer, Società Edison-Clerici, Milan. Siemens & Halske became, through Osram and their Swiss holding company, the major shareholder in the new firm, closely followed by AEG and General Electric.[90]

An extremely interesting case proves to be the Milan firm of OLAP (Officine Lombarde Aparecchi di Precisione), founded by Siemens in 1927, which was to produce equipment for target fixing and firing co-ordination for the Italian Navy.[91] Unfortunately this sector produced heavy losses during the first seven years of the firm's existence, and from 1935 the German government urged Siemens to reduce OLAP's activity in this field, since this transfer of know-how now interfered with its own rearmament programme.[92] Originally, this production had been built up in Italy, and even earlier in the Netherlands, in order to avoid the limitations on armament production imposed upon Germany by the Versailles Treaty.[93] From 1930/31 OLAP, however, also assembled radio sets, at the beginning importing most of the components from Germany. Autarky measures led to a rapid increase of the share of Italian-made parts, as is the case for telephones which had to be entirely manufactured in Italy after 1934.[94] Thus a foreign subsidiary founded for quite a different purpose proved to be extremely helpful when the multinational mother company had to cope with increasing transactions costs which, in the long run, threatened to exclude it completely from that particular foreign market.

Conclusion

This chapter, therefore, has examined the strategies of the German electrotechnical multinationals in the Italian market over the long term. It has been argued that the ownership advantages of the German firms such as Siemens and AEG before the First World War lay not only in their superior management and technology, but in their marketing and after sales service. The German firms also pursued the distinctive *Unternehmergeschäft* strategy to virtually create their own markets in Italy, as elsewhere. German business strategies were badly interrupted by the First World War, but subsequently there was a very flexible response to the changed environmental circumstances. The performance of the German electrotechnical firms in Italy in the inter-war years illustrates the continued vitality of multinational business even during the adverse conditions of these years.

Notes

1. These figures are based on weight, but since the Italian tariff was a weight tariff during that period they can be accepted as an indicator of imports (Giannetti, R., *Tecnologia. imprese e mercati: un profilo della industria elettromeccanica italiana (1883–1940)*, unpublished manuscript, Firenze (1988), table 9b.
2. Giannetti, R., 'Tecnologia, scelte d'impresa ed intervento pubblico: l'industria elettrica italiana dalle origini al 1921', *Passato e Presente*, 2/1982, p. 69.
3. Schumpeter, J.A., *Konjunkturzyklen*, vol. 1, Göttingen, 1961, p. 450.
4. US Department of Commerce, Bureau of the Census, *Historical statistics of the United States*, part 2, Washington, DC, 1975, p. 820; Ott, H. (ed.), *Statistik der öffentlichen Elektrizitätsversorgung Deutschlands 1890–1913* (Historische Energiestatistik von Deutschland), vol. 1, St Katharinen, 1986, p. X (the German figures refer to 1913); Mitchell, B.R., *European Historical Statistics*, 2nd ed., London, 1981, p. 501; Giannetti, R., *La conquista della forza. Risorse, tecnologia ed economia nell' industria elettrica italiana (1883–1940)*, Milano, 1985, p. 253.
5. Czada, P., *Die Berliner Elektroindustrie in der Weimarer Zeit*, Berlin, 1969, p. 138.
6. Jacob-Wendler, G., *Deutsche Elektroindustrie in Lateinamerika: Siemens und AEG (1890–1914)*, Stuttgart, 1982, p. 11; 'Die Elektrizität auf dem Weltmarkt', *Elektrotechnische Zeitschrift*, 1913, p. 1016.
7. Czada, idem note 5, p. 137 ff; Jacob-Wendler, *Deutsche Elektroindustrie*, idem note 6, p. 11; see also the statistical tables in Siemens-Archiv, München, SAA 11/LB 581 (Liedtke).
8. Jacob-Wendler, 'Die Elektrizität auf dem Weltmarkt', idem note 6; Reid P.P. *Private and public Regimes: International Cartelization of the Electrical Equipment Industry in an Era of Hegemonic Change. 1919–1939*, PhD thesis, The Johns Hopkins University School of Advanced International Studies, Washington, DC 1989, p. 19. This latter source has calculated slightly different figures, attributing a value of 25 per cent to the share German firms exported out of their total production whereas the corresponding figure for British industry would have been 26 per cent and the American percentage only 10 (all these figures refer to 1913).
9. Verein zur Wahrung gemeinsamer Wirtschaftsinteressender deutschen Elektrotechnik, *Die Geschäftslage der deutschen elektrotechnischen Industrie im Jahre 1904*, Berlin, 1905, p. 48.
10. Verein zur Wahrung gemeinsamer Wirtschaftsinteressender deutschen Elektrotechnik, *Tabellarische Übersicht über den auswärtigen Handel Deutschlands mit elektrotechnischen Erzeugnissen im Jahre 1913*, Berlin, 1914, *passim*.
11. Dunning, J.H., *International Production and the Multinational Enterprise*, London, 1981, p. 27.
12. As to Germany, in 1886 sales of electrotechnical goods were still equally divided between high-voltage and low-voltage products. In 1890, high-voltage products had already attained a share of 75 per cent; in 1898, finally, the high-voltage sector's share had risen to no less than 92

per cent (von Peschke, H.-P., *Elektroindustrie und Staatsverwaltung am Beispiel Siemens 1847-1914*, Frankfurt/Main and Bern, 1981, p. 168).

13. Wißner, A., 'Entwicklungslinien der Starkstromtechnik', *Technikgeschichte*, 1966, XXXIII, p. 391; Dettmar, G., *Die Entwicklung der Starkstromtechnik in Deutschland*, vol. 1, Berlin, 1940, p. 32 ff.; Bowers, B., *A History of Electric Light and Power*, Stevenage/New York, 1982, pp. 82ff.

14. Siemens, G., *Geschichte des Hauses Siemens*, vol. 1, München 1947, pp. 86 ff., 135 ff; Allgemeine Elektricitäts-Gesellschaft (ed.), *50 Jahre AEG*, printed manuscript, Berlin 1956, Kocka, J., 'Siemens und der aufhaltsame Aufstieg der AEG', *Tradition*, vol. 17, 1972, pp. 125–42.

15. Nussbaum, H., *Unternehmer gegen Monopole*, Berlin (DDR), 1966, p 84.

16. Siemens-Archiv, München (quoted from now on as, SAA), SAA 68/Li 174.

17. Ibid. 'Sales figures of Siemens representatives, Moleschott and Moleschott & Schilling.

18. Hertner, P., 'Il capitale tedesco nell'industria elettrica italiana fino alla prima guerra mondiale' in B. Bezza (ed.), *Energia e sviluppo. L'industria elettrica italiana e la Società Edison*, Torino, 1986, pp. 225 ff.

19. Hertner, P., 'German multinational enterprise before 1914: some case studies', in P. Hertner and G. Jones (eds.), *Multinationals: Theory and History*, Aldershot, 1986, p 128; but see above all Liefmann, R., *Beteiligungs- und Finanzierungsgesellschaften. Eine Studie über den modernen Kapitalismus und das Effektenwesen*, 2nd ed., Jena, 1913, pp. 103 ff.

20. Hertner, P., 'Financial Strategies and Adaptation to Foreign Markets: the German Electrotechnical Industry and its Multinational Activities: 1890s to 1939' in A. Teichova, M. Lévy-Leboyer, H. Nussbaum (eds), *Multinational Enterprise in Historical Perspective*, Cambridge, 1986, pp. 146 ff.

21. Fasolt, F., *Die sieben grössten deutschen Elektrizitätsgesellschaften. Ihre Entwicklung und Unternehmertätigkeit*, Dresden, 1904, p. 160 ff.; Jörgens, M., *Finanzielle Trustgesellschaften*, (PhD thesis, University of Münich), Stuttgart, 1902, pp. 117 ff.

22. Strobel, A., 'Die Gründung des Züricher Elektrotrusts. Ein Beitrag zum Unternehmergeschäft der deutschen Elektroindustrie' in H. Hassinger, (ed.), *Geschichte - Wirtschaft - Gesellschaft. Festschrift für Clemens Bauer zum 75. Geburtstag*, Berlin, 1974, pp. 303–32; Grossmann, H., *Die Finanzierungen der Bank für elektrische Unternehmungen in Zürich*, PhD thesis, University of Zürich, 1918; Hafner, K., *Die schweizerischen Finanzierungsgesellschaften für elektrische Unternehmungen*, Jur. Diss., University of Fribourg, Geneva, 1912, pp. 32ff.

23. Idem note 18, pp. 218 ff.

24. Confalonieri, A., *Banca e industria in Italia 1894–1906*, vol. 3, Milano, 1976, pp. 217 ff.

25. Idem note 18, pp. 242 ff.

26. Idem note 18, pp. 256.

27. Giarratana, A., ' Le reali condizioni dell' industria idroelettrica in Italia', *Le industrie italiane illustrate*, June 1918, **2**, (6), 56.

28. See, for instance, Wilhelm, K., *Die AEG*, Berlin, 1931, pp. 51 ff.

29. Idem note 8, pp. 47 ff. 54 ff.

30. Pavese, C., 'Between Financers and Entrepreneurs: Some Notes on the Growth of Electric Industry in Italy from the Origins to the World War I', *Annali della Facoltà di Scienze Politiche*, vol. 1, Milano, 1981, p. 377 ff.

31. Einhart, J.G., *Die wirtschaftliche Entwicklung und Lage der Elektrotechnik in der Schweiz*, Jur. thesis, University of Tübingen, Worms, 1906, pp. 10 ff; Ziegler, W.H., *Die wirtschaftliche Entwicklung der A.G. Brown, Boveri & Cie., Baden, des Brown-Boveri-Konzerns und der A.G. Motor-Columbus*, Jur. thesis, University of Berne, Brugg, 1937, pp. 136 ff.; Licini, S., 'Ercole Marelli e Tecnomasio Italiano dalle origini agli anni trenta: un tentativo di comparazione, in Assi, Fondazione (ed.), *Annali di storia dell'impresa*, 5/6, 1989/90, pp. 299-321; Wegmann, A., *Die wirtschaftliche Entwicklung der Maschinenfabrik Örlikon 1863–1917*, Jur. thesis, University of Zürich, Zürich, 1920, pp. 59 ff; Segreto, L., 'Capitali, tecnologie e imprenditori svizzeri nell'industria elettrica italiana: il caso della Motor (1895–1923), in Bezza, idem note 18, pp. 173–210; Hertner, P., 'Les sociétés financières suisses et le développement de l'industrie électrique jusqu'à la Première Guerre Mondiale', in F. Cardot, (ed.), *1880–1980. Un siècle d'électricité dans le monde*, Paris, 1987, pp. 341–55.

32. Allievi, L., 'Regime doganale dei prodotti della industria elettrica meccanica', *Rivista delle società commerciali*, 1916, pp. 112–17; Norsa, R., 'Il macchinario elettrico e la sua industria', in *Nel cinquantenario della Società Edison 1884/1934*, vol. 1, Milano, 1934, p. 304 .

33. Ziegler, *idem note 31*, p. 115; Licini, S., 'Ercole Marelli e Tecnomasio Italiano dalle origini agli anni trenta: un tentativo di comparazione', *Annali di storia dell'impresa*, V/VI, 1989/90, pp. 310 ff.
34. *Bollettino ufficiale delle società per azioni*, 22, 1904, fasc. 13quater, pp. 3 ff.; the *Société Thomson Houston de la Méditerranée* had been established in Brussels in 1898 with a majority of French capital guided by the French Thomson-Houston company; a minority participation was held among others by Thomson-Houston International, the foreign branch of General Electric (Lanthier, P., *Les constructions électriques en France. Financement et stratégies de six groupes industriels internationaux, 1880–1940*, PhD thesis, University of Paris, X, vol. 2, Paris 1988, p. 369).
35. *Electrical World and Engineer*, 16 April 1904, **43**, (16); *50 Jahre AEG*, p. 156.
36. Confalonieri, A., *Banca e industria in Italia dalla crisi del 1907 all'agosto del 1914*, vol. 2, Milan 1982, p. 245; Associazione fra gli industriali metallurgici italiani (ed.), *The metallurgic Industry in Italy: Description of Some of the Principal Works*, Milan (1912?), pp. 285 ff.
37. Ziegler, idem note 31, p 116.
38. SAA 11/Lb 58 ('Einige Angaben über den AEG-Konzern in Italien ...', 22 July 1919).
39. Siemens, idem note 14, vol. 2, pp. 79 ff.
40. Bottiglieri, B., *STET. Strategie e struttura delle telecomunicazioni*, Milano, 1987, p. 38.
41. Ibid., pp. 39 ff.
42. SAA 12/Lk 801 (Grabe).
43. In 1894, Western Electric purchased an interest in Officina Elettrica Nazionale, Milan; in April 1913 its participation was extended to 100 per cent and the firm transformed into Western Electric Italiana with a nominal capital of 950 000 Lire (Bell Laboratories Archives, Warren, New Jersey: Weco 87-08-24, folder 2; Weco 90-08-116, folder 2, 'Some facts about the International Western Electric Company and affiliated companies'). There was a branch at Rome, 'to handle the requirements of the Italian Government', and a manufacturing branch at Milan of which not much is known for the years before the First World War ('Our activities abroad', *Western Electric News*, March 1912, pp. 5–6; Leigh, W.E., 'Some Features of our Foreign Business as it is To-day', ibid., October 1913, pp. 1–3).
44. The re-establishment of official economic relations between Italy and Germany was realized only in August 1921 when the two countries concluded a provisional trade agreement (Muhr, J., *Die deutsch-italienischen Beziehungen in der Ära des Ersten Weltkrieges (1914–1922)*, Göttingen, 1977, p. 204.
45. See provisional contracts of 16 October and 27 November 1919 (SAA 11/la 137 (Jessen), vol. 11).
46. Ibid: memo of 4 July 1923 by Grabe.
47. SAA 68/Ld 851: *Geschichte des Hauses Siemens im Ausland*, part B, vol. 9: Wegner, J., *Italien*, Erlangen, 1977, p. 117; idem note 40, p. 48; according to Bottiglieri, Siemens would have joined SIRTI only in 1924 (ibid., p. 77).
48. Idem note 40, pp. 61 ff.
49. SAA 11/la 137 (Jessen), vol. 11: list of 12 March 1930. The position of Siemens as a supplier was particularly strong with the STIPEL company to which the telephone service in the economically most important area, Piedmont and Lombardy, had been assigned (Bottiglieri, B., *SIP. Impresa, tecnologia e stato nelle telecomunicazioni italiane*, Milano, 1990, pp. 93, 104).
50. International Western Electric was taken over by ITT in 1925 (Bell Laboratories Archives, Weco 90-08-116-02: 'Memorandum covering main points of proposed arrangement with the International Telephone and Telegraph Company covering the purchase of certain International Western Electric assets', dated 7-8-25); one might therefore suppose that its Italian branch was merged with the Face Standard company of Milan which operated a factory in that same city previously owned by the Fratelli Gerosa firm. *Face Standard* exchanges were particularly frequent in the concession zone of East Central Italy (Bottiglieri, *SIP*, idem note 49, pp. 84, 104).
51. Attman, A., Kuuse, J., Olsson, U., *LM Ericsson 100 Years*, vol. 1, Örebro, 1977, p. 332.
52. SAA 68/Ld 851: Wegner, *Italien*, p. 97 ss; SAA 68/Li 174: reports of 23 June and 18 August 1923; SAA 47/Lk 843: report on the development of Siemens-Milan of 9 September 1944.
53. Bell Laboratories Archives, Weco 90-08-116-02: DuBois, C.G., 'The Foreign Business of the Western Electric Company', dated August 1923.
54. Idem note 40, pp. 61, 69; idem note 51, vol. 1, p. 332.
55. Schröter, V., *Die deutsche Industrie auf dem Weltmarkt 1929 bis 1933. Außenwirtschaftliche Strategien unter dem Druck der Weltwirtschaftskrise*, Frankfurt, 1984, p. 423.

56. Cited ibid. Looking back to experience undergone in the past, Felix Deutsch, successor to the two Rathenaus at the leadership of AEG, stated also that only in cases where there had been strict protectionism in a country, either the foreign business had to be given up or part of production had to be shifted to the country concerned ('Zum 70. Geburtstag Dr. Felix Deutsch', *Die AEG-Umschau*, 16 May 1928, p. 33 ff.).
57. Sielcken, W., *Die deutsche Telephon- und Telegraphen- Industrie*, Jur. thesis, University of Hamburg, 1929, p. 74.
58. Glardon, A.R., *Die deutsche Elektroindustrie und der Absatz ihrer Erzeugnisse in der Nachkriegszeit*, Hamburg, 1933, pp. 61, 117.
59. Gapinski, F., *Die Stellung der deutschen Elektro-Industrie innerhalb der internationalen Elektrowirtschaft in der Gegenwart*, PhD thesis, University of Köln, Berlin, 1931, p. 86.
60. McLean, H.C., *Electrical Equipment in Italy*, United States Department of Commerce, Trade Information Bulletin no. 151, 15 October 1923, Washington, DC 1923.
61. Pescarolo, A., *Riconversione industriale e composizione di classe*, Milan, 1979, p. 73.
62. Ibid., p. 287.
63. Idem note 60, p. 14.
64. Ibid., p. 15.
65. Idem note 20, p. 153; among others see also Toggweiler, J., *Die Holding Company in der Schweiz*, Zürich, 1926, pp. 136 ff.
66. Waller, E., *Studien zur Finanzgeschichte des Hauses Siemens* (typescript kept in the Siemens archives, München), part V, 1960/61, p. 151 ff; idem note 55, p. 394 ff.
67. Idem note 59, pp. 105, 114 (note 29); idem note 55, pp. 258; according to Reid (idem note 8, p. 212) General Electric's total holding in AEG amounted even to 'around 30%'.
68. For concrete examples of such initiatives of German industry during the 1920s and 1930s see Schröter, idem note 55, pp. 422 ff.
69. SAA 11/Lf 289 (Köttgen); SAA 11/Lf 471 (Köttgen).
70. SAA 11/Lf 477 (Köttgen).
71. Calculated from SAA 15/Le 270 (Graupe).
72. Cohen, J.S., 'The 1927 Revaluation of the Lira: a Study in Political Economy', *Economic History Review*, 2nd Ser., XXV, 1972, pp. 642-54; Toniolo, G., *L'economia dell'Italia fascista*, Roma and Bari, 1980, pp. 102 ff.
73. The agreement became applicable only for 'non-exclusive' areas, i.e. essentially for all extra-European countries with the exception of the USA, Canada, Turkey and Japan (Reid, idem note 8, pp. 264 ff; Schröter, idem note 55, p. 292).
74. See the detailed description of this so-called ANIEM agreement in Doria M., 'Una "via nazionale" all'industrializzazione: L'Elettrotecnico Ansaldo dall'inizio del secolo alla Seconda Guerra Mondiale', in Associazione di Storia e Studi sull'Impresa (ed.), *Annali di Storia dell'Impresa*, IV, 1989, p. 201, and particularly note 82; see also Licini, idem note 33, p. 316 ff. Negotiations for the ANIEM agreement ('in order to discipline prices and sales') had already started at the beginning of 1929, but the final accord was concluded only by 8 April 1931 (Minutes of the Council of Administration of the *Compagnia Generale di Elettricità* of 12 March 1929 and 10 April 1931. I am most grateful to Dr Licini for having put copies of these documents at my disposal).
75. Banca Commerciale Italiana, *Movimento economico dell'Italia. Raccolta di statistiche per l'anno 1928*, vol. 18, Milano, 1929, p. 262; Banca d'Italia, *L'economia italiana nel sessennio 1931–1936*, part II, vol. 2, Roma, 1938, pp. 1299, 1331.
76. Idem note 58, p. 85.
77. Toniolo, idem note 72, p. 277 ss; Guarneri, F., *Battaglie economiche tra le due grandi guerre*, Milan, 1953, vol. 1, p. 298 ss., vol. 2, pp. 1 ff.
78. SAA 15/Lk 696, pp. 30 ff.
79. AEG, in order to avoid sequestration of AEG Thomson-Houston during the First World War, had ceded its 50 per cent participation to the Banca Commerciale Italiana group (SAA 68/Li 174: 'strictly confidential' memo of 27 March 1919). It seems that the entire firm, which by then had changed its name to Officine Galileo Ferraris, was sold in 1918 to the machine builder Tosi (SAA 11/Lb 58 (Haller): 'Einige Angaben über den A.E.G.-Konzern in Italien...', memo of 22 July 1919). A year later, General Electric 'signed a new contract with Tosi which granted the latter exclusive rights to manufacture and sell GE equipment and apparatus in Italy and Albania, and began negotiating the purchase of the Italian firm's electrical business' ((idem

note 8, p. 112). In 1921, General Electric, as mentioned, 'purchased roughly 50% Tosi, subsequently renamed Compagnia Generale di Elettricità' (ibid., p. 145). According to the shareholders' register, the International General Electric Company, owned 66.6 per cent of a nominal capital of 40 million lire to which the company's capital had been increased a few months after its foundation (Società Sadelmi-Cogepi, Milano, Libro Soci della Compagnia Generale di Elettricità, No. 1: registration of 30 August 1921).

80. Idem note 55, p. 258.
81. Minutes of the Council of Administration of the Compagnia Generale di Elettricità of 31 August 1923 and 28 May 1924.
82. Ibid: minutes of 13 March 1933.
83. SAA 15/Lk 696, pp. 39 ff.
84. Ibid., p. 50; Rafalski, T., *Italienischer Faschismus in der Weltwirtschaftskrise (1925-1936). Wirtschaft Gesellschaft und Politik auf der Schwelle zur Moderne*, Opladen, 1984, pp. 168 ff.
85. SAA 68/Ld 851: Wegner, idem note 52, p. 106 ff; SAA 4/Lt 398 (I): contract on the foundation of Siemens-Plania AG together with Rütgerswerke AG, p. 10; in April 1931 Siemens-Plania AG, after having bought further shares of Elettrocarbonium, owns 72.4 per cent of this Italian company which operates two plants, one at Narni in Umbria and one at Ascoli Piceno in the Marches (SAA, 4/Lt 398 (IVb), no. 51, p. 8); Marianeschi, E. *et al.*, *La grande industria a Terni*, Terni, 1986, p. 317.
86. SAA 68/Ld 851: Wegner, idem note 52, p. 109 ff.; Associazione fra le Società italiane per azioni, *Società italiane per azioni*, XIV, 1934, p. 945; Archivio Centrale dello Stato, Roma (abbreviated below as: ACS): Servizio Osservatori Industriali, busta 24, fasc. 484.
87. SAA 68/Ld 851: Wegner, idem note 52, p. 108 ff.
88. SAA 15/Le 270: Monthly reports of Siemens-Milan for November 1924, March 1926, April 1926, June 1926, April 1927.
89. Ibid: Monthly reports for April 1928, November 1928, July 1929. Construction of meters had been started at Isaria-Milan in 1925; in 1927 the firm had 50, and in 1930, 132 employees (ACS, Servizio Osservatori Industriali, busta 23, fasc. 473).
90. SAA 68/Ld 851: Wegner, idem note 52, pp. 108 ff; idem note 55, pp. 260 ff; Siemens, G., *Der Weg der Elektrotechnik. Geschichte des Hauses Siemens*, 2nd ed., Freiburg i.B. and München, 1961, pp. 53 ff; in 1934 the Milan firm Società riunite Osram-Edison-Clerici numbered 553 employees, with management almost exclusively German (ACS, Servizio Osservatori Industriali, busta 23, fasc. 471).
91. For a more detailed treatment of this specific case see Hertner, P., 'Un investimento tedesco in Lombardia tra le due guerre mondiali: La Officine Lombarde di Apparecchi di Precisione, *Storia in Lombardia*, 1986, pp. 7–37.
92. SAA 68/Li 182: Blattman, A., *Zur Entwicklung der Siemens Apparate und Maschinen GmbH (SAM) und ihrer Vorgeschichte*, typed manuscript, vol. 1, Münich 1976, pp. 5 ff; SAA 4/Lt 398 (VI): minutes of the supervisory board of Siemens & Halske on 29 January 1936; memo on the joint meeting of the supervisory boards of Siemens & Halske and Siemens-Schuckert on 31 October 1935.
93. SAA 68/Li 182: Report on SAM of 12 December 1945.
94. SAA 47/Lk 843: Report on Siemens in Italy of 9 September 1944.

8 The internationalization of West German banks, 1945–87

Richard Tilly

This chapter has two goals. The first is to provide a rough description of when and how West Germany's commercial banks internationalized their business after the Second World War. Secondly, some of the more obvious causes and consequences of that internationalization are discussed. Given the complexity of the topic, a brief treatment is inevitably a superficial one. A further limitation of the present chapter is that it considers only the large commercial banks – the 'Big Three' (Deutsche Bank, Dresdner Bank and Commerzbank). However, this procedure is partially justified by the fact that the 'Big Three' were far more important in the areas of international banking than any other West German bank group. Nevertheless, this limitation needs to be recognized in the following discussion.

The internationalization of German banking after 1945

Although the larger German commercial banks had been major actors in the international banking community before 1914, the First World War and the inflation which followed it left them weakened for years. Thereafter, events – the world financial crisis and depression, the Third Reich, and the Second World War prevented those banks from recapturing their pre-war position.[1] In the immediate post-1945 period, their primary concern was survival, for wartime finance had weakened them once more and they faced, in addition, the threat of break-up posed by Allied deconcentration plans. By 1952, however, the worst was over. A law of 29 March of that year definitely limited deconcentration and even provided, at least implicitly, a legal basis for reconcentration.[2]

The banks began rebuilding their international connections almost as soon as the West German economy started to revive, for the latter required imports, exports and credits related thereto. Initially, this meant establishing or renewing links with correspondent banks in the countries which supplied or bought from West Germany. This was a return to the traditional or classical way of financing the country's international business – through the construction of a network of correspondent banks in foreign countries by means of which trade credits (via

173

letters of credit, bills of exchange, etc.) could be mobilized - and it remained for at least a decade the primary form through which German banks conducted their international transactions.[3] In the early 1950s West German bankers had reason to be satisfied with such arrangements, for economically their country's scarce supply of foreign exchange and exchange controls probably limited the scale of their foreign operations, while politically, maintenance of a low profile must have seemed advisable for business in countries which only a few years earlier had been enemies or vassals.[4] Export success and the related liberalization of import and exchange controls soon eliminated the economic constraint. No doubt cold war considerations were the main factor behind the weakening of political constraints, but one should nevertheless also stress the immediate value in this respect of a concrete step – the London Debt Agreement negotiated in 1952 and 1953 – for it embodied helpful signs of international co-operation and, in particular, clear proof of West Germany's willingness to play the role of reliable international debtor.[5]

Despite the constraints mentioned, the banks began experimenting in the early 1950s – even before the European Economic Community or establishment of currency convertibility – with additional institutions for the conduct of their international business. One of the earliest of such institutions was the Ausfuhr-Kredit-AG (Export Credit Corporation), jointly founded in 1952 by the commercial banks for the purpose of providing long-term finance for exporters of investment goods, that is credits, the tenor or riskiness of which went beyond what the banks themselves felt ready to extend. It was (and is) a back-up institution, which supplied in effect refinancing for the commercial banks' trade finance business (and also access to special rediscount facilities of the Bundesbank). Strictly speaking, however, it was and is a German-based, and not an international, institution.[6]

More truly international in character were the representational offices (or *Repräsentanzen*) the banks began opening up in foreign countries in the 1950s. These carried out no banking business themselves but collected information, directed potential customers either to the German home office or a correspondent in the host country, and sought, in general, to promote the home bank's 'goodwill' abroad. The first such *Repräsentanz* was founded in 1952 by the Dresdner Bank in Istanbul. Many others followed. By the late 1960s (1967) the Dresdner Bank maintained 18 such offices (the Deutsche Bank 11 and the Commerzbank 8).[7] The idea was that if business potential developed sufficiently, a more substantial connection, such as a subsidiary or branch office, would replace the *Repräsentanz*. This began to happen in the late-1960s.[8]

In a rough chronological sense, the next international step most frequently taken by the banks was the establishment of subsidiaries – created by acquiring a controlling share (or sole ownership) of a foreign bank. One should note that a few important subsidiaries with foreign operations had survived from earlier times, for example the Deutsche Bank's German Overseas Bank (Deutsche-Überseeische Bank) which, itself German-based, owned or controlled a number of South American banks. Of similar status was the Dresdner Bank's German-South American Bank (Deutsch-Südamerikanische Bank). These are worth mentioning here since the scale of their operations did continue to grow throughout much of the period.[9] The main story, however, involves the new acquisitions. They were important because they offered a full complement of financial services and not just trade credits. The West German banks began founding subsidiaries in the late-1960s, the first and most important location being the Grand Duchy of Luxembourg. The first was founded by the Dresdner Bank in 1967. The Commerzbank followed in 1969 and the Deutsche Bank in 1970.[10] Here the idea was to exploit that country's liberal banking laws and to tap the growing funds and flexible financial devices of the burgeoning Euro-dollar or Euro-capital markets.[11] Such access enabled the West German banks to provide their own German customers – who increasingly operated internationally – with better and cheaper financial facilities. Moreover, they began to capture a share of non-German business as well.

The decisive shift in emphasis to foreign operations among West German commercial banks which marked the late-1960s and 1970s was by no means confined to the creation of Luxembourg subsidiaries, although these long remained the most important. The German banks founded, helped found, or acquired significant equity interests in many foreign countries. In 1967, for example, the 'Big Three' had 16 such equity interests (one full subsidiary) in banks in 15 countries. By the end of the 1970s these had grown to more than 60 (10 full subsidiaries) in over 20 countries.[12] In addition, the banks also founded or acquired important equity interests in investment finance companies – to some extent as adjuncts of their banks, in any case as part of a worldwide trend through which involvement in Euro-financial markets could be strengthened or specialized types of activity obtain funding. Among the more important were foreign bank institutions established in London and New York. The former facilitated participation in the Euro-dollar and Euro-finance markets, the latter allowed closer links to the US financial market *per se* and also the provision of facilities to the growing numbers of German enterprises which were operating there.

As one reconstructs this movement, however, one notes that the German banks did not always move into foreign centres alone, at least not initially. The Commerzbank's entry into London in 1967, for example, was a co-operative venture involving four other banks, two of them American, one British, the other from Hong Kong. The Deutsche Bank first entered New York in 1968 in association with three other European banks, while the Dresdner Bank went into Singapore in 1973 by founding a bank with six other partner banks (from six major countries).[13] In fact, one must stress that the early stage of internationalization of German banks followed largely co-operative lines involving banks of several countries and broad, if vague, programmes of co-operation. The first of these, the so-called EBIC group, was founded in 1963 by four major European banks, the German one being the Deutsche Bank.[14] The second group formed in 1970, the German side represented by the Commerzbank, its partners the Credit Lyonnais and (a bit later) the Banco di Roma. The third major group, the ABECOR (Associated Banks of Europe Corporation), came into being in 1971. It united the Dresdner Bank with another German bank (the Bayerische Hypothekenbank), the Banque Bruxelles

Lambert SA and the Algemene Bank Nederland. Besides regular consultation, joint security issues, joint control of foreign banks, and joint training and exchange programmes, the agreements sought to place the payment and other services of each bank's domestic and international organization at the disposal of customers of the other banks. The hope was to ease the execution of large-scale projects and to lower the costs of international credit and payments transactions.[15]

Such agreements, however, do not appear to have fulfilled their founders' hopes. Quite a list of joint projects and activities could be constructed for the 1970s and 1980s. One typical example: in 1978 the Europartners, led by the Commerzbank, launched a New York investment bank, the Europartners Securities Corporation, for the purpose of participating in trading and new issues on the New York stock exchange. In 1979 the firm obtained membership in that exchange, and in the 1980s was reportedly 'doing a good business'.[16] Nevertheless, not even the 'Europartner' group came close to the 'merger-like' arrangements the original agreement had pointed to.[17] Primary loyalties came to rest elsewhere in the 1980s,

Table 8.1. Foreign bank establishments of Big Three and all German banks, 1967–87 (by type)

	1967	1973	1980	1987
Big Three				
Repräsentanzen	37	40	64[2]	52
Participations[1]	16	33	26	30
Subsidiaries	1	4	10	22
Branches	–	6	32	52
All Banks				
Repräsentanzen		–	101[3]	–
Participations[1]		–	84[3]	–
Subsidiaries		27	52	76
Branches		23	74	102

Note
1.   At least 10 per cent of equity of foreign bank.
2.   Including South American offices shared with subsidiaries.
3.   1979 (Büschgen, H., 'Zeitgeschichtliche Problemfelder des Bankwesens der Bundesrepublik Deutschland', *Deutsche Bankengeschichte*, vol. 3, p. 396).

Source
Author's calculations.

as competition in banking intensified. 'Merger-like' moves proved to be much less than mergers.[18]

More important as a vehicle for international banking – indeed, ultimately most important – were the West German banks' own foreign branches. Their expansion lagged a few years behind the other institutions described, catching up by the end of the 1970s. Table 8.1 shows development of branches and the other institutional forms over the 1967–87 period. The pattern is clear. Thus in 1967 the Commerzbank had no foreign branches, but quite a few *Repräsentanzen*. By 1980, however, it had 11 foreign branches, and its presence in major financial centres such as London, New York or Tokyo was secured by these, rather than the other institutions. The same applies to the Deutsche and Dresdner Banks. In many countries, to be sure, the branch offices supplemented, rather than totally replaced the other institutions. Thus, in France, both the Commerzbank and the Dresdner Bank held on to the French banks they controlled after opening up branch offices there.[19] Nevertheless, the greater reliance placed upon branch office growth everywhere suggests that the latter embodied cost advantages over the other institutions.[20]

It may be useful at this point to speculate a bit more specifically about some of the quantitative dimensions of these foreign operations. The annual reports of the Big Three, publications of the German Bundesbank and a miscellany of other sources can permit a few crude bench mark estimates. For a start one may take M. Pohl's estimate (presumably for the early 1980s) according to which one-third of the banks' business represented international operations.[21] Some further clues derive from reports on the Luxembourg subsidiaries.[22] At the beginning of the 1970s the Luxembourg subsidiaries of the Big Three reported total assets then worth around 2 milliards DM, and by 1972 they had reached an estimated 8.3 milliards. This latter figure probably approximated about one-half of all German bank assets in Luxembourg. For 1977–78 the official '*Studienkommission*' investigating bank concentration estimated Big Three assets then at around 35 milliard DM, again about one-half of the suspected total for all German banks.[23] In 1987 the Big Three banks reportedly held assets roughly worth 72 milliard DM (and the same market share). Combining these estimates with other scattered figures contained in the Big Three's annual reports and the Bundesbank data, we arrive at the estimates shown in Table 8.2.[24] These are 'guestimates', of course, but they can serve the rough purpose at hand. That is to indicate orders of magnitude, for example that foreign expansion in the period exceeded its domestic counterpart; and also that the 'Big Three' played a prominent role in this field of banking growth.

Causes and consequences

The figures in Table 8.2 lead us to the consideration of the consequences and causes of the internationalization of German banking. By comparing those figures with other data one can begin to assess their significance, which does imply discussing the underlying causes and related consequences. First, it seems clear, as

*Table 8.2. Total assets and total foreign assets of foreign branches and subsidi-
aries of Big Three and all German banks, 1971–87 (in milliard DM)*

	1971/2	1973	1980	1987
Big Three				
Total assets	143[1]		400[1]	637[1]
Total foreign assets of foreign branches and subsidiaries	10.0		109	204
All German banks				
Total assets	1000	1200	3400	4100
Total foreign assets of foreign branches and subsidiaries	20.0		160	427

Note
1. *Konzernbilanzsumme.*

Source
Annual reports of Deutsche Bank, Dresdner Bank and Commerzbank; Deutsche Bundesbank, *40 Jahre Deutsche Mark*, Frankfurt, 1988; Pohl, M., 'Die Entwicklung des privaten Bankwesens nach 1945; *Deutsche Bankengeschichte*, vol. 3.

*Table 8.3. Share of Big Three banks in domestic commercial banking business,
1950–87 in % of total*

	1950	1960	1970	1980	1987
Non-bank deposits	25	18.5	16.5	14	9.5
Credit outstanding, non banks	26	17.5	14.5	12.5	9.0
Total assets	25	16.4	14	12.5	6.0

Note
1.   Excludes private bankers, branches of foreign banks and all special-purpose banks.

Source
Deutsche Bundesbank, *40 Jahre Deutsche Mark*, Frankfurt 1988.

suggested above, that the Big Three took the leading role among German banks operating abroad. Their (German) market share here remained a good deal higher than that realized in most domestic banking activities (see Table 8.3). Foreign expansion could thus be viewed as a means for offsetting declining market shares at home. Second, however, one must doubt the effectiveness of such a compensatory strategy, for the quantitative dimensions were too limited. In 1987 total foreign assets held by all German banks amounted to around 800 milliard DM, probably less than one-fifth of the value of all German bank assets (without the Bundesbank).[25] Such balance sheet figures, to be sure, do not capture off-balance sheet activities and advantages related thereto, so this judgement could require supplementation. In any case, the figures cited do not mean that the strategy itself was wrong, for given increasing competition in international banking, there was no alternative, and the appropriate measure of 'success' would necessarily involve comparison of ex-post results with some plausible counterfactual.

Third, assessment of West German bank expansion abroad – and also the construction of counterfactuals – calls for an examination of the profitability of international banking operations. Unfortunately, such an examination cannot be undertaken here, for it would require mastering the difficult terrain of bank balance sheet and profit and loss statements. Nevertheless, one may note that a few such studies of the matter have concluded that profit margins on international transactions, if anything, are and have been considerably lower than on domestic business. Krüger, for example, found the following rates of return for German banks and their Luxembourg subsidiaries for the years 1978–87 (annual surplus before taxes in per cent of total assets): domestic Banks – 0.52; Luxembourg Banks – 0.22.

The difference is unmistakeable. At the same time, the level of risk on international transactions was probably higher.[26] On the other hand, consideration of all costs (and not just interest rate spreads and commissions on individual transaction types) suggest little difference in net returns in the early 1980s.[27] Moreover, the possibility remains that foreign outposts contributed to their home banks' well-being in ways which elude such direct profit calculations. In fact, it seems clear that one of the principal functions of the foreign apparatus has been to generate information on investment and borrowing possibilities and to attract business which strengthens the home bank's overall position – including its domestic one. Such effects – corresponding to synergy effects, externalities or scale economies – are unfortunately not easy to quantify.

Discussing consequences of the internationalization of German banks inevitably means considering its causes, at least implicitly. They deserve an explicit treatment, however. Take the problems of market shares. The continuing fall in the share of the Big Three in domestic business, it was suggested above, could have motivated their internationalization. The banks themselves frequently associated that decline with legal and tax advantages which benefited their domestic competitors, and these advantages weighed but little in the different legal environment prevailing abroad.[28] There is something to this argument, no doubt.[29] However, neither the decline at home nor expansion abroad is interpretable solely in terms of *relative* legal and fiscal disadvantages – which were declining in importance over time in any case.[30] And this factor does not well explain the timing of internationalization. It is thus necessary to look further – to the internationalization of the German economy itself and to growing international competition in banking.

Several factors contributed to the development outlined: (1) the penetration of Western Europe and especially of Western Germany by US multinational enterprises in the 1960s (partly in response to the EEC), which served as a model of internationalization, initially for German non-bank enterprises, and which stimulated a demand for German banks to follow the latter abroad; (2) the emergence of chronic balance of payments deficits in the US in the late 1950s and resultant 'dollar glut' which led – in conjunction with US banking regulations - to offshore banking and the development of the Euro-financial markets (at first the Euro-dollar money markets, then the Euro-bond market, Euro-capital market, etc.) which offered alternative sources of financial services and new financial opportunities to West-German enterprises; and (3) the parallel emergence of chronic export and balance of payments surpluses for West Germany, which produced a considerable capital export potential and eventually - together with (2) – uncertainty about the future viability of the Bretton Woods international currency system.

Such factors, however, do not satisfactorily answer the question of timing: why West German banks shifted emphasis to international operations so markedly in the late 1960s and 1970s. This shift had, it can be argued, two primarily German sources. First, the West German economy registered the effects of a deep structural change in these years: what has been called 'the end of the reconstruction phase' and the end of 'catching-up growth', which produced a decline in domestic investment opportunities, a shift to services, and enhanced interest in foreign investment.[31]

Second, this period (and especially from 1968 to 1973) was one of repeated international currency crises and in West Germany was associated with a fear of inflation (and especially of 'imported inflation') which led the German Bundesbank (and eventually the German government) to enact measures to curtail domestic and especially commercial bank liquidity. These included measures to restrict access to foreign capital, for example by means of reserve requirements (for example in November 1968, in June 1972, or in January and February of 1973) which were only partially effective. The 'systemic solution' came with the abandonment of fixed exchange rates in 1973.[32] But in the meantime the German banks became acutely aware of the closeness of the links between national banking operations and international currency and capital markets and, in particular, of the discrepancy between the limitations of a mainly domestic banking business, burdened as it was with onerous central bank and government regulations, and the possibilities of more flexible operations abroad. In addition, this period of crises and fluctuating exchange rates stimulated customer demand for hedging facilities which the German banks felt best able to provide through their own foreign networks.[33] Internationalization of their operations thus continued.

Conclusion

In closing, it is necessary to return to a point made earlier: that the German banks were reacting to 'exogenous' events. By doing so, one is reminded of the fact that economic history, like all history, can easily become 'just one damned thing after another'. In the case at hand, internationalization of German banking, a fuller account would properly stress the oil crises of the 1970s and demand for recycling of the so-called 'petrodollars', the greatly increased bank lending to Third World countries from the 1970s to 1982 and the International Debt Crisis from 1982 on; and the worldwide trend toward deregulation of financial markets and increasing mobility of capital in the 1980s. Those facts, however, do have some analytical sense, for German banks, obviously, could not avoid being deeply affected by such changes. Maintaining their own market shares at home required their 'going international'; and each additional bank that entered into international operations represented an additional reason for the others to also do so.

Notes

1. See Born, K-E., 'Vom Beginn des Ersten Weltkrieges bis zum Ende der Weimarer Republik'; Wandel, E., 'Das deutsche Bankwesen im Dritten Reich', both in *Deutsche Bankengeschichte*, Vol. 3. Edited by the Institut für Bank-historiche Forschung, Frankfurt, 1983. For a succinct summary of the pre-1914 operations of German banks abroad see Hertner, Peter, 'German Banks Abroad before 1914', in Jones, Geoffrey (ed.), *Banks as Multinationals*, London, 1990.
2. Pohl, M., 'Die Entwicklung des privaten Bankwesens nach 1945', *Deutsche Bankengeschichte*, vol. 3, pp. 231–9. See also OMGUS, 'Ermittlungen gegen die deutsche Bank (1946–47)', in H.M. Enzensberger (ed.), Die andere Bibliothek, Nördingen, 1985, esp. pp. 13–17 and 291–300, for US views as of 1947.
3. Büschgen, H., 'Zeitgeschichtliche Problemfelder des Bankwesens der Bundesrepublik Deutschland', *Deutsche Bankengeschichte*, vol. 3, p. 386. See also Annual Reports of the Dresdner Bank, 1954 and 1955, or of the Commerzbank, 1953 to 1958.
4. The confiscation of foreign assets after two world wars was probably an additional constraint worth mentioning here.
5. See on this Pohl, M., *Wiederaufbau. Kunst und Technik der Finanzierung; 1947–1953*, Frankfurt, 1973, pp. 137–45. Also Seidenzahl, F., *100 Jahre Deutsche Bank*, Frankfurt, 1970, pp. 391–5; and Stolper, Gustav, Häuser, Karl and Borchardt, K., *Die deutsche Wirtschaft seit 1870*,. Tübingen, 1966, pp. 259 ff. Of importance were the facts that: (1) West Germany assumed responsibility for repayment of German foreign debts incurred in the 1920s and frozen in the 1930s, (2) the US cancelled part of its claims against West Germany; (3) one of Germany's leading commercial bankers, H.J. Abs, led the German negotiating group.
6. Pohl, M., idem note 2, p. 255. Over 30 banks participated in its founding. In 1969 it was converted into a GmbH.
7. Büschgen, idem note 3, p. 387; Annual Reports of the Dresdner Bank for 1954 and 1967; Annual Reports of the Deutsche Bank and Commerzbank for 1967.
8. It did not always happen. In 1987, for example, the Dresdner Bank still maintained its Istanbul *Repräsentanz*; and subsidiaries or branches were also founded where no *Repräsentanz* had existed.
9. In 1980 the Dresdner Bank's Deutsch-Amerikanische Bank had total assets worth c. 5.6 milliard DM – approximately 4.5 per cent of the Dresdner's consolidated balance sheet total. (Annual Report of Dresdner Bank for 1980). In 1977 the Deutsche Bank totally absorbed the Deutsche-Überseeische Bank, which disappeared. The Deutsche Bank set up its own branches in South America to supervise the older network of offices which existed as before. They held

assets reportedly worth about 500 million DM at this time. See Pohl, M., *Deutsche Bank Buenos Aires 1887–1987*, Mainz, 1987.

10. Annual Reports of these banks for the years cited.
11. Subsidiaries in Luxembourg, for example, were not subject to equity capital rules or reserve requirements on deposits as stringent as those in force in West Germany; nor were taxes as high.
12. 'Significant' means at least 10 per cent of total equity of the foreign bank.
13. Annual Reports of the three banks for the years cited.
14. The others were: the Amsterdam-Rotterdam Bank NV, the Midland Bank and the Belgian Société Générale. EBIC stands for European Banks International Company (SA, Brussels).
15. The Commerzbank creation was eventually called Europartners. The initial agreement of 14 October 1970 is summarized in the Commerzbank's Annual Report for 1970. See also the Annual Report of the Dresdner Bank for 1971; and also Pohl. idem note 2, p. 240.
16. Annual Report of Commerzbank, 1980 and 1983.
17. Annual Report of Commerzbank for 1970.
18. See Büschgen, idem note 3, p. 395.
19. For example, Annual Reports of Commerzbank and Dresdner Bank for 1978.
20. This applies to all commercial banks and not just the Big Three. By 1987 102 West German foreign branches held assets worth roughly 228 milliard DM as against 76 subsidiaries holding 193 milliard DM. These estimates by the Deutsche Bundesbank, *40 Jahre Deutsche Mark, Frankfurt*, 1988, pp. 90–3 and 316–17.
21. Pohl, idem note 2, p. 240. This estimate probably excluded foreign business done from German offices. In the early 1980s this roughly equalled that executed by foreign subsidiaries.
22. Taken from the Annual Reports of the Big Three.
23. See Bericht der Studienkommission 'Grundsatzfragen der Kreditwirtschaft', in *Schriftenreihe des Bundesministeriums der Finanzen*, part 28, Bonn, 1979.
24. The Big Three's reports contain various point estimates of total 'foreign assets' held, assets held by branches, and foreign loans outstanding for domestic and branch offices. There are also estimates of total assets held by subsidiaries – but not always for the same years as the other figures. Estimates here are built on the consistently available figures for assets held by Luxembourg subsidiaries and linked those to other subsidiaries at various points in time to get total assets of subsidiaries for the years covered by the Table. Plausible estimates for 1980 were extrapolated to 1987 for the Dresdner Bank and Commerzbank by the ratio of total assets 1987 to 1980. The Deutsche Bank had an estimate for 1988 which was extrapolated back to 1987. An appendix replicating the steps in these estimates is available on request.
25. Deutsche Bundesbank, *40 Jahre Deutsche Mark*, Frankfurt, 1988, pp. 90–1 and 316–17. But see Monatsbericht der Deutschen Bundesbank, *Langfristige Entwicklung des Bankensektors und Marktstellung der Kreditinstitute*, April 1989, where a comparison between 1988 and 1978 suggests a significant slowdown in the rate of decline. Here, however, special-purpose banks are excluded.
26. Krüger, Ralf, 'Die Bedeutung des internationalen Bankgeschäfts für die Rentabilität einer Geschäftsbank', in Hans Büschgen and Kurt Ridoll (eds), *Handbuch des internationalen Bankgeschäfts*, Wiesbaden, 1989, pp. 315–40; Brützel, Ch., *Offshore Banking deutscher Banken*, Frankfurt, 1985, pp. 298–318. Risk is measured here by the write-offs and reserve levels maintained by the banks.
27. Baumanns, Franz T., *Faktoren einer Internationalisierungsentscheidung der Kreditinstitute*, Frankfurt, 1983, pp. 40–53. In addition, it is of some interest to note that as late as 1978 and 1979 the rate of return for the Luxembourg subsidiaries was higher than that of their German parents. See Krüger, idem note 26, p. 324.
28. See for example, Floitgraf, H., *Steuerprivilegien und Wettbewerb im Bankwesen der Bundesrepublik Deutschland*, Frankfurt., 1964; and Ashauer, G., 'Entwicklung der Sparkassenorganisation ab 1924', *Deutsche Bankengeschichte* 3, 1983, pp. 322–3.
29. See Brützel, idem note 26, especially pp. 331–5 for a critical assessment.
30. Ashauer, idem note 28, p. 323.
31. For a discussion of the West German growth pattern and its causes see: Dumke, Rolf, 'Reassessing The Wirtschaftswunder: Reconstruction and Postwar Growth in West Germany in an International Context', *Oxford Bulletin of Economics and Statistics*, 1990, **52**, (2) 451–91; Helmstädter, Ernst, 'Soziale Marktwirtschaft. Die ordnungspolitische Grundlegung und der Wandel der Anforderungen an die Wirtschaftspolitik', in W. Weidenfeld, and H. Zimmermann,

(eds), *Deutschland-Handbuch. Bundeszentrale für politische Bildung*, Stuttgart, 1989; and Glastetter, Werner, Paulus, Rüdiger and Spörel, Ukich, *Die wirtschafftliche Entwicklung in der Bundesrepublik Deutschland 1950–1980*, Frankfurt, 1983.

32. For an 'insider's' description of this period see Emminger, Otmar, 'Deutsche Geld-und Währungspolitik im Spannungsfeld zwischen innerem und äußerem Gleichgewicht (1948–1975)', in Deutsche Bundesbank, (ed.), *Währung und Wirtschaft in Deutschland 1876–1975*, Frankfurt, 1976, pp. 514–33. The idea is that a central bank has no autonomy under a fixed exchange rate regime. Under the circumstances of the late 1960s, with German surpluses and revaluation expectations abroad, the Bundesbank was losing control over the economy. Emminger wrote: 'The foreign money markets have ... become a kind of substitute central bank (for Germany)', ibid., p. 523.

33. This is a continual theme in the reports of the Big Three in the early 1970s. See, for example, Annual Reports of Commerzbank and Dresdner Bank for 1973, where the importance of the Luxembourg facilities for this purpose is stressed (as well as the income derived therefrom).

9 The development of Pirelli as an Italian multinational, 1872–1992[1]

Angelo Montenegro

Italy, like Japan, was a latecomer to large-scale foreign direct investment (fdi). The Dunning estimates given in Table 1.2 (see p. 10) show that, even in the early 1980s, Italy was less important as a home country for multinational investment than much smaller European economies. However, over the last decade, this situation has begun to change. Figure 1.2 (see p. 13) demonstrates the fast growth of Italian fdi in this period. By the beginning of the 1990s, the country had acquired a new position as one of the larger direct investors in Europe, and perhaps the most dynamic one.

The success of modern Italian business has puzzled many Anglo-Saxon observers, who have been distressed by that country's inefficient state bureaucracy, and – as in the case of Japan – found it hard to appreciate that a business culture very different from their own could also be more competitive and successful. Michael Porter's recent book is a noteworthy exception to this generalization, for he ranks Italy alongside Japan as one of the world's most successful economies in the recent past.[2] The evident international competitiveness of Italian companies in, among other sectors, consumer electrics, clothing, cars, shoes and textiles has indeed been a striking feature of contemporary European business.

This chapter provides a case study of the multinational growth of one of the most important Italian manufacturing enterprises, Pirelli. It offers some insights into the competitive advantages of Italian firms, although it must be admitted that the Pirelli case is in some respects exceptional. Although Italy was a latecomer to multinational activity, Pirelli invested abroad very early, and can lay claim to be the first Italian multinational. The early history of Italian-based multinationals remains almost unknown,[3] and it is hoped that this case study will help to shed light on a distinctive form of European direct investment.

The Growth of Pirelli before 1914

Pirelli was founded in 1872, about 25 years after the discovery of the process of 'vulcanization', which had allowed the industrial use of natural rubber.

Giovanni Battista Pirelli, after having obtained a degree in engineering in Milan, travelled to Switzerland, Germany, Belgium and France in order to attain the essential knowledge of this type of production. He returned with the firm intention of establishing a rubber industry in Italy. In 1872, thanks to the support of some Milanese industrialists, he managed to raise a capital of 215 000 Lit. (Italian Lire), with which he founded the limited share partnership company 'G.B. Pirelli & Co.'.[4]

During the first years of activity the production of the firm was limited to medical and sporting articles, waterproof fabrics and to various other commercial products which covered a big part of the Italian market. Exports began in 1875, mainly to Switzerland, and later to France and Spain. But the volume was very modest, and in 1883 the level destined for export was still only about 4 per cent of total turnover.[5]

The turning point in the history of the company could be said to have been 1879, when Pirelli started the production of insulated electrical conductors. This was to be one of the factors leading to the firm beginning multinational production at the beginning of the next century. This sector of production would flank that of rubber over the years, constituting one of the strategic bases for the future development of the firm. The rapid growth of this production, due to the progressive electrification of Italy, rendered it necessary to restructure the organization and partnership of the firm, which in 1883 was transformed into the joint stock company Pirelli & Co., with a capital of 2 million Lit.

Another decisive step was made in 1886 with the construction of a plant for the production of submarine cables. The first Italian telegraphic network which connected Italy to its islands was realized by a British enterprise which was the first in Europe to carry out this type of work. When it became necessary to integrate this network with 12 new submarine cables, Pirelli managed to win the contract from the Italian government to construct and lay the cables. Pirelli was given the responsibility for maintaining the new network, as well as the previously laid one, for the following 20 years.[6]

Pirelli entered into a branch of production technically far advanced for that era, establishing itself as the only firm in its field in Italy, and one of the very few in Europe. Such a radical step required a further increase in company capital, which was raised from 2 to 5.5 million Lit., and the issuing of debenture bonds for 3 million Lit. The need for sophisticated technology also induced Pirelli to seek collaboration with certain British companies. In particular, technical help was received from Eastern Telegraph Co. and Henley Telegraph Works, and this collaboration continued even after the technological gap between the Italian firm and the British ones had been filled.

Over time, considerable sums were invested in laboratories, and in the training of specialized personnel and research. The volume of government orders increased sharply as Italian colonial operations in East Africa intensified, enabling Pirelli to expand production. The success of the first accomplishments and growing prestige opened the way to new markets. Particularly important was a contract signed with the Spanish government to furnish and lay down submarine cables. In 1892 the level represented by the cables and conductor sectors was 21.5 per cent of the entire production. It reached a peak of 53.7 per cent in 1912. Exports, which in 1889 represented 18.1 per cent of total turnover, reached 32 per cent in 1900.[7]

At the beginning of the 20th century, Pirelli presented itself on the world market with a technology in the field of conductors equal to that of its Anglo-American rivals. In the very high tension cable sector, it could indeed boast a worldwide supremacy, as was shown at the electrotechnical congress of St Louis in 1904. It was recognized by the American Electrical Society which awarded Pirelli substantial orders for these cables in 1905.[8]

From 1890 Pirelli also entered into another branch of production, that of tyres for velocipedes, which after the first application by John Boyd Dunlop in 1888 had spread rapidly. In 1896 production started on a new kind of bicycle tyre which was patented by Pirelli itself. In 1906, after a difficult start, production began on automobile tyres.

By the beginning of the century the three main branches of Pirelli production were well defined: electrical conductors, miscellaneous rubber articles and tyres. The basis had been laid for the firm to become a multinational.

The first direct investments abroad: 1902 to 1920

From the beginning of its development, Pirelli was driven towards expansion abroad because of the insufficiency of its home market. In the words of Alberto Pirelli in 1946, 'We found ... in the extending of our activities abroad those bases which our stronger foreign competitors have already in their internal market'.[9] The limits of the national market were made still more narrow by Germany's predominant financial and industrial presence in Italy, particularly in the electrical and electrotechnical sector, which is examined by Peter Hertner in Chapter 7 in this book. German companies were equally active in countries such as Spain and Argentina, which represented important export markets for Pirelli. For example, one-half of the electrical products imported into Argentina between 1903 and 1913 came from Germany.[10]

In Italy, Pirelli followed a similar policy to the German companies of buying substantial shares in existing electrical companies, and promoting new ventures. In 1883 G.B. Pirelli became one of the founders of Edison, which was destined to become within a few years one of the major electrical companies in Italy. Pirelli in 1897 became part of the administrative board of directors of the Credito Italiano, a business bank second only to the Banca Commerciale, which had been founded with a substantial amount of German capital. Both the Banca Commerciale and the Credito Italiano owned substantial shares in Italian electrical companies.

These strategies strengthened Pirelli's position in the Italian market, but could do little to combat the fierce German onslaught on its traditional export markets, above all in Latin America. A more radical strategy was required, and this was to engage in production abroad.

The first important direct investment was made in Spain. The rising custom duties on conductor wire convinced Pirelli in 1901 to construct a plant to manufacture electrical conductors at Villaneuva y Geltrú in 1901. It began production in the following year. This initiative was preceded by an agreement with the Société Française pour l'Industrie et les Mines de Paris and the Spanish Compagnie Asturienne, controlled by the former. This agreement provided for the supply of copper for the electrical conductors by the Compagnie Asturienne at a particularly favourable price in exchange for participating shares in the new firm. [11]

In 1911 Pirelli also purchased a share in Sociedad Italo-Argentina de Electricidad, in collaboration with the firms Franco Tosi and Motor, the latter controlled by Brown Boveri. This Italo-Argentinian company was founded in that year to open a way into the Argentinian market, and to counteract the 'financial influence of ... many competitors, especially German ones'. [12] In 1913 all shares were concentrated together in a Swiss financial holding company, the Columbus, which had the objective of acquiring shares in Latin American electrical companies. This initiative made it possible for Pirelli to effect business alliances with some important players in the Swiss financial world; while it also allowed the Italian firm to penetrate Paraguay, Venezuela and Peru. In those countries, shares were bought in electrical companies, which then gave preference to Pirelli products.

The policies adopted on the important British and American markets were different, however. In the first case, Pirelli had had an agreement with the General Electric Company (GEC) of London since 1895 which gave the British firm exclusive rights to distribute Pirelli products on the British market. This accord was consolidated over the years, and led to the establishment in 1909 of Pirelli Ltd, a trading company to sell Pirelli products and to purchase raw materials 'for the whole group'. [13] The volume of business grew to such an extent that it became more convenient to produce directly in Britain. So in 1913 the Pirelli General Cable Works Ltd was founded, as a joint venture with a cable and conductor production plant at Southampton. The capital was divided in half between Pirelli Ltd and GEC. Pirelli was thereby able to widen its market further, taking advantage of being able to share costs and risks, and gaining access to GEC's extensive commercial network and participation in many other electrical companies. In return, Pirelli offered the British company its avant-garde technology, an already tested management, and an assurance of a dividend not less than 6 per cent as established in the contract. [14] The advantage of one complemented the other, and the constant increase in production, which in some years exceeded that of the Pirelli Italian factories for the same category of products, was a confirmation of the success of the enterprise.

In the United States, Pirelli followed the same strategy, collaborating with local partners. Particularly close technical relations were established with the General Electric Co. of New York. General Electric was granted a licence to produce Pirelli's patented fluid oil high-tension cables, so that Pirelli's supremacy in this field of production on the world market was confirmed. This new type of cable could double the running tension of cables, and was installed in 1927 in Chicago for Commonwealth Edison Co., and also in New York for New York Edison Co. In all, 87 km of fluid oil cable carrying 140 000 volts was laid. Half the cable was manufactured in Milan, and the other half in the United States by General Electric from Pirelli's patent design.[15]

Substantial agreements were also reached with some American multinational enterprises (mnes) active in the telephone industry. Through these, for example, Pirelli formed a syndicate in 1920 with Western Electric Incorporated of New York to install the interurban telephone line in Spain and Spanish overseas possessions.[16] In 1921, in participation with a branch of the American ITT, SIRTI (Italian Interurban Telephone Network Company) was formed. This reinforced Pirelli's position in the field of telecommunications and led to the securing of a contract for the production and installation of an underground telephone cable between Turin, Milan and Genoa.[17]

Reorganization after the First World War

On the eve of the First World War, Pirelli's international presence as a multinational was well established. Foreign expansion had accelerated the growth of the firm. Company capital rose from 7 million Lit. in 1904, to 17.5 million in 1912, and 21 million in 1914. Turnover rose from 31.5 million Lit. in 1911, to 42 million in 1912, and to 47.5 million in 1914, one-quarter of which was from exports. Dividends were maintained at an average of 9 per cent, reaching 11 per cent in some cases, up until 1913.

The enormous growth of internal demand brought on by the war further increased production. The Italian plant supplied a large part of the Italian armed force's total consumption: 80 per cent of the electrical wire for field telegraph and telephones; pneumatic, semi-pneumatic and solid rubber tyres for military vehicles, bicycles and aeroplanes; and a wide variety of miscellaneous articles for marine, aviation and army use.[18] Pirelli's turnover increased from 64 million Lit. in 1915, to 90 million in 1916, 165 million in 1917, and to 190 million in 1918. The number of employees rose from 3500 in 1914 to 10 000 in 1918. Foreign factories not only almost doubled their turnover, but in some cases considerably widened their range of production. The plant at Villaneuva y Geltrú, for example, started production of solid rubber tyres in 1917, and in the following year had a lamination and wire drawing mill in operation, which could reduce copper ingots to a thread of 0.08 mm in diameter.[19]

This big growth both in Italy and abroad revealed that the organizational structure of Pirelli, which had changed very little since the firm began, was inadequate. The structure was based on a rather simple scheme, and was strictly functional. The firm was divided into departments of production in terms of product, with a sales department, a purchasing office, a technical department, and so on. The directors of these departments had only technical duties, while the management controlled production and sales following an out-moded 19th-century organization.

This sort of structure was not well-suited to the strategies of diversification and vertical integration that Pirelli was pursuing. A radical structural reorganization began during the war, and progressed in stages until the beginning of the 1920s. The first step was the setting up of a 'central directorate for conductors'. This put together all the divisions and offices connected with production and sale of electrical conductors, becoming an organization complete within itself, with its own internal budget. In the choice of the 'technical director', strict production considerations had prevailed, but in the appointment of the 'director general' it was managerial qualities that were more valued. Shortly afterwards, and on a similar basis, a 'central directorate for tyres' was set up, to bring together production and sales of tyres and miscellaneous rubber products.[20] Considerable decentralization was achieved with production subdivided into categories of diverse products, promoting in this way higher responsibility in the technical staff, and utilizing managerial capacity to its optimum.

The consequences of the war made themselves felt also within the international organization of the whole group, which by now was becoming too big to be entirely controlled from Milan.

From 1902 the factories constructed abroad were directly and legally dependent on Pirelli & Co., as were all other Italian factories. The only difference was in the fact that they were placed under the control of a Milan-based 'foreign office', which dealt directly with almost all problems of management of these factories. All technicians and managers were Italian, while local workers were recruited for less qualified work. The growth during the war years placed this type of relationship between the parent company and its branches under strain. New problems arose of a fiscal kind and some difficulty in the relationship with local administrations was also encountered. The centralized management structure could not cope with the new demands of co-ordination and programming on an international scale. All these facts induced the management of Pirelli to reorganize the foreign subsidiaries, and the relationship between them and the parent on a new basis.

In 1917 a new company was formed, Productos Pirelli SA. This company, based in Barcelona, was legally autonomous from the Italian parent. In order to emphasize its Spanish character, well-known local financiers were invited to join the board of directors. A similar initiative was adopted in Argentina, where in the same year the branch office at Buenos Aires was transformed into a shareholder company registered as Pirelli Platense SA. Meanwhile in Britain more local personnel were engaged, both workers and managers.[21]

In 1920, a new financial company was formed, the Compagnie Internationale Pirelli. This was registered in Brussels, and it assumed control of the entire foreign operations of the group. Alberto Pirelli, second son of Giovanni Battista, was called to preside over the new company, assuming, in this way, the main responsibility in setting the development strategy of the foreign group. Each foreign company was given greater autonomy, both operational and managerial, especially in decisions affecting the market in which they operated. In 1921 a convention was signed between the Italian parent and all the foreign subsidiary companies. Under this agreement, the limits of operative autonomy were set and the boundaries of the market pertaining to each subsidiary were set.

Another aspect of the reorganization was the formation of a new joint-stock company, the Società Italiana Pirelli (SIP), in 1920 with a company capital of 1 million Lit. This became the biggest production company and the centre 'of the technical development of the group'.[22] Pirelli & Co. assumed control over both the Compagnie Internationale Pirelli and SIP. Between 1925 and 1927 Pirelli & Co. took majority control over SIP, while the latter gained control over CIP. In this way, all the shares owned by the Pirelli family members were concentrated in Pirelli & Co., the true holding company of the group, while SIP assumed operative, financial and productive functions. SIP's board of directors was increased to include, apart from Giovanni Battista Pirelli and his two sons Alberto and Piero, the three most senior central directors, Emilio Calcagni, Fabio Palandri and Guiseppe Venosta.

The inter-war years

The reorganization of the group and its new internal structure was in a certain sense a watershed between the first and second phases of multinationalization of Pirelli. While the first phase was, as we have seen, characterized by direct investment abroad in the field of cables and electrical conductors, in this new phase there was a new emphasis on tyres. This posed new investment strategy problems, and modified the face which the foreign operations of the group had had up to the end of the First World War.

In the years preceding 1914, tyre production represented about 25 per cent of Pirelli's total turnover, whilst cables and conductors represented 50 per cent. At the end of the 1920s, the relationship between the two branches had radically changed. In 1929 tyres represented 47 per cent of Pirelli's Italian production, while cables and conductors went down to 33 per cent and miscellaneous articles settled at around 20 per cent. About 40 per cent of this output was destined for export.[23]

In the 1920s a score or so of companies virtually dominated world trade in tyres. These companies had all arisen and been consolidated before the First World War. After the war, only a very few companies managed to enter the narrow circle of 'first movers' who had an already consolidated position and an international reputation. Tyre production required heavy capital investment to maintain costly research laboratories, extensive plantations in the Far East, and a widespread distribution network which had to satisfy the demands of millions of consumers. All of this required a degree of concentration and integration that only a very few enterprises, already established on the world market, were able to accomplish. Consequently, it was the same pre-war established companies which contended for the international market during this period when the headlong rise in demand, connected mainly to the development of the automobile sector, created new needs and problems in the field of technology, and of the organization of production and distribution.

After the First World War, Pirelli's position in the international motor vehicle tyre market was handicapped by its backward technology in comparison with its competitors. During the course of the war, financial resources had been concentrated almost entirely on products destined for the Army, allowing Pirelli to keep pace with competitors only in the semi- and solid rubber tyre field used mainly by heavy vehicles. No significant technological development had been made in car tyres during that period. After the war, exports to America in this sector had to be abandoned, as the market had become dominated by the huge world rubber giants. To regain competitiveness, Pirelli launched a series of initiatives designed to place itself once more at the top. In Milan the company instituted a central research laboratory, to which some of Italy's best chemists were recruited. In 1920 it bought plantations in Malaya, and on the island of Java in the Dutch East Indies, in order to secure reliable supplies of raw rubber, and to experiment with new grafts and cultivation techniques which would improve the quality and durability of the finished product.[24] Great efforts were made to rationalize the distribution network, and to relaunch its image with a publicity campaign considered avant-garde in those years.[25] On the production front, new work methods and other reorganizations significantly reduced costs.

These measures produced notable results. According to studies conducted by the US Department of Commerce, in the 1920s the international tyre trade consisted mainly of a 'competition between American and Canadian companies on one side and Franco-Italian on the other'.[26] From such data, it appeared that Italy's share of the world tyre trade rose from 7.1 per cent in 1920 to 13.3 per cent in 1924, surpassed only by France (35.4 per cent) and the USA (24.6 per cent). Italy achieved a greater share than Britain, Canada or Germany. Within Italy, Pirelli held about 65 per cent of the market, while the remaining 35 per cent was held by imports, Michelin Italia, and by small minor Italian producers. In the 1930s, due to the autarky policy adopted by the Fascist state and the consequential restrictions on imports, Pirelli's share of its home market reached about 80 per cent, with only 15 per cent remaining for Michelin Italiana. The French company continued to be Pirelli's strongest competitor throughout the inter-war years, both on the home market and in Europe.

Fdi in tyres began in the first years of the 1920s. In 1923 a new Spanish company was established, Nacional Pirelli, with a tyre factory at Manresa; in 1929 a new plant was erected in England at Burton-on-Trent; in 1930 Industrie du Caoutchouc Souple was formed in France, with the participation of Société Tréfileris and Laminoirs du Hâvre, with plants for the manufacturing of semi-pneumatic and solid rubber tyres. Other factories for tyre production and miscellaneous rubber articles were constructed in Argentina, Brazil and Belgium during the 1930s.

In some cases Pirelli took advantage of its management and organization expertise to take over small companies on the edge of bankruptcy and reorganized them on a more sound basis. This happened, for example, in the case of the Spanish plant at Manresa and also in Belgium, taken over in 1935 by Société pour le Commerce et l'Industrie du Caoutchouc (SACIC) of Brussels. After a reconstruction exercise, Pirelli merged SACIC with the Société Belge Pirelli, from which Pirelli-Sacic was born in 1939. This new company ended its first year of operation with the distribution of a dividend of 7 per cent .[27]

In Britain, the formalities and motivation for direct investment were different. In this case the drive came from the high British customs tariffs in 1927, which created huge problems for the export of tyres to this important market. The leading American tyre producers, Goodyear, Firestone and Goodrich, also established British factories at this time.[28] However, even before 1927, a project to construct a tyre factory in England had existed. Alberto Pirelli believed it indispensable to invest in what he considered 'the major competitive market in the world', even if it meant sustaining losses for some years. A presence in that market, the company believed, was important to continually test Pirelli's capabilities against major international manufacturers, and so keep alive the spur of progress, and also to acquire 'sure and opportune information'.[29] After a difficult start, by 1930 Pirelli held 1.5 per cent of the British tyre market, and 7 per cent of the semi-pneumatic and solid rubber market.[30]

If we analyse these fdis, taking the previous phase into account, it is clear that they were located in those countries where Pirelli was already established in the cable and conductor sector. In the first phase the investments in local electrical companies and updated technology had given Pirelli the main advantage over local competitors, creating favourable conditions for fdi. In the inter-war years, the main advantage against local competitors in the tyre field was due to the fact that Pirelli was an established mne. The presence in Britain, Spain, Belgium and South America of Pirelli's own cable and conductor factories and its trading companies, permitted the exploitation in tyres of good market knowledge and the prestige of a known trade-name. Moreover, the possibilities of a wider distribution of losses and cost saving due to the utilization of established structures already operating on those markets (administration, personnel, supplies, etc.) reduced risks and possible initial losses.[31]

In countries where Pirelli was not already established and/or where strong competitors operated, direct investment in the tyre industry was more problematic. Such was the case in France, the home of Michelin, one of the biggest European tyre producers. Pirelli was impeded in increasing its share of the tyre market in France both because of the high level of tariffs and the strong position of Michelin. To overcome these problems, the Milan company tried to increase exports by lowering production costs. For this purpose a tyre factory was built in Egypt in 1921. It was hoped that the low cost of labour and some raw materials would reduce the production cost so as to balance the French customs tariff.[32] But this initiative failed to deliver the desired results. In 1930 Pirelli opted for direct investment in France together with a local partner, to produce semi-pneumatic and solid rubber tyres, a sector in which Pirelli was very competitive. But in the nine years of Pirelli's management of the plant at Pont-de-Chémy, the economic results were most unsatisfactory, and the operation was sold in 1939.[33]

At the end of the 1930s the tyre sector equalled 50 per cent of total turnover, while in the foreign group of Pirelli it managed only 15 per cent. For the foreign group, the conductor sector remained the sector of strategic expansion abroad, where it represented 74 per cent of total turnover.

In 1929 Pirelli achieved the best financial results in its history. Sales exceeded 400 million Lit. Net profit reached 28 million Lit, giving a dividend of 60 Lit. per share – the highest ever registered. A good part of the profit was invested abroad. CIP increased its capital from 30 to 50 million Belgian francs. Furthermore, Pirelli established, together with the participation of Banca Sarasin & Co. of Basel, another new company in Zurich called 'Volta', the Société Anonyme pour Enterprises Electriques et Industrielles. The objective of this company was to operate in the electrotelephonic sector in international markets. In 1930 Pirelli SA, Companhia Brasileira of San Paolo in Brazil was formed in Capuava, with the minor participation of a branch of General Electric Co. of New York, to produce telephonic and electric cables. A few years later a small tyre production plant was built at the same place. In Britain a second cable plant started production in 1927 at Eastleigh.

In 1931 Pirelli joined the International Rubber Thread Association (Irta) which was constituted by all the world producers of elastic thread for textiles. Pirelli had been producing elastic thread since 1883. The substantial technical and organizational capacity required made it very difficult to produce this thread, so that only a few very big firms in the world were able to realize it. In fact, only 11 members made up this syndicate which covered almost the whole world market. Pirelli allied with the United States Rubber Co., the manufacturers of the elastic thread Revere. Pirelli-Revere was founded, and was allocated the biggest share of the European market (21.04 per cent).[34]

In the late 1930s a large-scale reorganization of Pirelli's foreign operations was undertaken, which involved a shift in the centre of control from Belgium to Switzerland. In December 1937, together with the Banca Sarasin of Brazil, Pirelli Holding was founded with its seat in Brazil. This company started off with a capital of 12 million Swiss francs, which was increased to 18 million Swiss francs a short while later. In 1938 Pirelli Holding merged with Volta and officially replaced CIP in 1940 as the controller of all the foreign operations. In 1941 Societá Italiana Pirelli changed its trade name to Pirelli Spa (joint stock company). This operation was not only allowed more space for the financial participation of Swiss partners, but through a complex mechanism of equity exchange, Pirelli reduced its participation inside the Swiss holding of 30 per cent, while still holding management control over it. This new structure allowed Pirelli to survive the war years without a major crisis. This was because *de jure* Pirelli was a minority shareholder of the holding which controlled the foreign group of the company. It was only because of this that the Allied governments recognized the Swiss 'status' of the enterprise so, as Alberto Pirelli wrote, 'they did not take any hostile measures against the foreign companies controlled by Pirelli Holding'.[35]

The 'economic miracle' years

In spite of the damage suffered by the Milan factories during the Second World War, Pirelli owned 12 plants in five different countries when the conflict ended. After the damaged plants' reconstruction, Pirelli enjoyed a remarkable growth, especially in the 1950s and 1960s. Italy experienced fast growth rates in these years, as did most Western European economies apart from Britain, and there was a marked restructuring of the economy, with a shift of workers out of agriculture.[36] The consequent expansion of the domestic Italian market, above all in the automobile, agricultural and industrial vehicle sectors, enabled Pirelli Spa, to start mass tyre production for the first time. Both in Italy and abroad, large sums were invested in building new plants and improving research and development potential in order to meet increasing market demand volume and to offer more competitive products. The new series of truck tyres, Anteo, Atlante and Zeus were successful during the 1950s. The Rolle, Stelvio and Sempione series 'introduced the concept of mass production, that is: one product available for every car size, overcoming the old concept of one tyre for each type of car'.[37]

Pirelli's presence abroad, through directly-owned factories, was powerfully strengthened in every sector, even though cables and conductors continued to predominate. Investment abroad was particularly great during the 1960s. In 1962 the Italian government nationalized all electrical companies, creating ENEL (the National Electrical Energy Corporation). All the alliances and financial structures that the Pirelli family had forged for almost a century with the biggest electrical companies were, as a result, upset. However, although Pirelli suffered a short-term financial shock, the 7 billion Lit. received in compensation was available to be invested abroad.

During the 1950s and 1960s, resources went largely towards strengthening Pirelli's position in regions where it already had a base. Among these were Argentina, Brazil, Spain, Britain and Belgium. Plants were multiplied and diversification of products was undertaken. Investments in new areas were also made, however. In Latin America, Pirelli's presence reached Peru, where a cable plant was constructed. In Mexico, Condumex was founded in alliance with Anaconda Cables with three cable plants. For the first time direct investments were made in North America. Pirelli Canada Co. was constituted in St Johns, Quebec, and by the close of the 1960s it controlled four cable plants.

In tyres, direct investment was undertaken in Greece and Turkey. Both markets showed good potential for expansion due to the general post-war economic recovery and low labour costs. Pirelli Hellas was founded in Athens and Turk Pirelli Lastikleri in Istanbul. But the most important investment was made in Germany during the first years of the 1960s, with the merger between Pirelli and Veith Gummiwerke. From this transaction, Pirelli Veith was founded with a capital of 24 million DM. The European Community (EC), established in 1957, initiated a process of European economic integration. For large and solid European companies such as Pirelli, technologically and financially well placed to confront the continental market, this provided a good opportunity for growth. But smaller companies like Veith Gummiwerke, operating almost exclusively on their national market, could not cope or stand up to these changes. The only alternative was to merge with the bigger producers or abandon the market altogether. With this transaction, Pirelli increased its share of one of the largest European markets, undermining even the position of Continental, the German giant, and laying down a solid basis for further expansion towards northern European and Eastern markets. Also in France, Pirelli France was established, with a plant to produce foam rubber.[38]

The pre-war corporate structure was changed again. In 1954 Pirelli Holding SA, based in Basel, became Société Internationale Pirelli (SIP), holding control over the foreign operations of the group. During the 1960s, SIP ceded to Pirelli Spa control over plants seated in EC countries against a compensation of shares. The exchange of shares between the two companies, and between them and Pirelli & Co., became more intertwined. In April 1965, Alberto Pirelli left his son, Leopoldo, to preside over Pirelli Spa, which was still the true parent company of the group.

By the end of the 1960s, the Pirelli group employed 76 000 people, had a total turnover of 700 billion Lit., and owned 82 plants in Italy and abroad. Cable production represented 40 per cent of total group production, tyres 45 per cent, and miscellaneous articles 15 per cent. Within the foreign group, controlled by SIP, cable production was the dominant activity with 60 per cent of the total production, compared to 30 per cent for tyres, and miscellaneous articles 10 per cent. In Pirelli Spa activities, tyre production prevailed with 45 per cent, cables 35 per cent and miscellaneous articles 20 per cent.[39]

Nevertheless, even at the end of the 1960s, Pirelli had not yet reached the dimensions comparable to those of its strongest world competitors. Furthermore, the liberalizing of the European market had attracted considerable investments from American multinationals such as Goodyear, Firestone, Uniroyal and Goodrich. In particular, Firestone and Goodrich had invested in Italy, establishing plants in the central and southern areas. These two companies were true world giants whose total turnovers reached respectively US$ 3215.3 and 2278.9 million, against Pirelli's US$ 1067.1 million in the rubber sector.[40] To keep pace with such competitors, both on the home and world markets, it was necessary to reach a size large enough to allow decreasing unitary costs, scale economies and an intensification of research and development efforts. There was a pressing need, therefore, for Pirelli to grow in order to attain a level closer to that of its American competitors.

In order to achieve this objective, one route was to associate Pirelli with another big industrial group, in the hope of creating a European rubber giant which was competitive on the world market. The only company in Europe in possession of the required characteristics for such an operation was Dunlop, with whom Pirelli had already established a good relationship. During the 1960s Dunlop had passed through rather similar problems to Pirelli, and it needed to achieve a greater size in order to maintain itself at the frontiers of technology in tyres. The apparent synergy between the British and Italian firms led to the merger of the two companies, which was accomplished in December 1970, giving birth to the giant Pirelli-

Dunlop Union. It acquired third place in the world industry, after Goodyear and Firestone, and with plants spread on all continents. Pirelli's dowry was its technical know-how and productive capacity, plus a sound worldwide prestige in the tyre and cable sector. Dunlop could supply its recognized excellence in the field of natural and synthetic rubber, together with the mechanics of application.

As a consequence of the merger, within the Pirelli group another company was founded: Industria Pirelli Spa (joint-stock company). This company took over the management of all industrial activities in Italy, and the control over their associated companies in France, Belgium and Germany, as well as over all activities not included in the Pirelli-Dunlop Union. Pirelli Spa also became a holding company which, together with SIP, co-operated to maintain control over all foreign companies outside the EC.[41]

The difficult years – 1970s

After the expansion of the 1960s, the world tyre market went into recession in the following decade. The world oil crisis of 1973–4, with its accompanying increase in raw material costs, decrease in car production, and market saturation, reduced world demand. There was a new emphasis on cost-saving technologies, to which some firms responded more effectively than others. Michelin had pioneered the longer-wearing radial tyre in the post-war decades, and demand for this soared in the United States in the 1970s. Goodyear also moved successfully and rapidly into radial production, but other American firms such as Firestone floundered and lost market share. In contrast, the Japanese tyre company, Bridgestone, flourished, and embarked on fdi in the United States.[42]

In this challenging era for the tyre industry, neither Pirelli nor Dunlop fared well. They were extremely slow to respond to the American demand for radials. The terms of their alliance were extremely complex, and worked to prevent serious integration between two groups.[43] They always retained their own trade-marks and internal structures. Pirelli passed through a crisis period of grand proportions in the tyre sector between 1971 and 1975. It lost market share in the world market and suffered a decrease in overall production of 20 per cent.[44] Furthermore, the critical situation of the Italian economy, harsh union struggles, and, above all, erroneously placed investment programmes in tyre development deepened the crisis even further. Dunlop initially enjoyed more success, but by the end of the 1970s was also in great difficulties. This situation weakened the reciprocal trust between the partners leading to the dissolution of the Union in 1981. Meanwhile Dunlop never recovered from the disastrous Pirelli alliance. In the early 1980s it sold most of its European tyre facilities to Sumitomo, formerly its own Japanese affiliate, and in 1985 the remainder of the group was acquired by the British conglomerate BTR.[45]

If Pirelli's foreign group of companies had not held its place well during the 1970s, and not continued to produce profits, especially in the conductor and cable sector, the crisis for Pirelli might also have been terminal. However, Pirelli's substantial investment in R. & D. in this sector yielded substantial rewards, allowing targets to be reached in both very high-tension cables and in telecommunications. Optic cables were devised which could carry 16 000 possible contemporary communications, compared with only 2500 using the traditional system, opening up big market opportunities.

Pirelli was able to further enlarge its presence abroad in this sector. In 1978 Pirelli Enterprise was founded in the United States. This company bought the five plants of General Cable Co., putting them under the control of Pirelli Cable Co. In 1979, seven cable plants were bought in France from Trefilmétaux, plus another on the Ivory Coast. Together, those eight plants were put under the control of Treficable Pirelli. These and other acquisitions made Pirelli the world leader in cable production. With SIP, the share of cable production in total Pirelli production reached 71 per cent in 1980, while tyres dropped to 23 per cent. The geographical distribution of assets also changed, with a new emphasis on Europe, the United States and Australia, and decreasing investment in South America.[46]

A high-level strategy choice was changing SIP's dimension and role within the group. This was marked by the fact that Leopoldo Pirelli, the grandson of the founder of the group, took over the position of Vice President. In addition, a redefining of the relationship between this and the other Pirelli group companies could no longer be postponed. The relationship between SIP and Pirelli Spa had become particularly unbalanced especially in relation to the specific competence traditionally assigned to each of them. Pirelli Spa, which had always carried out the role of parent company, had been badly hit by the tyre crisis. It was now surpassed by SIP, both in volume of business and availability of resources. To balance this disequilibrium within the different centres of the group, a redesigning of the company structure was necessary. To this purpose, Pirelli Société Générale (Psg), was constituted. It was seated in Basel, with a capital of 135.1 million Swiss francs, divided between SIP and Pirelli Spa. Through the interchange of shares, Pirelli Spa and SIP arranged the equalizing of their own participation in all companies throughout the group. In this way, both companies now became the parent company, leaving Psg the task of co-ordination and strategy definition.[47]

Recovery in the 1980s

After the difficulties suffered during the 1970s, the reformation and recovery of the tyre sector posed the crucial test for the adequacy of the new corporate structure. Big investments were made to diversify production and improve quality. Both in Italy and abroad, large investments were put into the telecommunications and electronic fields. Pirelli acquired, during the first years of the 1980s, 5 per cent of the Italian national telephone corporation which was controlled by the finance company Stet. In the United States, it assumed control of David System in Silicon Valley, producers of technologically-advanced communications systems. A majority share of 60 per cent was also bought in Focom System, a British company specializing in data collection and transmission.

The previous investments of more than US$ 100 million in research and development in the tyre sector began to bear fruit. A new series called 'large' was launched on the market. Its innovative characteristics allowed Pirelli to challenge all its major competitors, and to considerably increase sales on the international market. Net profit reached 140 billion Lit. in 1984, double that of the previous year. Total turnover attained 6800 billion Lit., with an increase of 14 per cent against 1983. During this same period former giants such as Dunlop were destroyed, and Pirelli's achievements were considerable.[48]

Another new reorganization of the company was undertaken in 1988. SIP became the financial company of the entire group, taking control over Pirelli Spa. All the other companies operating throughout the world came under the control of Pirelli Spa, including Industrie Pirelli Spa which controlled all the Italian activities of the group, and Pirelli Tyre Co., which grouped all the tyre-producing companies together.

In spite of the big growth in the tyre sector, the management continued to believe that to hold a strong position on the world market in the near future, it was necessary that Pirelli grow as large as possible, ideally to match the size of Michelin. After the failure of the Dunlop merger, Pirelli succeeded, not without a struggle, to achieve fifth place in the world. But this was not enough. The desire to grow remained. The last years of the 1980s saw an unsuccessful attempt to acquire Firestone. This was followed, in 1990, by a disastrously unsuccessful takeover bid for Continental of Germany in an ambitious strategy to create a European rival to Michelin. Pirelli's misjudgement of German business practices and culture resulted in the failure of the bid, and in losses in 1991 of hundreds of millions of US dollars through indemnities offered to Pirelli's allies in the abortive offer.[49] The fiasco revealed, if nothing else, the continuing substantial differences in the business cultures of different European countries, even as they approached the Single Market.

Conclusion

This chapter has examined the international growth of Pirelli, a pioneer Italian multinational whose first fdi took place before the First World War. Like many Dutch and Swedish firms, Pirelli was initially prompted to engage in fdi by the limitations of its domestic market, which was a relatively low per capita income one before the First World War, and one which had to be shared with powerful German firms. The firm acquired ownership advantages through a long-term willingness to engage in applied research, and it also developed managerial advantages. This private firm was organized through, to Anglo-American eyes, a confusing and complex system of holding companies, but in a long-term perspective it can be seen that corporate structures were regularly renewed in response to changing environmental circumstances. Pirelli's organizational capability was considerable, enabling it both to transfer ownership advantages developed in one industry to other activities, and to survive a major political trauma such as the Second World War with a minimum of disruption.

Nevertheless, there were evident limitations to the organizational capability of the Italian firm. In particular, its attempts to grow through cross-border merger and acquisitions in the 1970s and the 1980s were regularly undermined by organizational and cross-cultural problems. Like many Italian firms, Pirelli found it difficult to forge the international alliances used by other European, American and Japanese multinationals in the contemporary period to enhance their competitive advantages. Arguably Pirelli's problems at the beginning of the 1990s, like those of Fiat and Olivetti, were an indication that the Italian tradition of family capitalism was, finally, becoming a grave disability in the era of global business.[50] However, the continuing international competitiveness of other Italian family enterprises, such as Benetton and Ferruzzi-Montedison, made a final verdict on this matter impossible.

Notes

1. I would like to thank the editors for rewriting an earlier version of this chapter.
2. Porter, M. *The Competitive Advantage of Nations*, London, 1990, pp. 421–53.
3. Hertner, P. and Jones, G., 'Multinationals: Theory and History', in P. Hertner and G. Jones, (eds), *Multinationals: Theory and History*, Aldershot, 1986, p. 9. There is data on the pre-1914 direct investments of Fiat in the United States in Wilkins, M., *The History of Foreign Investment in the United States to* 1914, Cambridge, Mass, 1989, pp. 420–1, 423.
4. Pirelli, A., *La Pirelli. Vita di una azienda industriale*, Milan, 1946, pp. 11–12.
5. Bezza, B., 'L'attività multinazionale della Pirelli (1883–1914)', *Società e Storia*, 1987, **35**, (9), 55.
6. Idem note 4, pp. 25-6.
7. Idem note 5, p. 69.
8. Idem note 4, p. 44.
9. Idem note 4, p. 60.
10. Hertner, P., 'German Multinational Enterprises before 1914. Some Case Studies', paper presented to a workshop on 'The early phase of multinational enterprises in Germany, France and Italy, held at the European University Institute, Florence, in 1983.
11. Idem note 5, pp. 71–2.
12. Idem note 4, p. 116
13. Idem note 4, p. 63.
14. Archivio storico delle industrie Pirelli, document (doc.) 944. See also Jones, G., 'Foreign multinationals and British Industry before 1945', *Economic History Review*, 2nd ser., 1988, XLI, 3, p. 431.
15. Idem note 14, Note illustrate sugli impianti di cavi ad altissima tensione in esercizio a New York e Chicago, doc. 1508.
16. Idem note 14, Agreement for the formation of a Syndicate for the study and solution of problems relating to the installation and operation of interurban telephone lines in Spain, Spanish Colonies and Spanish possessions, doc. 1219.
17. Idem note 14, The National City Company, The Pirelli Company of Italy: An Unbroken Dividend Record for the Last Thirty-Seven Years, New York, 1929, doc. 1598. See also Chapter 7 in this book.
18. *Pirelli e C. nel suo cinquantenario, 1872-1922*, Milan, 1922, pp. 35, 42-3.
19. Idem note 14, Stabilimenti di Villaneuva y Geltrù, doc. 1323.
20. Idem note 14, doc. 1087.

21.   Idem note 14, Viaggio in Inghilterra del Sig. Alberto Pirelli, January 1917, doc. 1132.
22.   Idem note 14, Convenzione fra la società Pirelli e C. e le società da essa derivate, 1921, doc. 1298.
23.   Montenegro, A., 'La Pirelli tra le due guerre mondiali' in P. Anelli, G. Bonvini, A. Montenegro, and P. Bolchini, *Pirelli 1914-1980. Strategia aziendale e relazioni industriali nella storia di una multinazionale*, vol. 1, Milan, 1985, p. 43.
24.   Idem note 14, Note generali di carattere economico sulle piantagioni, 10 December 1944, file 2181.
25.   Idem note 14, doc. 1598.
26.   Quoted in ASP, idem note 14, doc. 1422.
27.   Idem note 14, CIP, Rapports présentés à l'Assemblée générale ordinaire, 12 March 1940, doc. 2096.
28.   Jones, G., 'The Multinational Expansion of Dunlop, 1890-1939', in G. Jones, (ed.), *British Multinationals: Origins, Management and Performance*, Aldershot, 1986, p. 33.
29.   Idem note 4, p. 61.
30.   Idem note 14, Relazione del viaggio in Inghilterra del dott.Luzzatto, September 1930, doc. 65.
31.   Concerning this kind of advantage see Dunning, J.H., *International Production and the Multinational Enterprise*, London, 1981, p. 27.
32.   Idem note 14, Confronto fra i costi di produzione delle coperture auto in Egitto ed in Italia, 28 September 1921, file 1296.
33.   Idem note 14, CIP, Rapports présentés à l'Assemblée générale ordinaire, 17 March 1938, doc. 1996.
34.   Idem note 14, Statuto sociale della International Rubber Thread Association, doc. 1666.
35.   Idem note 4, pp. 61–2.
36.   Castronovo, V., 'La storia economica' in *Storia d'Italia. Dall'Unità ad oggi*, vol. 4, Turin, 1975, p. 402.
37.   Bolchini, P., 'Il gruppo Pirelli-Dunlop: gli anni più lunghi', in P. Anelli, *et al.*, *Pirelli 1914–1980*, idem note 23, vol. 2, p. 18.
38.   Bolchini, P. 'Lo sviluppo economico e finanziario del gruppo Pirelli', *Critica marxista*, 1964, **6** (2), pp. 39–61.
39.   Idem note 37, p. 17.
40.   'Fortune's Directory of the 500 largest U.S. Industrial Corporations for 1969', in *Fortune*, May 1970; 'Fortune's Directory of the 100 Largest Industrials outside the US', in *Fortune*, August 1970.
41.   Idem note 37, pp. 46–50.
42.   Stopford, J. and Turner, L., *Britain and the Multinationals*, Chichester, 1985, pp. 86–7.
43.   Ibid.
44.   Idem note 37, pp. 103–5, 108–11.
45.   Idem note 42, p. 87. Dunlop's relationship with Sumitomo is discussed in Davenport-Hines, R.P.T. and Jones, G., 'British Business in Japan since 1868', in R.P.T. Davenport-Hines and Geoffrey Jones, (eds), *British Business in Asia since 1860*, Cambridge, 1989, pp. 225–6, 233, 237, 242.
46.   Idem note 37, pp. 148–9.
47.   Idem note 37, pp. 161–3.
48.   La Ferla, M. and Sisti, L. 'Miracolo a Milano', *L'Espresso*, 17 March 1985,**11** (31).
49.   'Pirelli falls into a hidden chasm', *Financial Times*, 4 December 1991.
50.   'Leaders that have lost their way', *Financial Times*, 21 January 1992.

10 Agfa-Gevaert and Belgian multinational enterprise[1]

Greta Devos

Belgium has not usually been regarded as one of the smaller European economies, such as the Netherlands or Switzerland, which have been prominent in generating multinational enterprise (mne). In fact, before the First World War, Belgium was an extremely active foreign investor, and a considerable amount of this seems likely to have taken the form of direct investment. However, after 1918, Belgian direct investment became far less extensive. In striking continuity up to the present day, Belgian multinational investment remained relatively small, with much of it clustered in the extractive and service sectors, and in the form of holding companies.

This chapter begins with a survey of the history of Belgian multinationals, drawing attention to the considerable gaps in our knowledge. It then provides a case study of the firm of Gevaert, which can be taken to represent some 'typical' features of Belgian international business activity. This firm grew to be a leading player in the European photochemical industry and engaged in successful international expansion. Then, after some extraordinary decades, there was a decline of competitiveness. The firm entered a pioneering transnational merger with the German company Agfa, only to pass under full German ownership in the 1980s.

Belgian mne in perspective

There is a large literature on Belgian business and financial activity in foreign countries in the 19th century, but much of it is hard to relate to modern concepts of the mne.[2] Most authors do not distinguish between portfolio and direct investment. In part, this is because much of the research is based on the published statutes of the numerous limited companies founded to operate abroad under the liberal Belgian company legislation of 18 May 1873. Belgium had a special legal status for a *société anonyme* which carried out most or all of its activities abroad. Nearly 14 per cent of all Belgian limited liability companies created between 1874 and 1914 carried out their activities abroad. The information in the published statutes does not permit an easy classification into direct or other investments. It also exaggerates the amount of Belgian capital because foreign interests, especially

French, often made use of Belgian corporate entities because of the liberal legal framework.

The distinction between direct and other investments is further complicated by the important role of the 'mixed' banks in Belgium. The growth of Belgian investments abroad was largely supported by the development and important role of these 'mixed' banks. As institutions they issued long-term claims to hold long-term industrial assets, and at the same time they engaged in the typical activities of a commercial bank. Through financial subsidiaries they held controlling interests in some big industrial corporations, and helped those companies financially to carry out their industrial activities and investment projects in Belgium and abroad by providing them with funds in current account.[3] The activities abroad of such 'mixed' banks were particularly important from the last quarter of the 19th century onwards. Besides such purely financial aid, they also offered technical expertise and commercial guidance in foreign markets to their industrial affiliated companies. This was especially helpful in periods of strengthened protectionism in the host countries. However the multinational character of these investments, especially those of the autonomous holdings, is at times difficult to detect.

Nevertheless, a general outline of Belgian direct investment can be established. The country became a large foreign investor in the 19th century. It would seem that much of this investment was direct, but, as in the British case, this often took the form of 'free-standing' companies and other forms of corporate structure rather different from the classic, American-style, multinational. Direct investment activity became noteworthy in the middle of the century, particularly in the mining sector. The increasing shortage of national deposits of minerals forced the metallurgical industry to go and search for raw materials first in neighbouring, and later in more distant, countries. This tendency should not be generalized, though. The large non-ferro metals firm Vieille Montagne, which settled in Prussia in the early 1850s, did not do this with the sole purpose of exploiting ore mines, but also wanted to establish a presence in a region that was being hit by the 'railway mania', and which promised to become a considerable market for the future. The reorganization of the Silesian zinc industry by Vieille Montagne also indicated a desire to control the zinc market, an aspiration strengthened by the very early international cartel movement that it initiated between the zinc producers of the Rhineland, France, Silesia and Belgium.[4] By 1870 two Belgian multinationals, Vieille Montagne and La Providence (iron and steel) had 21 separate direct investments in foreign countries.[5] The close alliance between 'haute finance' in Brussels and the rapidly developing heavy industry in Wallonia helps to explain why Belgian investments abroad were so strongly biased towards the mining, iron and steel and non-ferro sector. Before 1905, upwards of 70 per cent of all Belgian direct investment abroad was connected to the mining sector and heavy industry.

From the 1870s, investments in public utilities, especially the tram and railway sector, were added to those in the mining sector. At first, these took the form of equity participation in foreign enterprises. In the next stage, the delivery of rails and vehicles was carried out against the payment of shares and obligations of those foreign tram and train companies. Due to the liberal company legislation of the early 1870s, investments in the public transport sector assumed a Belgian juridical structure as well. Some of them were 'tied investments', including managerial contacts at least for the duration of the loan.[6] Often these initiatives were led by 'mixed' banks or specialized holding companies. There were important service sector investments related to transport. The Belgian firm Wagon-Lits, which operated international rail services, was well-established on its international career by the time of the First World War.

Belgian direct investment in industry was not confined to the metallurgical sector, but included investments in the mirror and glass, chemicals, electrotechnical, gas and electricity industries. Schröter has recently calculated the number of Belgian direct investments in industry, and the number and geographical distribution of these are shown in Table 10.1. Schröter defines a multinational, for the purposes of his estimate, as a company with direct investment in at least two different foreign countries, or three separate investments in the same country.

Table 10.1   Fdi in industry by Belgian multinationals, 1870–1914

	1870	1880	1890	1900	1905	1910	1914
France	5	16	17	22	25	27	34
Germany	5	5	8	12	13	16	23
Italy	9	9	18	18	20	20	21
Britain	–	6	10	10	11	11	13
Russia	–	–	4	9	10	11	11
Austria-Hungary	–	–	6	6	6	6	7
Luxembourg	1	1	1	7	7	7	7
Spain	–	–	–	2	4	5	5
USA	–	–	1	3	3	3	3
Sweden	1	1	1	1	1	1	1
Netherlands	–	–	–	–	–	–	1
Total	21	38	66	90	100	107	126

Source
Schröter, H., *Multinationale Unternehmen aus kleinen Staaten bis 1914*, forthcoming.

The most attractive areas for Belgian investment, in general, in the period 1874 to 1914 were Russia (22.9 per cent), southern Europe (16.3 per cent), South America (13.8 per cent) and neighbouring European countries (12.1 per cent).[7] In this latter category, investments in France dominated. Belgian-French co-operation and French participation in Belgian companies was very strong throughout the 19th century.[8] Schröter's data show the considerable importance of France as a host country to Belgian industrial direct investment, and, conversely, the remarkably small investment in the neighbouring Dutch economy. The United States, too, attracted little Belgian investment of this kind.[9]

The First World War and its aftermath caused a major disenchantment with fdi. Belgium lost all of its 160 or more companies located in Russia following the Bolshevik Revolution. Certain investments in Germany had been taken over during the war. The increasing nationalism in Italy in the 1920s caused even more losses. During the War, the German occupier had also dismantled part of Belgian industry. As a result, investment was needed to rebuild the national industry. The grip of the mixed banks tightened, especially in the traditional sectors like coal, steel and non-ferrous metals, and there was some concentration to produce larger companies, which were better equipped to fight foreign competition on the domestic market and abroad. Firms often preferred to participate in cartels rather than undertake the risks of foreign investment. The amount of foreign capital invested in Belgian firms also declined, particularly because the revision of the legislation on limited liability companies in 1913 had made a Belgium-registered company less attractive to foreign investors.

The result was stagnation in Belgian multinational activity. During the inter-war period, only 13 new Belgian enterprises with activity abroad were founded under Belgian law. Geographically, these were oriented mainly to Central Europe.[10] Occasionally the protectionist environment of these years did prompt direct investment. For example, British tariffs encouraged Bekaert, the steel wire specialist, to open a new wire drawing unit near Sheffield in 1933.[11] However, as far as can be established, Belgian foreign investment was largely portfolio in this period, with a focus on the exploitation of colonial riches meaning that the mining sector exerted the greatest attraction to investors. In so far as there was any expansion of outward direct investment in this era, it was largely located in the extractive sector of the Belgian Congo.[12] It needs to be added, however, that only a limited amount of research has been undertaken on Belgian investment in the inter-war years, and these generalizations might yet be overturned by new empirical research.

The number of Belgian industrial investments abroad increased after the Second World War, but they accounted for less than one-third of inward direct investment in Belgium for most of the 1960s and 1970s. Conversely, Belgian indirect and portfolio investments were over ten times the level of foreign portfolio investment in Belgium.[13] Outward direct investment in manufacturing began to accelerate in the 1970s. The pioneering research carried out by Van den Bulcke and his team in the mid-1970s produced some hard data on the state of Belgian mne in this stage. This research focused on 1224 Belgian companies in manufacturing which had over 100 employees. If we consider an equity participation of at least 10 per cent in a subsidiary abroad as direct investment, then 96 of the Belgian companies with over 100 employees controlled a total of 609 industrial subsidiaries abroad in 1976. In addition, 'industrial holding companies' owned 138 industrial outlets. Including the 44 establishments abroad in the construction and engineering sector, this amounted to a total of 1026 industrial affiliates abroad in the mid-1970s.[14] Most of these investments were located in neighbouring countries.[15] France attracted most, followed by the Netherlands and West Germany. Two-thirds of Belgian enterprises abroad was settled in the EC. Developing countries (not counting Zaire) accounted for only 13 per cent. Belgian direct investment appeared very concentrated, with the five biggest enterprises combined representing no less than 43 per cent of the industrial subsidiaries abroad.[16] With regard to sectors, the metallurgical and the chemical industries were the most active.

A further perspective on Belgian direct investment came with the research published by the Institut Royal des Relations Internationales in 1987. While the Van den Bulcke project was based on data collected from companies, this new study included information from Belgian embassies abroad, as well as Belgian companies, in a survey covering the 1978 to 1983 period. It included both Zaire and the agrarian and the service sector in its investigation. The research indicated the importance of direct investment in the service sector, which was greater than in industry, and the concentration of investment in Europe, Canada, the US and Japan. The enterprises in the agrarian sector, in its broad sense, were located mainly in Africa, more specifically Zaire, yet even there Belgian enterprises in the industrial or service sectors predominated.[17]

In the early 1980s Belgium counted for a modest 1.2 per cent of the stock world fdi (see Table 1.2, p. 10) Dutch fdi was over five times larger. There was undoubtedly a range of explanations for the modesty of Belgian direct investment, but the traditional heavy industrial bias of the economy is a possible explanation.[18] Also important was the fact that Belgium still possessed few very large companies, in contrast to the more concentrated business sectors in some other smaller European economies. In 1991, the largest Belgian company (by market capitalization) was Petrofina, but it was ranked only 58th in the list of the 500 largest European companies.[19] Belgian companies often appeared modest in their international ambitions, the smaller enterprises satisfying themselves with a commercial office abroad.

The growth of Gevaert

The Gevaert company had a very modest origin. Its founder, Lieven Gevaert, was the son of a gilder and picture framer. At the age of 21 he became established as an independent portrait photographer, especially known for printing photographs on ceramics and china. This speciality led him to manufacture collodion materials of higher quality. As a self-made man he experimented with various kinds of paper and chemical products and he succeeded in developing high-quality photographic paper called Calcium on a rapidly-growing scale, due to his invention of a simple semi-automatic machine for coating paper with emulsion.[20]

With the financial support of some local moneylenders, a kind of partnership limited by shares, L. Gevaert & Cie, was founded in 1894.[21] Its limited capital of

20 000 BF was meant to achieve an output of Calcium paper on a larger scale. The initial customers were local photographers. The domestic market position improved quickly. Out of the eight enterprises that operated in the Belgian photochemical industry in 1896, six focused on manufacturing photographic plates. They were not competitors because the more plates they sold, the more print and developing paper was needed.[22] Some new competitors did appear before 1914, but they never reached the same output level.[23] Gevaert's competitive advantages lay initially in the restriction of the product range to a well-tested product and the maintenance of strict manufacturing standards, together with a heavy emphasis on quality and service. As such, it is not surprising that Gevaert paper soon found an entry into foreign markets.

In this respect, also, Gevaert was different from its Belgian competitors. Having originally imported its raw materials from Germany, the company soon engaged in international business. In 1894 it started exporting to the Netherlands. The following year it began exporting to France, Germany, Switzerland, Italy, Portugal and Luxembourg. It appears from the accounts that sales of Gevaert paper were concentrated in the smaller provincial towns. Within a year of the foundation of Gevaert, more than one-half of its photographic paper sales were to customers outside Belgium. Competition with established brands such as Kodak was deliberately avoided.

The first foreign representation was a depot established in Paris in 1895. Agencies appeared in other extensive markets as well, including Vienna (1901) and Berlin, Milan and Moscow (all in 1906).[24] In the course of time, some of these outlets became locally-registered companies in their host countries. Thus the German GmbH Gevaert Werke was created in 1908, followed by the English Gevaert Ltd, one year later. A French company followed suit in 1914, and an Italian one in 1915. According to the management, the creation of these independent companies improved relationships with both customers and host public authorities.[25]

Prior to the outbreak of the First World War, a systematic export policy was also developed for extra-European markets. After the turn of the century, the Defender Photo Supply Co. of Rochester, NY gained exclusive US distribution rights for Gevaert products. These agreements lasted until 1907. A proper sales subsidiary in North America was established after the war. South America, which had always attracted the attention of Belgian financial circles, apparently offered bright perspectives to Gevaert as well. Sales agencies and depots were organized in Buenos Aires in 1913 and in Rio de Janeiro in 1914.

During the pre-war decades the company substantially extended its product range, its equity and its international standing. Calcium paper was but the first type in a long series. Only as late as 1910 did Gevaert include photographic plates in its range. However, the full-scale production did not start before 1918. The extension of manufacturing capacity within Belgium involved capital increases, but Gevaert's cautious management avoided drawing on the firm's financial reserves. Step by step capital was raised to BF 1 million. In the world industry, and using an index of 100 to measure turnover, the Belgian company was ranked second only to

Eastman Kodak (431), while it had a larger business than Ansco (71) and Farbenfabriken Bayer Photoabteilung (14).[26] The turnover of the Gevaert company itself grew from 10 000 square metres of paper in 1895 to 1 200 000 in 1905, and to 3 200 000 in 1913.[27]

The outbreak of the First World War caused losses to many of the foreign sales subsidiaries due to the lack of supplies from Antwerp. In the parent company, however, a limited production continued under German supervision. Due to export restrictions, special attention was given to exports to neutral countries.

After the war, the Belgian firm faced a severe competitive struggle to regain its prominent position in the world market. Major markets like Russia, Germany and Austria-Hungary were lost, at least temporarily. Protectionism on the part of the United Kingdom, France and the United States hindered sales. The unstable currency situations in numerous countries handicapped international transactions. Moreover, the Belgian market was flooded by German photographic products sold at prices below Gevaert's. Nevertheless, Gevaert managed to expand the production of photographic plates and paper and, at this time, also film, due to an increase of capital arising from a restructuring of the enterprise in 1920 into a limited liability company, Gevaert Photo-Producten NV. Its capital was raised to BF 15 million, no less than nine million of which derived from its own resources.[28] This was an indication of the conservative financial policies which the firm had followed in its early years.

Gevaert responded to the challenges of the inter-war years with a strong international marketing drive. The reduction of market potential in Europe appeared a strong incentive to promote Gevaert products in the United States. The new sales subsidiary in New York – the Gevaert Company of America Inc., established in 1920 – acquired branches in Canada and Mexico. At the end of the 1920s, market studies of South-East Asia and Africa triggered the appointment of exclusive distributors in those parts of the world as well. Gevaert was represented in 74 countries by the eve of the Second World War. Like many firms in many industries, it also became active after 1924 in international cartel agreements.[29]

In the middle of the 1920s, and after the external value of the Belgian currency had been stabilized, Gevaert started production abroad, beginning with Spain, a country with particularly high tariff barriers. The sole Spanish producer of photographic paper had been founded at the beginning of the First World War, but it was still struggling with technical difficulties in the 1920s. Gevaert exploited this situation, and in 1928 it acquired a 75 per cent equity participation in the venture, which was incorporated as Industria Fotoquimica Nacional SA (or Infonal).

To a company like Gevaert, whose exports accounted for about 90 per cent of its turnover, the world crisis in the late 1920s came as a severe blow. Photographic products were not necessities. Growing protectionism, successive devaluations, currency inconvertibilities, competition and low sales prices resulted in a sales reduction of 25 per cent, and a profit reduction of almost 80 per cent, in the first half of the 1930s. The fact that as few as possible employees were dismissed, and that technicians were kept on the payroll as long as possible, was due to Lieven

Gevaert's strong social commitment. Under the motto 'selling and selling again, prices are of secondary importance',[30] Gevaert tried to hold ground in the world market.

This economic environment led to further investment in multinational manufacturing. In order to keep a steady control on business, the distance between subsidiary and parent company was considered as a major criterion.[31] This led the firm to consider either France or the United Kingdom as preferred locations. After the devaluation of the Belgian currency and the sudden death of the founder, Lieven Gevaert, in 1935, the wheels were put in motion. France was chosen, and a factory was built at Pont-à-Marcq near Lille. Again, in order to bypass the import restrictions of Germany, existing distribution facilities were expanded at Spindlersfeld (Berlin) in 1935. Gevaert entered a joint venture with the German Voigtländer und Sohn AG, to operate a factory designed to produce photographic paper, plates and films. As a supplement to the direct supplies from Belgium and within the context of increasing trade restrictions, it was also decided in 1939 to build a factory for paper and film coating in the US at Williamstown, Massachusetts. The Gevaert Company of America Inc. had already built up a network of sales offices in New York, Boston, Chicago, Philadelphia and Los Angeles. A Canadian branch had also been incorporated as Gevaert Canada Ltd, with offices in Montreal, Toronto and Winnipeg.

In its home country, Gevaert was the sole major producer by the end of the 1930s, for the economic crisis had led to the dramatic rationalization of the photochemical sector. Fotobel, based at Evere near Brussels, was potentially a major competitor, being a subsidiary of the chemical company Union Chimique Belge. It had a very modern factory which manufactured photographic paper and others. But the world crisis took the company by surprise while in its infant stage. As a result it had to radically reduce its product range, and in 1938 it closed down.[32] On the other hand, foreign competition on the Belgian market continued. Kodak had a retail and wholesale branch in Brussels, and in the 1930s the Ilford-Selo SA competed with Gevaert in its home territory.[33]

During the Second World War Belgium was again occupied by Germany, but once more this did not prevent a limited production from continuing. Gevaert Ltd in London functioned with the aid of materials supplied by Ilford when Belgian imports were cut off. The London subsidiary also served as the distribution centre for the Gevaert subsidiaries in Allied territories. The factory at Williamstown also became self-supporting during the war.[34]

The end of the war caused further disruption to the Belgian company. The Berlin factory was expropriated and dismantled by the Soviet forces, although business relations with Voigtländer continued. The latter marketed Gevaert products in Germany until 1957, and other German connections were developed. An agreement with Zeiss Ikon AG of Stuttgart introduced Gevaert's amateur products into the West German market under the Zeiss label. In collaboration with Voigtländer AG Braunschweig, Gevaert Technik GmbH was also founded in 1956 to market professional products.

Gevaert recovered quickly from the post-war dislocations, and its turnover increased regularly from 1949 onwards. Profits did not rise at the same rate, however, due to fierce competition, low prices and other problems. In this respect, a weak year like 1955 showed an increase in production and sales of 8 per cent over the previous year, but an increase in profits of only 2.5 per cent.[35] As before the war, there was a strong emphasis on international markets. By 1957 an export level of 90 per cent of the total production was reached again. Almost two-fifths of these exports went to the six members of the European Community, with the West German market alone accounting for 17 per cent.

There was an evident loss of competitiveness at Gevaert in this period. The firm focused increasingly on the production of photographic materials for medical and graphic-industrial use, which kept its R. & D. spending low, but meant that it was not an active participant in the dynamic amateur photography market. It was a small player in the world market compared to Kodak, which had a share of around 56 per cent of world sales in 1964. The competitive environment of the Belgian firm was also changed as, for example, the European photographic industry underwent a process of concentration as small and medium-sized companies merged into large chemical concerns. Adox joined Dupont and Ferronia and Bauchet joined 3M.[36]

This was the background to the historical transnational merger between Gevaert and Agfa in 1964. Agfa had originated as a German medium-sized high-quality speciality dye manufacturer, which had diversified into photographic film in the late 19th century. It set up a photographic department in 1888, supplying developers and fixers, and in 1893 started making plates. Later, the German firm developed Agfa cinefilm, which went into manufacture in 1909, and which made it a highly successful company. The company was a constituent of I.G. Farben, formed in 1925, and when this was broken up after the end of the Second World War, Agfa continued under the ownership of the Bayer chemical company.[37] Unlike Gevaert, it focused on amateur photography in the post-war period. It, and other Bayer subsidiaries, held 7 per cent of the world market in 1964, compared to Gevaert's 6 per cent, and there was a considerable synergy between the two enterprises. Agfa absorbed seven other smaller German producers as a prelude to its merger with Gevaert.

Negotiations started in 1958 and resulted in the merger of the two biggest European photo-producers. Agfa AG and Gevaert Photo-Producten NV were turned into holding companies. They created two new operating companies – Gevaert-Agfa NV Mortsel and Agfa-Gevaert AG Leverkusen – with a 50 per cent participation for each. These came under a joint general management direction with common members. This form of merger was chosen because a juridical merger was impossible due to a lack of conformity in European company legislation. The problem of overlapping foreign subsidiaries and distributorships was a complex one. The Gevaert network was most developed of the two with 16 subsidiaries or agencies in 122 countries. After the merger, the Agfa-Gevaert group was represented in 144 countries.

As so often, the gains from merger were, at least initially, less then expected. The process of integration in the European operations was difficult. Nevertheless, the group engaged in vigorous new direct investment, adding two new factories in France, one in India, one in Spain and one in Brazil in the years after the merger.[38]

In 1979 a new corporate structure was implemented, and an increase in capital led to Bayer acquiring an equity interest of 60 per cent in both the German and Belgian holding companies. Two years later, after the silver crisis provoked by the Hunt brothers, Bayer provided another infusion of share capital, and took over the minority interest (then 37.5 per cent) held by the Belgian holding company. Thus, Bayer became the sole owner of Agfa-Gevaert in 1981. It became, in effect, a German multinational, although with a continuing large Belgian production base.

Conclusion

Belgium is an intriguing case in the story of the rise of continental multinationals. In the 19th century, it was one of the most dynamic host economies. There was extensive direct investment in extractives, services and manufacturing, adopting a range of corporate forms. By 1914, 126 cases of Belgian fdi in industry have been identified. Belgian business in this period had organizational and technological advantages which could be, and were, exploited in foreign markets.[39]

From the First World War onwards, however, Belgium has not been a dynamic home economy for multinationals, especially in manufacturing. At least from the formation of the European Community, Belgium was more noteworthy for serving as an attractive host economy for foreign multinationals. By 1978 the stock of inward direct investment in Belgium was estimated as being twice as high as the stock of Belgian outward investment, while in the same year 45 per cent of Belgium's 522 largest manufacturing companies were foreign affiliates.[40]

Nevertheless, Belgium has in this century possessed some important international enterprises. Gevaert was a highly international, if not multinational, enterprise from its very beginning. It became, along with Kodak, Agfa and Ilford, one of the select group of companies which dominated the photochemical industry, at least until the arrival of Japanese firms such as Fuji on world markets from the 1950s. The firm was no doubt prompted to internationalize by the smallness of the Belgian market. Its foreign activities developed stage by stage. The sales network abroad was developed first by appointing independent distributors, then by building depots, and then by creating sales subsidiaries. The parent company preferred for a long period to retain production in Belgium. Then, in the difficult climate of the inter-war years, foreign manufacturing started.

Gevaert developed firm-specific ownership advantages by producing high-quality goods developed by applied research. Five years after the firm's foundation, the first university graduate was hired to do research. A laboratory came next in 1908, and a centre for chemical research in 1939. Subsequently, the technical department developed progressively. In the mid-1950s about 5 per cent of turnover was spent on R. & D., more than the average R. & D. expenditure of Belgian mnes, although not really unusual in the chemical sector.[41] Lieven Gevaert was not an original inventor, but drew his strength from quickly exploiting new inventions by adding quality and service. Quality, service and innovation through applied research remained at the heart of the firm's growth.

Notes

1. I would like to thank Dr L. Roosens of the Agfa-Gevaert historical archives for his hospitality and kind and helpful comments. I would also like to thank the editors for revising this chapter for publication.
2. Dumoulin, M., *Les relations économiques italo-belges (1861–1914)*, Brussels, 1990, pp. 115–24; Stols, E., 'Colonisation et intérêts culturels belges en Argentine (1830–1914)', in J.A.O. Schneider, *et al.*, *Wirtschaftskräfte und Wirtschaftswege IV*, Frankfurt, 1978, pp. 287–312; Kurgan-Van Hentenryk, G., *Léopold II et les groupes financiers belges en Chine*, Brussels, 1972, pp. 43–8; Devos, M., *Kapitalverflechtungen in der Montanindustrie zwischen dem westlichen Deutschland und Belgien von etwa 1830 bis 1914*, Bonn, 1986, *passim;* and Kurgan-Van Hentenryk, G. and Laureyssens, J., *Un siècle d'investissements belges au Canada*, Brussels, 1986, *passim.*
3. Daems, H., *The Holding Company and Corporate Control*, Leiden, 1978, pp. 8–9. For the growth of the mixed banks, see Cameron, R., 'Belgium, 1800–1875', in R. Cameron, *et al.*, *Banking in the Early Stages of Industrialization*, New York, 1967, and Kurgen-Van Hentenryk, G., 'Finance and financiers in Belgium, 1880–1940', in Y., Cassis, (ed.), *Finance and Financiers in European History, 1880–1960*, Cambridge, 1992.
4. Devos, idem note 2, pp. 274–5.
5. Schröter, H., *Multinationale Unternehmen aus kleinen Staaten bis 1914*, forthcoming, p. 46, Table 3.5
6. Wilkins, M., 'Modern European Economic History and the Multinationals', *Journal of European Economic History*, 1977, **6**, 586–7.
7. Dumoulin, idem note 2, p. 123.
8. For the case of China, for example, see Kurgan-Van Hentenryk, G., 'Les associations d'intérêts franco-belges en Chine de 1896 à 1914', in *Centre des Recherches Relations internationales de l'Université de Metz, 4. Travaux et Recherches*, 1973/1, pp. 15–25.
9. However, in the chemical sector, there is an extremely valuable discussion of the Solvay direct investment in the United States before 1914 in Wilkins, M., *The History of Foreign Investment in the United States to 1914*, Cambridge, Mass, 1989, pp. 402–6.
10. Alloo, R., 'Le rôle des banques et des capitaux belges dans le développement économique des pays étrangers', *Revue de la Banque*, 1953, 3–4, p. 340.
11. Deloof, J., '100 jaar Bekaert Zwevegem', in L. Kympers *et al.*, *Bekaert 100. Economische ontwikkeling in Zuid-West-Vlaanderen*, Tielt, 1980, pp. 272–3.
12. Van den Bulcke, D, 'Belgium', in J. H. Dunning (ed.), *Multinational Enterprises, Economic Structure and International Competitiveness*, Chichester, 1985, p. 250. This chapter contains a valuable survey of both inward and outward direct investment, with a focus on the contemporary period.
13. Haex, F. and Van den Bulcke, D., *Belgische multinationale ondernemingen*, Diepenbeek, 1979, p. 32.
14. Haex, F. and Van den Bulcke, D. (1978), *De Belgische industriële investeringen in het buitenland. Een oriënterend onderzoek*, Diepenbeek, 1978, pp. 32–3.
15. Ibid., p. 26.
16. Ibid., p. 37.
17. Commission d'étude de l'IRRI, 'Les investissements directs belges à l'étranger', *Studia Diplomatica*, 1987, 1, p. 24.
18. Caves, R., *Multinational Enterprise and Economic Analysis*, Cambridge, 1982, drew attention to the importance of its 'particular' complement of industries in explaining Belgium's low

foreign capital stock, but this raises further questions, as Mira Wilkins has observed (Wilkins, M., 'The History of European Multinationals: A New Look', *Journal of European Economic History*, 1986, **15**, 3, p. 509 n. 71)

19. The European Top 500, *Financial Times*, 13 January 1992. See also Table 1.5 (p. 22). For the more recent growth of concentration in the Belgian economy, see Vincent, A., *Les groupes d' entreprises en Belgique. Le domaine des principaux groupes privés*, Brussels, 1990.
20. Roosens, L., 'De foto – en filmindustrie', in R. Baetens, (ed.), *Industriële Revoluties in de provincie Antwerpen*, Antwerp, 1984, pp. 148–50.
21. It was founded according to Belgian law as a *'société en commandite par actions'*.
22. Nooyens, F., 'Lieven Gevaert & Cie en de Belgische fotochemische industrie in 1896', in Mortsels Heemkundige Kring (ed.), *Jaarboek 1989*, p. 93.
23. Idem note 20, pp. 159–60.
24. Roosens, L. and van Deuren, K., *Lieven Gevaert 1868–1935. Herdenking van de 50e verjaardag van zijn overlijden*, Antwerp, 1985, pp. 16, 28.
25. Agfa-Gevaert Historical Archives (AGHA), D 195, Annual Reports, 1915.
26. Idem note 20, p. 159.
27. Alt, L., 'The Photochemical Industry: Historical Essay in Business Strategy and Internationalization', unpublished Massachusetts Institute of Technology PhD, 1986, p. 76.
28. Idem note 25, D195, 1920.
29. Heens, L.J., 'Industrie en Handel der Belgische Foto-Produkten', *Licht en Schaduw*, 1936–7.
30. Idem note 25, D 195, 1934.
31. Idem note 25, D 250, Note of 15 October 1933 on subsidiaries abroad.
32. Gevaert, C., 'De Fotographische Nijverheid in België', *Economische tijdingen der Kredietbank*, 1938, p. 223.
33. Idem note 27, p. 9; Hercock, R.J. and Jones, G.A., *Silver by the Ton. The History of Ilford*, London, 1979, p. 71; Collins, D., *The Story of Kodak*, New York, 1990, p. 94.
34. Idem note 25, D 195, 1945.
35. Idem note 25, D 195, 1955.
36. Idem note 25, D 941, Competition – Note on the Competitive Position, 4 December 1967.
37. Chandler, A.D., *Scale and Scope*, Cambridge, Mass, 1990, pp. 474–5, 479, 571, 583–4; Alt, L., 'The Photochemical Industry: Historical Essays in Business Strategy and Internationalization', *Business and Economic History*, 1987, 16, p. 186.
38. Alt, idem note 27, pp. 119–20.
39. See van der Wee, H., 'Investment Strategy of Belgian Industrial Enterprise between 1830 and 1980 and its Influence on the Economic Development of Europe' in G. Verbeke, (ed.), *Belgium and European Integration. Belgium and Europe – Proceedings of the International Francqui-Colloquium. Brussels-Ghent, 12–14 November*, Brussels, 1981, pp. 75–93.
40. Idem note 12, pp. 251, 253.
41. Wilsdon, M., 'Gevaert – The story of an Industry', *Perspective*, 1960, 2, p. 16; idem note 13, p. 96.

Index

ABN 87
    see also Nederlandsche Handel-
        Maatschappij
AEG 38, 155ff
AEGON 87–8
AGA 101, 103, 105, 120
Agfa 31, 209ff
    see also Gevaert
Ahold 81
airlines 19, 38–9
Aker 133, 138–9, 140, 142–3
AKU 60, 73, 75, 77–8, 81–4,
    see also AKZO
AKZO 83–4, 86
    see also AKU
AL 140–41, 143–4
Alfa Laval 101, 104–5, 111, 123
Algemeene Maatschappij van
    Levensverzekening 70–71
Algemeene Norit Maatschappij 75–6
alliances, strategic 19, 85–6, 118, 124, 187,
    199
    see also cartels, international
Allianz 29, 37
Alpine Montan 32
Alusuisse-Lonza 53
AMEV 87–8
Ansaldo 164
anti-trust 7, 16, 117
Asea-Brown Boveri (ABB) 19, 24–5, 50, 101,
    103–4, 120, 124, 139, 160, 166, 187
Assi 120
Astra 120
Atlas Copco 120–21, 123
Australia 115–16, 144, 147, 197
automobiles 17, 24, 29, 36, 38–9, 43–4,
    108, 120, 124, 184, 191

Baltic 101
Banca Commerciale Italiana 186
banks
    and industry 16, 19, 102, 105, 122, 125,
        141, 158, 186, 202–204
    multinational 18, 29, 36–7, 44, 58–9,
        68–9, 86–7, 132, 136, 173ff
Banque de Paris et des Pays-Bas 69, 93
Bantam Books 40
BASF 36, 40
Bayer 31, 33, 36, 40, 42–3, 209
Beiersdorf 36
Bekaert 204
Belgian Congo (Zaire) 204–205
Benedetti, Carlo De 20
Benetton 199
Bensdorp & Co. 68
Bertelsmann 17, 40
Biotechnology 40
BMW 39, 43
Bofors 32
Borregaard 139, 141
Bosch 38
Bridgestone 196
Bruning 85
BTR 196

Canada 36, 41, 69, 81, 108, 148, 191, 194,
    205, 208
Canadian Eagle Oil Company 79
Carbo Union 76
cartels, international 19, 30, 74, 76, 82,
    202, 204
Casson, Mark 5
Centra AG 72
Chandler, Alfred D. 6–7, 12, 16–17, 28, 30,
    38